Princeton Campus Plan

Princeton Campus Plan
The next ten years and beyond

Beyer Blinder Belle
Architects & Planners LLP

Nassau Hall, completed in 1756, reconstructed in 1855

CONTENTS

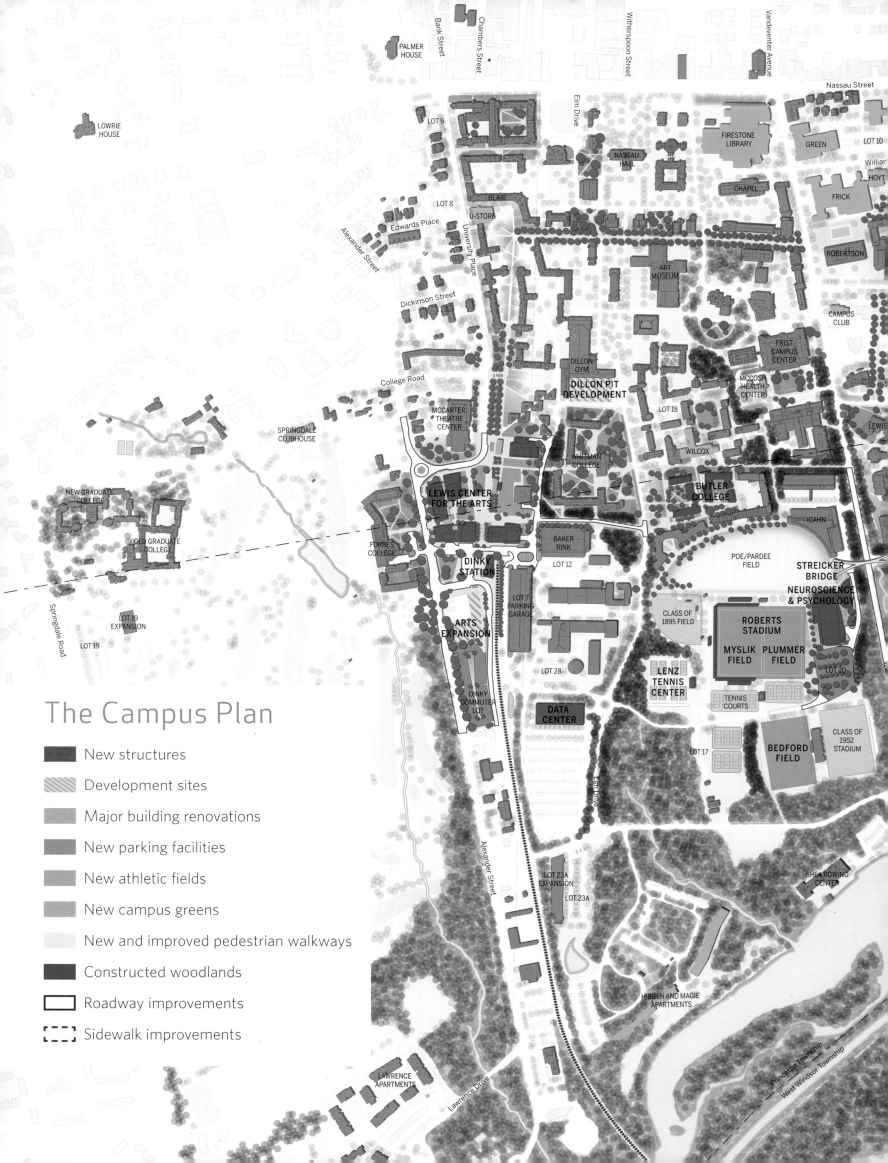

The Campus Plan

- ▮ New structures
- ▨ Development sites
- ▮ Major building renovations
- ▮ New parking facilities
- ▮ New athletic fields
- ▮ New campus greens
- ▮ New and improved pedestrian walkways
- ▮ Constructed woodlands
- ▭ Roadway improvements
- ┅ Sidewalk improvements

LOWRIE HOUSE

PALMER HOUSE

Bank Street

Chambers Street

Witherspoon Street

Vandeventer Avenue

Nassau Street

LOT 9

NASSAU HALL

FIRESTONE LIBRARY

GREEN

LOT 10

CHAPEL

HOYT

FRICK

William

LOT 8

BLAIR

U-STORE

ROBERTSON

Edwards Place

Alexander Street

University Place

ART MUSEUM

Dickinson Street

CAMPUS CLUB

College Road

DILLON GYM

DILLON PIT DEVELOPMENT

FRIST CAMPUS CENTER

MCCOSH HEALTH CENTER

SPRINGDALE CLUBHOUSE

MCCARTER THEATRE CENTER

LOT 18

LEWIS

WHITMAN COLLEGE

WILCOX

NEW GRADUATE COLLEGE

LEWIS CENTER FOR THE ARTS

BUTLER COLLEGE

OLD GRADUATE COLLEGE

FORBES COLLEGE

BAKER RINK

ICAHN

DINKY STATION

LOT 12

POE/PARDEE FIELD

STREICKER BRIDGE

LOT 7 PARKING GARAGE

NEUROSCIENCE & PSYCHOLOGY

Springdale Road

LOT 19 EXPANSION

ARTS EXPANSION

CLASS OF 1895 FIELD

ROBERTS STADIUM

LOT 19

LOT 28

MYSLIK FIELD

PLUMMER FIELD

LOT 20

LENZ TENNIS CENTER

DINKY COMMUTER LOT

DATA CENTER

TENNIS COURTS

LOT 17

BEDFORD FIELD

CLASS OF 1952 STADIUM

Elm Drive

SHEA ROWING CENTER

Alexander Street

LOT 23A EXPANSION

LOT 23A

HIBBEN AND MAGIE APARTMENTS

LAWRENCE APARTMENTS

Lawrence Drive

Princeton Township

West Windsor Township

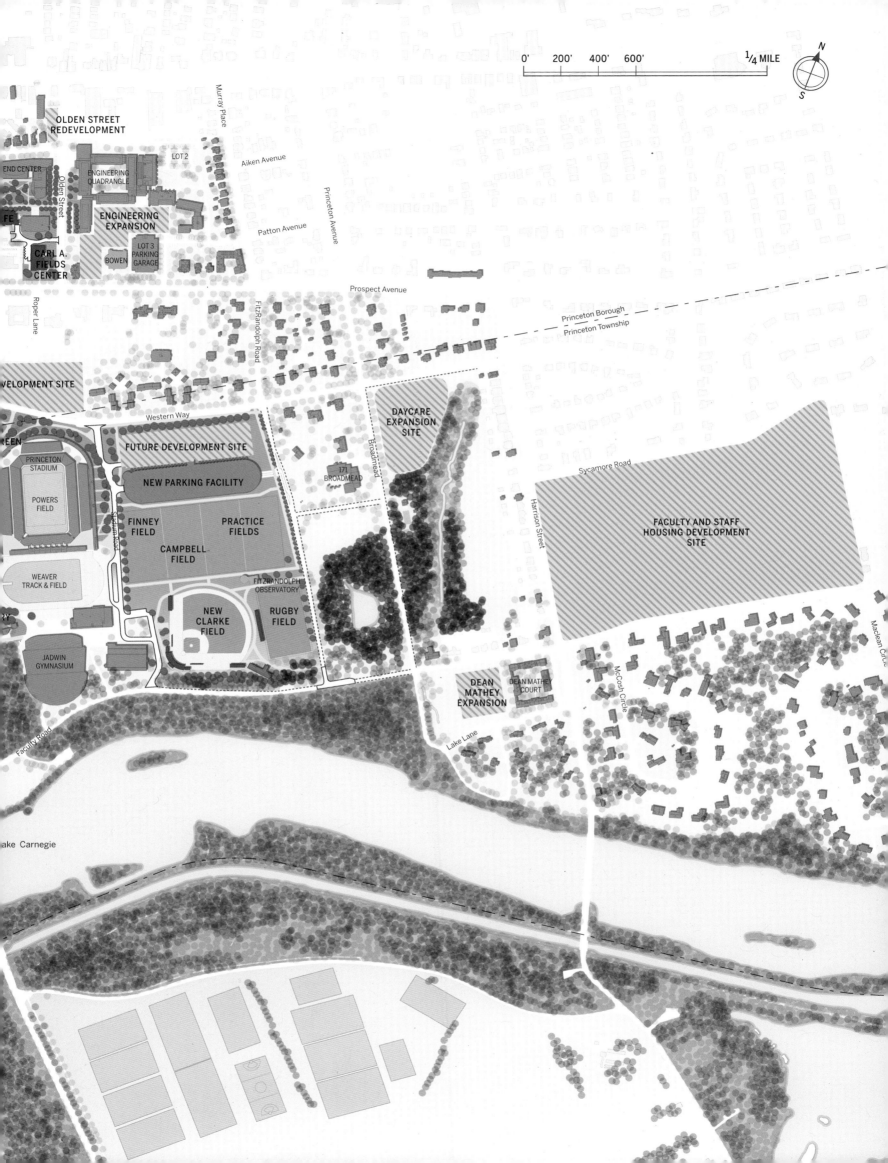

OLDEN STREET
REDEVELOPMENT

END CENTER

ENGINEERING
QUADRANGLE

LOT 2

FE

ENGINEERING
EXPANSION

CARL A.
FIELDS
CENTER

BOWEN

LOT 3
PARKING
GARAGE

Olden Street

Roper Lane

Murray Place

Aiken Avenue

Patton Avenue

Princeton Avenue

Prospect Avenue

FitzRandolph Road

Princeton Borough
Princeton Township

VELOPMENT SITE

Western Way

REEN

PRINCETON
STADIUM

POWERS
FIELD

WEAVER
TRACK & FIELD

JADWIN
GYMNASIUM

FUTURE DEVELOPMENT SITE

NEW PARKING FACILITY

FINNEY
FIELD

PRACTICE
FIELDS

CAMPBELL
FIELD

NEW
CLARKE
FIELD

RUGBY
FIELD

FITZRANDOLPH
OBSERVATORY

171
BROADMEAD

Broadmead

DAYCARE
EXPANSION
SITE

Sycamore Road

FACULTY AND STAFF
HOUSING DEVELOPMENT
SITE

Harrison Street

Maclean Circle

McCosh Circle

DEAN
MATHEY
EXPANSION

DEAN MATHEY
COURT

Lake Lane

Faculty Road

RY

Lake Carnegie

0'   200'   400'   600'   ¼ MILE

N
S

CHAPTER 1
THE CAMPUS AS A WORK IN PROGRESS

In 2005 Princeton embarked on a major campus planning initiative, the most comprehensive in its history. It began at a critical moment when the University needed to determine how it could accommodate significant academic expansion while preserving the historic beauty and walkability of the campus. What follows is the story behind this Campus Plan.

Physics class with Princeton physicist and Nobel laureate Joseph Taylor

McCosh Courtyard

The Campus as a Work in Progress

Why is a campus plan for Princeton University needed, and what kind of plan should it be?

Campus planning takes many forms, from the technical documentation of needs to aesthetic design considerations. The plan presented in the following pages offers a sweeping view of Princeton's campus as a web of interconnected systems. It weaves together policy, architecture, infrastructure, landscape, and environment, along with implications and opportunities for the surrounding community. It is the most comprehensive plan ever developed by Princeton, at a moment when taking such an integrated view has never been more important.

The fundamental planning challenge that now confronts Princeton is the intelligent use of diminishing available land for development on campus. Having passed its 260th anniversary, the University has faced this obstacle in earlier

times. But the constraints of space and infrastructure on the campus today are such that they impose significant strategic and aesthetic consequences on any new growth, requiring much more intensive consideration of the impacts of individual projects than ever before. Today, even the smallest intervention has long-range consequences that will either preserve or foreclose options in the future.

A seemingly easy solution would be to "jump" across Lake Carnegie to Princeton's long term land holdings in West Windsor Township. But, as this plan demonstrates, it is premature for such a move, which would fundamentally alter the University's distinctive academic culture. This opportunity, and its challenges, must be preserved for future generations.

Fitting growth into the seemingly crowded main campus is truly a difficult challenge. Significant expansion in Princeton's historic core campus is no longer an option. A place of sublime beauty, renowned for its "park-like" character, the core campus was formed largely by the vision of Presidents James McCosh and later Woodrow Wilson between the 1870s and 1930s. However, rings of postwar expansion have not always met the standards of the past, resulting in areas of undistinguished architecture lacking quality open space. Some new development is possible within these "middle rings" by recycling underutilized or outmoded sites, but most new growth is now beyond the postwar "ring," closer to the periphery of the campus. Some of these modern areas feel isolated and disconnected from the heart of campus, separated by distance and the barriers created by roadways and inadequate pedestrian paths.

This plan demonstrates that accommodating needed growth is not only possible, but necessary for Princeton to flourish, and can be done in a way that results in a better campus. Instead of imposing unwelcome densification and congestion on a beloved campus and neighboring community, the next ten years of development, if properly managed, presents an opportunity to tie the campus together, reinvigorate the landscape, improve the environment, and revitalize utilitarian sites as vibrant campus and community spaces. The plan is ambitious yet subtle: while nearly one-third of the 380-acre contiguous main campus may be rebuilt, the results will integrate the new with the old and weave modern development with the historic campus into a coherent whole. The Princeton campus of 2016 and beyond will have greater definition of the edges where it meets its neighbors; more opportunities for academic and interdisciplinary collaboration; improved facilities for students, faculty, staff, and visitors; more sustainable application of infrastructure; and fresh, innovative architecture that is well integrated into the campus and community setting.

Concentrating growth within a walkable distance of the center honors Princeton's unique academic culture and educational philosophy, which is manifested in the historic design of its campus. Perpetuating this tradition forward means that even as Princeton University becomes larger, it must continue to feel small. Even as the campus grows and adds more people and buildings, it must continue to possess the spirit of a pastoral and intimate place. It should continue to be distinguished by green, open spaces where professor and student meet and work face-to-face, and walk across campus in the ten-minute interval between classes.

To maintain this intimate character, the Campus Plan breaks down the scale of an increasingly large area through the identification of a series of "campus neighborhoods." While the campus must always function and be experienced as an integrated whole, without boundaries or divisions, the neighborhoods create local relationships within a greater sense of community. They are defined by commonalities of function or collaborative academic relationships, such as the Natural Sciences Neighborhood where various sciences will be concentrated, or of architectural and landscape character, creating a coherence of design within the vibrant diversity of the campus as a whole. To highlight the areas of greatest proposed change, and to ensure that new buildings are well integrated into their surroundings, the plan focuses on four emerging campus neighborhoods around the edges of the historic Core Campus.

Princeton's vision and commitment to this plan over the next ten years will foster a positive transformation. By leveraging growth, the University will create a harmonious, coherent, and environmentally sustainable campus, carrying the history of this sublime and inimitable place into a new phase of its gradual but continual evolution.

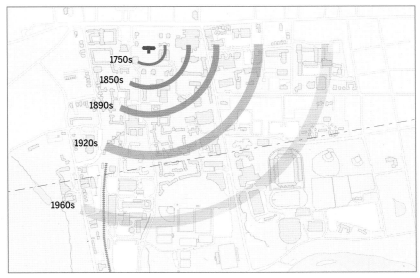

Historic rings diagram

Over the course of its 250-year history, Princeton's campus has generally grown in rings radiating outward from Nassau Hall.

PRINCETON AND CAMPUS PLANNING IN AMERICA TODAY

The growth of American higher education has driven an extraordinary demand for expansion, such that campus planning is one of the most active and important trends in planning and development today. Since universities inherently value the campus as an irreplaceable long-term asset, they are approaching planning with a high level of sophistication and strategic long-range vision.

As a result, universities are now leaders in experimental and innovative architecture, mixed-use development, transportation planning and policy, and large-scale environmental sustainability. This expertise often benefits academic goals; for example, sustainability efforts on campuses can be integrated into education and research in the environmental sciences and public policy.

Princeton's current phase of growth is driven by many of the same factors that influence university planning around the country.

The rapidly changing nature of the sciences

Older science buildings, many from the first half of the 20th century, can no longer support the requirements of modern research, so larger, more advanced technology buildings have become essential for campuses around the country. At Princeton, the planned Chemistry building will provide state-of-the-art facilities for a longstanding department no longer adequately served by the Frick Laboratory, built in 1929. The School of Engineering and Applied Science, located in the 1962 E-Quad complex, while not leaving its current building, will also benefit from a significant expansion that will provide space for the needs of modern research and equipment.

At the same time, emerging scientific disciplines and interdisciplinary collaborations call for completely new facilities and teaching methods. Princeton's Lewis-Sigler Institute for Integrative Genomics and planned Neurosci-

ence Institute represent cutting-edge cross-disciplinary developments driving major construction unimaginable even a few years earlier.

The rapid development of the sciences has created significant challenges for campus planning, for the simple reason that research laboratories require larger and more highly equipped buildings than ever before, which must often be integrated into traditional campus settings. A key challenge of Princeton's campus plan has been introducing new science buildings while maintaining the scale and character of the campus.

A new focus on student life

Competition for students, an increasing emphasis on a robust and well-rounded environment for student life, and a growing appreciation of the critical importance of extracurricular engagement also drive campus expansion. Student centers supporting a wide range of activities, more diverse athletic options, health and wellness centers, dormitories with diverse amenities, and expanded arts and cultural programs are integral features of the modern campus. Universities recognize that in the right campus setting, undergraduate education can prepare students for a multifaceted civic life by promoting social and cultural engagement and public service.

The "open" campus

Campus planning also reflects the changing role of universities within the public sphere. The historic model of the American campus—a rural environment to nurture the academic life of students and faculty—was pioneered at Princeton, where the location was chosen in part because it was, as Princeton President Aaron Burr Sr. described it, "more sequestered from the various temptations attending a promiscuous converse with the world, that theater of folly and dissipation." [1] Later, President Woodrow Wilson wanted students to play leadership roles "in the nation's service" after they graduated, but commissioned cloistered greens and neo-gothic walls to protect them during their student years from the influence of external distractions.

Today, this pedagogic ideal of the "ivory tower" has changed to that of the "open" and engaged campus, where academic work is connected to the outside world, and where colleges and universities increasingly make contributions to the nation's economic prosperity; to environmental, government, and public policy; to culture and the arts; and in many other areas. The outside world, once seen as a corrupting influence, is now a locus of real-world educational opportunity. Paradigms of campus planning, as well as the traditional image of the campus, are changing to reflect this transformation.

Thomas Lab, built in 1986 for the study of molecular biology

To strengthen ties, many universities are contributing to the well-being and quality of life of their home communities. While the precise nature of these contributions varies depending on the capacities of the institution and the needs of the community, it is widely recognized that in the most successful situations, institutions draw strength from their communities, and communities draw strength from their institutions. The most visible of these efforts are apparent at universities within urban settings. Yale, the University of Pennsylvania, and the University of Cincinnati, for instance, have become deeply engaged in the revitalization of their surrounding urban districts, partnering with community groups and local governments to create mixed-use developments that blend housing, neighborhood services, and facilities for academics and campus life. These collaborations blur the boundary line between academia and community, challenging the traditional definition of "campus."

Princeton University's planned Peter B. Lewis Center for the Arts provides such an opportunity to "open" an edge of campus. A hybrid space for both campus and civic use, the project mixes traditional classrooms and studios with public performance and exhibition spaces and retail spaces including a restaurant and café. A new multi-modal transportation plaza will serve the entire Princeton community as well as visitors to both campus and town.

Satellite campuses

Pressure to grow has prompted some universities to expand beyond their historic campuses. Recently several major universities have chosen to create satellite campuses on available land in new locations, separated from their historic centers. Harvard and Columbia are notable examples of this trend: both universities have strategically acquired land in nearby areas for later expansion, recently announcing major plans to develop entirely new campuses. In Philadelphia, the University of Pennsylvania has similar expansion plans for former industrial properties along the Schuylkill River. Development so dramatic in scale and ambition recalls earlier times when universities were being planned and designed from scratch, but in today's climate such development is inherently controversial within its surrounding communities.

FACING A STRATEGIC CHOICE

Early in Shirley M. Tilghman's presidency, Princeton University faced a similar decisive moment regarding expansion.

Between 1922 and 1948, with remarkable foresight, the University acquired nearly 400 acres of farmland in West Windsor Township across Lake Carnegie from its campus, an area almost as large as today's entire contiguous main campus.[2] This land now serves to buffer the campus from commercial development along Route 1. It also offers a memorable experience of arrival: leaving the strip malls

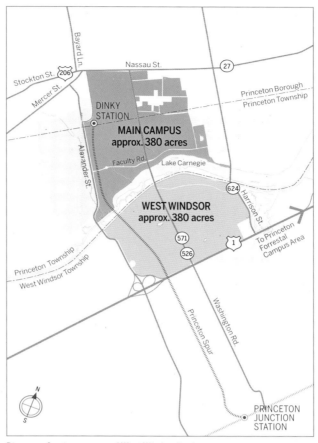

Diagram of main campus and West Windsor lands

The largely undeveloped property owned by the University in West Windsor Township is approximately the same size as the entire existing campus north of Lake Carnegie.

and office parks behind, visitors pass through open fields and a nearly mile long allée of 70-year old elm trees. Suddenly the scenic lake vista emerges, a sublime and calming transition providing a gracious sense of arrival to both campus and town.

For a number of years, the University contemplated developing a "mirror campus" across the lake, to the point of having discussions with local planning authorities about its general configuration. Since President Tilghman's major academic initiatives would require space for growth, she was compelled to study this option. She knew that such a move must be carefully considered and well-timed. Although it would provide significant expansion space, the option posed many challenges: it would require enormous upfront investment in supporting infrastructure; it would create two physically distinct campuses; and it could separate departments and weaken academic and interdisciplinary collaboration.

At Princeton or any other university, a thoughtful campus design should express and embody the institution's defining values. For us, the campus must reinforce our commitment to be simultaneously a great research university and a great liberal arts college—a commitment founded on the belief that teaching and research are not, as some would have it, competing projects, or mere supplements to one another, but rather mutually reinforcing enterprises. This special fusion of research, graduate teaching, and undergraduate teaching defines Princeton's mission and community, and it should inform our campus architecture, too.

—CHRISTOPHER L. EISGRUBER,
 PROVOST

Such debates would be even greater at Princeton, where the mirror campus concept runs counter to a distinctive academic culture that thrives on the close proximity of students and faculty to colleagues and classrooms. Princeton's interdisciplinary culture and compact, walkable campus would be very difficult to sustain in two physically separate locations. John Moran, former vice president for facilities, assessed the situation in 1966, and the same holds true today: "Despite this vast and valuable resource of land, it is very clear that we dare not squander it. Not only do we have an obligation to future generations, but we have an obligation to this generation to organize the parts of the University so that they support the academic objectives set down by the Trustees and the President."[3]

A campus culture suited to a compact, walkable layout
The difficulty of "dividing" the campus stems from a longstanding academic culture that is one of Princeton's most distinctive strengths. Compared to its peers, Princeton has always benefited from being small and remains so today, with a student population of only 7,128 and one of the lowest student-faculty ratios in the country, roughly five to one. The intense face-to-face contact and personal attention of faculty to students afforded by these proportions is a valued tradition of academic life. The University also has one of the highest ratios of space per student, over 1,400 square feet of academic, residential, and support space.
Princeton is unique among major research universities in its dedication to teaching, and to undergraduate education in particular. The traditional liberal-arts college education holds a place of honor in the University's culture,

as does a deep appreciation of the learning and personal growth that occurs from extracurricular activity and residential life. The University's exemplary graduate programs focus primarily on the PhD along with a few strong masters programs in selected fields, largely due to the University's choice not to establish the major professional schools which play significant, even dominant, roles at other universities.

Interdisciplinary collaboration is also encouraged, creating surprising breakthroughs and new fields of intellectual inquiry. Unique partnerships have developed between social scientists and engineers, visual artists and genetics researchers. This type of collaboration fosters emerging fields of inquiry at the intersections of traditional departments: during the last five decades, over 30 interdisciplinary programs have been created.[4] In this spirit, Operations Research and Financial Engineering, a program combining mathematics, engineering, and finance, will inaugurate a new building in the fall of 2008, located halfway between the school of engineering and the department of economics.

In another example of physical planning fostering academic collaboration, a new co-located and linked pair of buildings for neuroscience and psychology will leverage the strong connections between the missions and activities of these two interdependent departments, while maintaining the individual character and separate activities of each. Although the psychology department could have remained in its existing building far from the proposed site, the advantages of frequent face-to-face communication between faculties and shared space for research were persuasive. As a by-product, Green Hall will become available to accommodate the expansion needs of various departments in the humanities and social sciences.

All these characteristics have been nurtured by a campus design which, in more successful areas, encourages ease of movement, informal meetings, and casual interaction among faculty, but also among and with students. Outdoor spaces on campus and other "common" areas shape people's experience of Princeton's distinctive academic climate almost as much as classrooms and laboratories.

President Tilghman's challenge was to foster this climate while also meeting multiple needs for new and expanded space. In thinking about how to meet this challenge, the idea of the "walkable campus" came to be seen as a distinctive physical manifestation of Princeton's culture. As a result, the principle that no part of campus should be more than a ten-minute walk from the Frist Campus Center became a guiding concept for the planning process.

Choosing a path for growth
At this strategically critical moment, President Tilghman consulted with a wide range of advisors, including architects, planners, and educators, to focus on how to respond

to the University's need for growth. In 2003, she concluded that it was not yet time to create a "mirror campus" across Lake Carnegie, and that Princeton's academic culture would be best maintained by reinforcing the existing campus and accommodating additional growth within its boundaries. She believed that with careful planning, sufficient room still existed on the contiguous main campus to accommodate at least ten more years of expected growth, including some of her most important initiatives in the sciences and the arts.

This "generational" decision to preserve the opportunity of development in West Windsor for her successors immediately raised difficult conflicts. Adding new buildings on the existing campus would increase density and bring additional parking, traffic, population, and energy consumption, not to mention the potential loss of open space. In recent decades, the increasing density of the campus and perceived loss of green space have been growing concerns. Environmentally, increased density has both positive and negative consequences: it combines the benefits of concentration, which avoids detrimental effects of urban sprawl, with the costs of local impacts on the hillsides, streams, wooded areas, and other ecological areas of the campus. Finally, most new development would inevitably occur closer to the edges of campus, some of which are immediately adjacent to residential communities in Princeton Township and Princeton Borough, the two municipalities which the campus calls home.

Facing these complex challenges, and embarking on an ambitious building program, the University decided to retain a campus planning consultant to develop a comprehensive campus-wide master plan to predict, guide, and manage campus growth. The plan would maximize benefits and minimize impacts, ensuring that the next decade of development proceeds holistically within a coherent framework. To guide the planning process, President Tilghman articulated her goals in five "guiding principles." Notably, none of the principles is about growth itself: all are about protecting the values that could be compromised if growth is poorly planned.

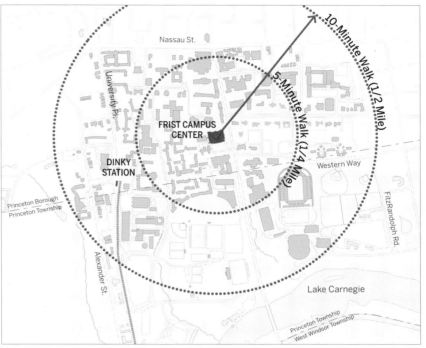

Ten-minute walk diagram

For the next two years, the planning team led by Beyer Blinder Belle focused on resolving the inherent tensions of this strategic direction, and on transforming a set of desires and constraints into a plan that would carry the campus through the next stage of its evolution.

This plan demonstrates that the hypothesis of the "pre-planning" phase was correct: not only can the campus support growth within its existing territory, but growth can be achieved in a balanced, well-designed, environmentally responsible, and integrated fashion.

The Five Guiding Principles:

- Maintain a pedestrian-oriented campus

- Preserve the park-like character of the campus

- Maintain campus neighborhoods while promoting a sense of community

- Build in an environmentally responsible manner

- Sustain strong community relations

In developing the five planning principles into a comprehensive plan, we confronted two challenges. The Princeton campus already stood as a model of open space that served teaching, research, and the public in extraordinary ways, and the planning exercise needed to coexist, even influence, significant construction projects already under way.

—MARK BURSTEIN,
  EXECUTIVE VICE PRESIDENT

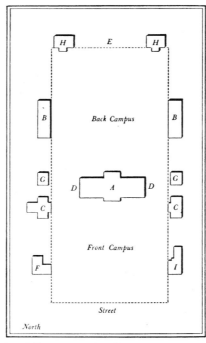
Joseph Henry master plan, 1830

Princeton's first documented campus master plan defined "front" and "back" campus greens on either side of Nassau Hall.

Aerial view of the Ellipse, 2004

The most recent campus plan, in 1996, created the Ellipse to define the symbolic southern edge of campus.

WHAT IS UNIQUE ABOUT THIS PLAN?

Surprisingly, the most constant aspect of Princeton's campus has been its continuous pace of change. Despite the sense of timelessness and permanence imparted by stone walls and majestic trees in the historic center, the campus has been a continuous "work-in-progress" since its inception. Unlike other historic sites, which live on mainly as ceremonial spaces or tourist destinations, Princeton's 250-year old campus houses a vibrant institution undergoing constant improvement, growing in pace with emerging fields of knowledge. Hundreds of buildings have been added since the completion of Nassau Hall in 1756, and many early monuments no longer exist, demolished to accommodate growth or simply in response to changing tastes.

Over its long history, Princeton University undertook six major planning initiatives to guide campus growth.[5] In between these periods, the campus grew more organically, under the stewardship of its trustees, administration, and staff. Comprehensive plans have been commissioned for one or both of two reasons: the need to plan for significant growth, or the desire to better reflect the image and identity of the institution. This plan is certainly intended to manage the next ten years of growth. While it is also intended to preserve and accentuate Princeton's unique qualities, it selectively adds new ones that build on the past, such as a reinvigorated approach to environmental stewardship, a new Arts and Transit Neighborhood that will bring together campus and community, and integration of sensitively designed modern architecture within the campus setting.

Planning for "smart growth"

The original College of New Jersey began with a seemingly unlimited supply of land, gradually acquiring farms and woodlands in the valley below its original four and one-half acre land grant from the FitzRandolph family. Over 250 years, the University would eventually come to occupy much of this territory.

The 1996 master plan, designed by Machado and Silvetti Associates, still had reasonable flexibility to locate buildings, even to create the Ellipse, a graceful arc of buildings introduced to form, if only symbolically, the southern "edge" of campus, beyond which lay "unfettered" nature (in actuality an area which included parking lots and athletics fields, but no buildings). Today, two major buildings for the sciences are already planned southeast of the Ellipse, redefining the edge of campus deeper into the valley based on needs not anticipated in 1996.

With diminishing space for development, what distinguishes the current period of campus planning is the increasing sensitivity of the campus, community, and natural environment to each new increment of growth. Each decision to locate a new building impacts future options, and thus must be thought of strategically, to preserve critical flexibility for academic expansion. "Highest and best use" projects must take precedence; support functions cannot occupy land needed to expand Princeton's core academic mission. As a result, some support and administrative functions must be located farther toward the edge of campus, or even off campus. To ensure a continuing sense of community, these developments will include valued amenities and improved transportation links back to the Core Campus.

The University must also consider aspects of development that seemed less critical in decades past, when there were fewer demands on resources and less awareness of environmental issues. The campus is located in a region with a rapidly increasing population and therefore rapidly increasing demands on infrastructure and the environment. The impact of constructing a building is felt well past its immediate surrounding area. It may have wider-reaching consequences on environmental systems, such as water quality and ecological balance, and infrastructure, including the regional traffic network and campus parking supply.

In response to these challenges, the planning team recognized that the traditional skills and fields of knowledge familiar to architects and campus planners would be inadequate to address the complex demands of planning Princeton's growth. The University is the long-term steward of a 380-acre site[6] which consists not only of buildings and cultivated landscapes, but also extensive roadways and parking facilities, a railroad station, a power plant, and, perhaps most significantly, the sweeping underlying hillside, forming a natural watershed for Lake Carnegie, with its surviving primitive streams coursing through wooded ravines.

Aware that each of these features interconnect, and that manipulating any one impacts the whole, Beyer Blinder Belle organized a team of experts to study the campus as a complex set of interdependent systems. The team included landscape architects, ecologists, environmental engineers, civil engineers, transportation planners, parking planners, wayfinding designers, and other specialists. While the core objective of a campus plan is the accommodation of space needs and the gracious arrangement of buildings, the team believed that many "invisible" factors, often left to technicians to solve later, must be incorporated as integrated aspects of the planning process.

The plan applies the principles of "smart growth" to Princeton's campus: maximizing the advantages of density to create efficiency in the use of infrastructure and resources; reducing dependence on automobiles by encouraging walking, biking, and use of transit; and preserving the natural environment by leveraging the construction of new buildings to restore local ecologies and reduce stormwater runoff.

It turns out that the University has more capacity for growth on campus than was recognized before this planning process began, so long as it is intelligently planned. The plan avoids the two extremes of over-densification and sprawl, and rather than proposing the use of all available opportunities for development, it succeeds in preserving a number of long-term expansion options within the campus. While protecting the University's West Windsor lands for future use, the plan demonstrates that the existing campus can support not only the next decade of academic expansion but quite possibly one or more beyond that.

WHAT HAS THE CAMPUS PLAN ACHIEVED?

The plan described in these pages documents the results of the two-year planning process, which studied a wide ranging set of issues affecting the entire campus. More than a collection of projects, the plan provides a comprehensive and integrated framework.

Early in the process, the University and the planning team observed a number of significant and unique challenges facing Princeton's campus, ranging from the experiential, such as the visitor's perception of arrival, to the functional, such as corridors of seemingly insoluble traffic congestion. The plan leverages proposed developments to confront these challenges, in the process creating dramatic opportunities to transform the experience of the campus and its surroundings.

Turning the "back" of campus into a new front

While Nassau Hall and FitzRandolph Gate will always mark the traditional "front door" of Princeton University, these landmarks are far removed from the parking and transit facilities where most commuters and visitors, including prospective students, are now directed, after passing through what appears to be the "back" of campus. Emerging from cars and trains, a lack of clear signage and pathways directing visitors to the Core Campus worsens their disorientation. The Campus Plan proposes to transform the experience of arrival, using development to create new gateways complementing the historic landmarks on Nassau Street.

A proposed multi-modal transportation hub, to be created in concert with a major new arts complex, will become a clear and welcoming point of entry to both the University and the township and borough of Princeton.

New Jersey Transit's Dinky train, connected to the Northeast Corridor rail line, is an extraordinary and unique asset for a major university. Established in 1839 to link the campus to New York City, the Dinky has also come to be an essential commuter service for local residents, and can

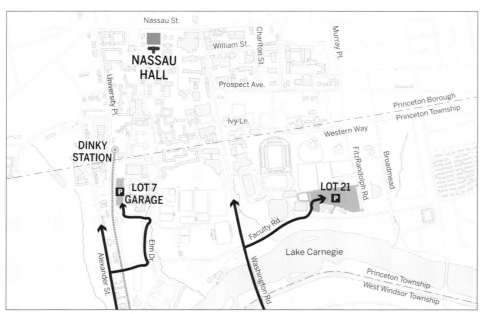
Diagram of roadways approaching the campus

Although Nassau Street and landmarks such as Nassau Hall are the traditional front of the University, many visitors now experience arrival to the campus from the south where the actual first impression is more likely to be the back of a parking garage.

Nassau Hall

Lot 7 garage

now help reduce the University's dependence on cars in an increasingly congested regional road system. A pedestrian-oriented transit plaza will include a new station and retail services, and connect rail travelers to local buses, jitneys, campus shuttles, taxis, parking, and bike facilities. New pathways, signage, and maps will direct visitors to destinations across campus and in the community.

At Washington Road, another important route of arrival, new buildings for the natural sciences, an elegantly engineered pedestrian bridge arching over the road, and a restored and extended woodland valley will create a dramatic visual gateway to both campus and community for drivers.

An arts plaza bridging campus and community

President Tilghman's creative and performing arts initiative signals a dramatic improvement of programs for the arts, with expanded academic offerings in music, theater, dance, visual arts, and creative writing, additional exhibition space for the Princeton University Art Museum, and performance facilities that range from a traditional concert hall to an "experimental media studio." These spaces will intensify the role of the arts in the life of Princeton students, supporting their artistic interests and endeavors even as they pursue degrees in other subjects, and preparing them for a lifelong appreciation of and involvement in all forms of artistic and cultural expression.

The planning strategy for arts on campus is twofold. Existing and expanded arts programs and facilities will continue to be distributed across the campus, infusing the University community with arts activities from edge to edge. At the same time, a robust new mixed-use arts neighborhood will be created at the west edge of campus, anchored by the existing McCarter and Berlind theaters, where Princeton's arts programs can foster a new relationship between the University and the public. Unlike some areas of study which benefit from the traditional sequestered space of campus, the arts thrive on intensive engagement with the outside world. A public presence will create energy and vitality for arts programs, and draw outside visitors to performances and exhibitions, enriching the cultural life of the Princeton community both on and off campus.

The complex will include academic buildings as well as performance and exhibition venues designed by different architects, creating aesthetic diversity and collaborative design innovation, all within the framework of a coherent plan. The focal point of the development will be a public plaza forming a new, more open relationship between the campus and the surrounding town, in contrast to the gothic walls, archways, and gates enclosing other parts of the campus. New restaurants and cafés on the plaza will serve patrons of the complex and of existing theaters, as well as students, faculty, commuters, and other riders of the trains and buses arriving at the nearby transit hub. The plaza and its surrounding activities, serving both the University and the public, will be a nexus of campus and community life, a space promoting cultural and social exchange.

Reinvigorating the campus landscape

The best-loved areas of Princeton's campus, created in the early part of the 20th century, resulted from the collaboration of building architects and landscape architects in equal partnership. While these historic spaces still make a beautiful and powerful impact, investment in landscape since the 1950s has been more limited and landscape has often taken a secondary role to the design of buildings. The results are apparent in the diminished sense of campus in some of the more modern areas, and in the uninviting gaps between the historic campus and recently developed districts.

The planning team recognized early in the process that landscape and nature form the connective fabric that binds diverse buildings into a coherent space and encourages the enjoyment of the outdoor environment as an integral part of campus life. Beatrix Farrand, the landscape architect of many of Princeton's beloved open spaces, believed that exposure to landscape and nature was essential to the mental and spiritual development of the student. Through the planning process, the University has developed a renewed appreciation of the fundamental role of landscape in establishing a campus setting that expresses the goals and values of the institution.

The plan provides for significant new investment in landscape projects across the campus, to reconnect campus neighborhoods back to the historic core and to extend a sense of campus character to areas which lack it. Combined with the landscaping associated with new buildings, a vast area of campus will be transformed over the next ten years. The pathway network will be expanded and woven through areas of new development to reinforce walkability, supported by a new system of subtly-integrated wayfinding signage. In addition to improved aesthetics, new landscapes will also be more resilient and self-sustaining, incorporating features such as passive irrigation and engineered soils. This work will also reassert the presence of nature and revitalize ecological areas as a defining part of the campus experience. While other universities are notable for their unique natural features, such as the gorges of Cornell or Strawberry Creek at Berkeley, Princeton's stunning wooded ravines can be barely noticed as part of the campus experience. As the campus grows into the valley, nature will become a stronger presence, conversely growing further into the campus.

The NJ Transit Dinky station provides rail service to the University and the Princeton community

The planning team tours a Beatrix Farrand-designed landscape in 2006

Leveraging a parking strategy to transform the eastern edge of campus

With planned buildings both increasing the population of the campus and displacing existing parking lots, the University faced a significant parking deficit for development projected by the plan. A comprehensive parking strategy was needed to meet the needs of the next ten years while supporting the principle of a walkable campus, and avoiding the negative impacts feared by the campus and neighboring communities.

The proposed strategy begins by reducing the amount of new parking needed through "transportation demand management" policies, which encourage alternative means of transportation including walking, biking, car pooling, and transit, as well as other specific policy decisions, such as limiting undergraduate parking. A redesigned campus shuttle system will improve existing service to parking areas, graduate student housing, other campus destinations, and off-campus sites, thus reducing the amount of local driving and its related demand for parking. Finally, a major new parking facility is planned to be located within convenient walking distance of the workplaces of a large number of University employees, minimizing reliance on shuttles and supporting the principle of a walkable campus. The environmentally sustainable parking facility will combine surface lots with a garage, incorporating innovative architecture and amenities.

While a parking project may not seem to be the most glamorous of campus planning initiatives, the proposed concept leverages this functional need to create a bold and strategic transformation of a large area of campus that could not otherwise be achieved. To enable the parking development, athletics fields will be relocated and improved, strengthening the athletics neighborhood and increasing utilization through improved surfaces and lighting. Campus-wide environmental benefits will include a stormwater retention system beneath the new fields and within parking areas, diverting runoff which currently overstresses nearby streams. Finally, the project generates a critical strategic opportunity for the future: the new parking area can support long-term academic development within walking distance of all of Princeton's academic neighborhoods.

Such a comprehensive and integrated solution is the result of a planning process that seeks to address multiple challenges with each concept. Once development occurs that precludes future flexibility and sustainability, it is extremely difficult to reverse. By addressing parking, walkability, open space, stormwater, and flexibility for future growth in a single move, the University demonstrates the priority it attaches to long-term sustainability and effective use of limited land.

As the planning process began, Lewis Library, designed by Frank Gehry, was already under construction.

Lewis Library under construction, 2007

A PLAN IN ACTION

This will not be the proverbial "plan on a shelf." The recommendations of the Campus Plan are being implemented even as this book is published, making the maps and images shown in the following chapters a snapshot at a point in time, as much as they are a guide for the future.

Planning in the midst of a construction campaign

Princeton could not afford the luxury of stopping its ongoing construction activity to engage in a multi-year planning process. The process itself began in 2005 and ended in 2008; when it began, the Whitman College residential complex and Lewis Library were already under construction. Architects and engineers were at work designing a new Chemistry building and pedestrian bridge across Washington Road. The University also needed immediate assistance selecting a site for new buildings for the expanded study of neuroscience and the associated relocation of the psychology department.

The challenge of planning a campus in the midst of such a dynamic environment was significant. These pressures proved inspirational, however: the planning team immediately saw opportunities to leverage these projects to effect a transformation of large areas of campus, and to road-test ideas that might later become campus-wide strategies. Each project could fit into the context of a larger vision, even if the Campus Plan was then only loosely defined.

The planning process was unique in its seamless integration with these ongoing development initiatives. From the beginning, the team was closely involved with projects at various stages of design, benefiting from the access granted by the University to the parties responsible for their implementation. The result has produced enduring benefits for both the historic and growing areas of campus. These opportunities may have been lost had the plan been conceived in isolation from the ongoing decision-making processes within the various departments of the University.

By the time work on the Campus Plan was completed, some of its recommendations had already become reality. For example, Whitman College has been elegantly integrated with its surroundings through the use of landscape and the historic Beatrix Farrand-designed landscape of Holder Court has been restored and upgraded. Other projects proposed or influenced by the plan were in various stages of implementation: construction had begun on the new Butler College and Chemistry buildings; and the Peter B. Lewis Center for the Arts, Neuroscience and Psychology buildings, and proposed new parking facility were in the process of design and implementation.

As a result of the Campus Plan, the landscape surrounding the planned Chemistry building has been designed as an environmentally sustainable stormwater management system.

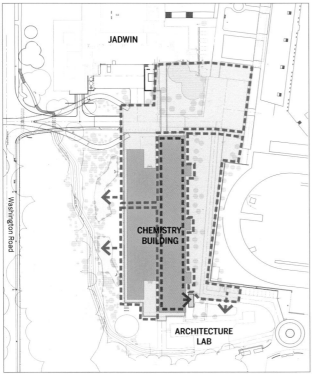

Chemistry building stormwater site plan

- Building site area
- Building roof area
- Biofiltration landscapes
- Water capture and reuse
- Stormwater drainage area

All of these elements are highly integrated: for new buildings to be occupied by their proposed opening dates, parking to support them must exist and necessary changes in the transportation network must be in place. Landscapes and pathways must permit students, faculty, and staff to walk to and from their new classrooms and offices to their dormitories and cars. Signage must direct visitors to new destinations. In addition, a complex sequence of public discussions and approvals is required before any project can move forward. Finally, each element has been scheduled to allow the whole campus to function during the course of ten years of construction.

From plan to action: the Chemistry building

One of the most successful examples of the integration of planning and implementation occurred with the new Chemistry building. The planning team observed that the proposed site lay close to a sensitive environmental area, including a stream and forested ravine, and hypothesized that the landscape and site engineering of the building could utilize an environmentally sustainable approach with wider campus benefits.

The project presented an opportunity to restore eroded stream banks and slopes, reduce sediments and pollutants in water flow to the lake, and strengthen the overall health of native woodlands. The resulting design includes, among other environmental strategies, a natural "biofiltration" system to manage stormwater runoff, using plants and landscapes to filter pollutants while beautifying the building's setting. These concepts complement the sustainabililty techniques planned by Hopkins Architects for the building itself.

The Chemistry building landscape plan would become one component of an integrated stormwater management strategy for much of the eastern campus, intended to reduce the impacts of upstream runoff sources on streams and natural areas. The system will protect the unique natural resources of the campus and mitigate the impact of the University's large landholdings on water quality in the Stony Brook/Millstone River watershed.

A work in progress continues

Thanks to a productive collaboration between the planning team and Princeton's staff and administration, hundreds of ideas representing wide-ranging aspects of campus policy now fit into the University's plans for the future. Some originated with the planning consultants, while others were inspired by longstanding concepts which have found a place in the larger planning scheme, or by the creative efforts of architects and designers working in parallel to the planning effort. The Campus Plan's major contribution is the consolidation of all of these initiatives into a coherent framework that guides their evaluation and execution so they work together seamlessly.

Throughout the process, studies and ideas were vigorously challenged and questioned, primarily through the forum of the monthly Campus Planning Steering Committee, chaired by President Tilghman, as well as in frequent sessions with the University's administration and staff, and periodic reviews with the Board of Trustees' Committee on Grounds and Buildings. The aim was to ensure that each problem had been thoroughly examined, the pros and cons of possible alternatives were understood, and every resulting concept was consistent with the culture and character of Princeton's physical and social landscape. No action would be taken that would not meet the highest standards of stewardship for the 250-year-old legacy of campus design that this generation has inherited and cherished. Princeton is very aware of the fact that the impact of today's decisions will be felt 20, 50, even 100 years from now. If a concept did not measure up to the highest standards, it would not be adopted. If it had merit but was not feasible or affordable, alternatives would be rigorously studied until a solution was found that was both visionary and practical.

While the plan seeks to be as comprehensive as possible, it is certainly not the end of the natural ongoing planning process at the University. Some areas which will be the subject of continued development in the short term include: improved accommodation of bicycles on campus; policies to consolidate loading, garbage collection, and deliveries in order to reduce the impact of vehicles on campus landscapes; preservation needs of the many historic buildings on campus; and the accessibility of all buildings and campus areas for the disabled, a particular challenge given the age of many of Princeton's buildings and its hillside location. The University's Office of Sustainability is also in the process of integrating the Campus Plan's recommendations into an overall campus sustainability strategy, which considers sustainability comprehensively across all campus policies, and connects practice with academic and research programs.

Looking beyond the ten-year horizon that is the core of this plan, every effort has been made to prepare for longer-term development, and to avoid precluding opportunities for future development through the overly expedient satisfaction of short-term needs. The plan has determined that after 2016, space remains for substantial growth within the compact, walkable space of the main campus north of Lake Carnegie. Many seemingly small choices within this plan are designed to maximize these opportunities, while maintaining a balance of open space and sustainable infrastructure. Rather than attempting to be overly specific, the plan seeks to preserve options and flexibility for future growth. Later planning efforts will build upon and modify these opportunities, solving problems and meeting needs that cannot be predicted today.

These future plans will begin to define a more complete vision for Princeton's main campus, for a time when all of its available sites have been developed. By maintaining a walkable campus for as long as possible, the opportunity, and the challenge, of expansion to remote sites is preserved for future generations, who will look beyond the campus boundaries to meet the ever-evolving needs of the University's academic and research mission. Even then, there will likely continue to be reason to revise, redevelop, and renew the main campus, which, as its history teaches, is a continual work in progress, undergoing constant change.

Students enjoy the walk to Lauritzen Hall in Whitman College

1 Raymond P. Rhinehart, *The Campus Guide: Princeton University* (New York, Princeton University Press, 1999), 2

2 Gerald Breese, *Princeton University Land* (New York, Princeton University Press, 1986)

3 Breese, 33

4 Don Oberdorfer, *Princeton University: The First 250 Years* (The Trustees of Princeton University, 1995), 224

5 Breese, 122-155

6 Contiguous main campus only, not including the Graduate College or other off-campus property holdings

Nassau Hall

HOW THE UNIVERSITY RELATES TO ITS CAMPUS

Princeton University's campus is one of its most precious assets. The first time I visited the campus I was captivated by the stately dignity of Nassau Hall and its canopy of trees, the eclectic collection of architectural styles that mysteriously fit together, and the way buildings define inviting green spaces, and paths create new vistas at every turn. My lasting impression was of a special place that had been lovingly stewarded by generation after generation.

My reaction is shared by many first-time visitors to campus, but it wasn't until I joined the faculty that I understood that our predecessors had been attentive to far more than aesthetics. They had purposefully designed the campus to support the University's most important goals. While the beauty of our campus inspires and refreshes us, it also opens our minds to new possibilities, and its intimacy advances our goal of integrating academic and extracurricular life. The campus is knit together to reflect a strong sense of community, with classrooms and cafés interspersed so that faculty and students may gather both formally and informally. It is a common sight on a fall or spring afternoon to see a precept on Cannon Green conclude, and be followed within minutes by students tossing frisbees.

There is also an elegant logic to the way the campus evolved to support the growth of academic disciplines. The natural sciences and engineering, with their need for large and sophisticated research facilities, have moved down and across Washington Road—first Palmer, Green, Frick, and Guyot Halls, and when they would no longer suffice for a world-class university, the E-Quad, Jadwin, and Lewis Thomas. The social sciences clustered around the fountain on Scudder Plaza, with the Woodrow Wilson School as the interdisciplinary glue. And of course the humanities, where the University began, maintain their place of honor on the historic campus near Firestone.

As we plan for the next decade of campus growth and add more space for the arts, we need to strengthen all these neighborhoods and their interconnections, even as we continue to express our highest aspirations in the buildings and green spaces we construct and preserve.

Shirley M. Tilghman
President of the University

THE FIVE GUIDING PRINCIPLES

Following the University's decision to grow within its main campus setting north of Lake Carnegie, President Tilghman articulated five guiding principles to steer the planning process.

MAINTAIN A PEDESTRIAN-ORIENTED CAMPUS

From the heart of the student-oriented campus, the Frist Campus Center, nearly all areas of the Core Campus are within a ten-minute walk. This "walkable" design is one of the campus' strengths, and a guide for future growth is to maintain that quality. This suggests a strategy of concentration and density rather than diffusion and sprawl.

PRESERVE THE PARK-LIKE CHARACTER OF THE CAMPUS

Princeton's characteristic combination of open spaces, gardens, and intimate courtyards creates "the revelation of the unexpected," in the words of the University's master architect of the early 20th century, Ralph Adams Cram. Preserving this park-like quality and extending it to more areas of the campus is a core principle in planning for the future.

MAINTAIN CAMPUS NEIGHBORHOODS WHILE PROMOTING A SENSE OF COMMUNITY

Future growth should respect Princeton's existing academic, residential, and architectural neighborhoods, providing each with a distinct identity while emphasizing the sense of an integrated campus community.

BUILD IN AN ENVIRONMENTALLY RESPONSIBLE MANNER

Building upon Princeton's extensive record in environmental sustainability, new development should be sensitive to the natural landscape, air and water quality, resource conservation, and energy efficiency in building design. Future growth must take into account aggressive measures to reduce the campus's greenhouse gas emissions to their 1990 levels.

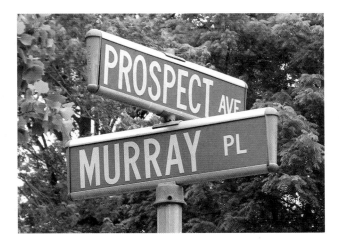

SUSTAIN STRONG COMMUNITY RELATIONS

Orderly growth will require that we sustain our historically strong relationships with the surrounding communities.

CHAPTER 2
CAMPUS AND COMMUNITY

To shape a realistic ten-year Campus Plan, Princeton had to balance the needs and desires of two interdependent communities. The University, a thriving community in itself, is home to a changeable population that interacts on many levels with the neighboring Princeton Borough and Princeton Township, a civic community of some 30,000 people including many longtime residents. These groups share a mutually beneficial relationship, and sustaining strong community relations became one of this plan's guiding principles. To this end, the University encouraged public dialogue among the planning team, stakeholders, and local citizens. Their feedback helped to shape the plan's approach to major issues—transportation, traffic, pedestrian safety, housing, and development along the campus edges—and also confirmed widespread support for environmental sustainability initiatives.

The FitzRandolph Gate at Nassau Street

Dialogue with Our Neighbors and the University Community

Joined by a common history dating to the pre-revolutionary colonial period, as well as numerous contemporary economic and social interrelationships, Princeton University and the Princeton community are indelibly linked. Although the University owns property in five municipalities, its main campus areas are located in Princeton Borough and Princeton Township, collectively home to just over 30,000 residents. Defined by its appealing and historic downtown, Princeton is one of the most compact and walkable town centers in New Jersey. According to a recent study, a remarkable 36 percent of residents walk to work compared to 3 percent statewide. The availability of retail, services, and even a railroad link to the Northeast Corridor within walking distance of residential neighborhoods makes Princeton a unique community.

Princeton University is one of the top five employers in the region, with over 5,000 full-time-equivalent workers. The University is located in two counties, Mercer and Middlesex, and in Mercer County alone it is estimated that in fiscal year 2005 the University's direct and indirect economic activity created $1.38 billion in spending, as well as 1,648 non-University jobs, and 429 construction jobs. In the same year, students spent $40 million in the local economy, and 700,000 visitors to the University and the McCarter Theatre Center spent an additional $39 million. The University is the largest taxpayer in both Princeton Borough and Princeton Township, and it makes an annual

(and increasing) voluntary contribution to Princeton Borough that in 2007 was more than $1 million. In recent years it also has made significant financial contributions to the school system, the public library, the hospital, the arts center, the first aid and rescue squad, and other organizations, and it has provided support for open space and affordable housing.

The University also subsidizes the local movie theater and the historical society, and recently took the initiative to make sure Princeton would continue to have an excellent independent bookstore right on Nassau Street. The campus provides green space, which is highly valued by residents of Princeton as a recreational asset and for its vistas and environmental benefits, as well as intellectual, cultural, athletic, and other activities and resources that are available to the public. These include the Princeton University Art Museum, the Cotsen Children's Library, the Chapel, a Community Auditing Program, and concerts and other programs in Richardson Auditorium. In the fall of 2007, students at the University founded a farmers market on campus that was open to all.

As with any relationship between a large university and its community, the University can also be a source of concerns, often centering on issues related to campus growth. Over time, as both the campus and the community see increased development, and as growth in the surrounding region puts increased pressure on already taxed road systems and infrastructure, such concerns are naturally heightened. Many of these concerns are shared by members of the University community, which consists of students, faculty, staff, and to some extent alumni and others who feel strong personal attachments to the campus. Members of both the on-campus community and the off-campus community are stakeholders in the process of planning for the campus of the future, and from the beginning opportunities were developed to provide information to them and seek their views.

One of the five guiding principles articulated by President Tilghman at the outset of the planning effort, "sustain strong community relations," signals the University's recognition that it does not—and does not wish to—live in an enclave behind ivy-covered walls, but rather that it is and aims to be a positive and respectful citizen of the communities in which it resides. With community relations established early as a priority for the planning process, the University and the planning consultants were able to engage in numerous public discussions and workshops, including an unprecedented public open house called "Plans in Progress" that was attended by nearly 900 people who provided significant input at the midpoint of the process. Following the open house, an interactive Campus Plan website provided a continuing forum for feedback from the community.

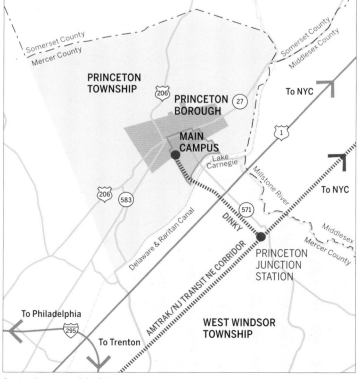

Regional context of the Princeton campus

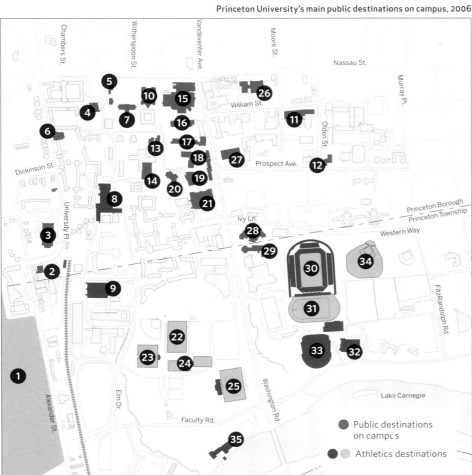

Princeton University's main public destinations on campus, 2006

● Public destinations on campus

● Athletics destinations

MAIN PUBLIC DESTINATIONS ON CAMPUS

1 Springdale Golf Course
2 Dinky station, Wawa, and commuter lot
3 McCarter Theatre Center
4 Richardson Auditorium (Alexander Hall)
5 Maclean House
6 University Store
7 Nassau Hall
8 Dillon Gymnasium
9 Baker Rink
10 Chancellor Green/East Pyne
11 Friend Center
12 Carl A. Fields Center

13 Murray/Dodge Halls
14 Princeton University Art Museum
15 Firestone Library
16 University Chapel
17 McCosh Hall
18 Architecture School
19 Woolworth Center of Musical Studies
20 Prospect House
21 Frist Campus Center
22 Roberts Stadium
23 Lenz Tennis Center

24 Tennis Courts
25 Class of 1952 Stadium
26 185 Nassau Street
27 Robertson Hall and Scudder Plaza
28 Lewis Library
29 Taplin Auditorium (Fine Hall)
30 Princeton Stadium
31 Weaver Track and Field
32 DeNunzio Pool
33 Jadwin Gymnasium
34 Clarke Field
35 Shea Rowing Center

For the Princeton University campus—as for many other campuses and the country as a whole—the late 1960s were a time of enormous intellectual, social, and political ferment. It was a transformational era for the country as opposition to the war in Vietnam intensified and battles for human and civil rights took on renewed urgency. It was also a transformational era for Princeton, with women admitted as undergraduates for the first time in 1969; students of color admitted for the first time in significant numbers; and governance changes that, among other things, added students to the annual budgeting process and young alumni to the Board of Trustees.

One of the most disturbing symbols of what many saw as Princeton's isolation from the world beyond its borders was the closed FitzRandolph Gate. The gate separated the campus from the community, and like the University's inward looking courtyards and its unmarked buildings and paths, it seemed to send a clear message that the campus was for insiders, and outsiders should remain outside. This view was roundly rejected by the campus community of the late 1960s and, in one of the more dramatic moments of that era, the graduating class of 1970 opened the gate and engraved in it the words "Together for Community." It has remained open ever since.

The opening of the gate marked the beginning of initiatives that continue today to connect the University with the community in multiple ways. Some of these are architectural, such as the more open lawns on Nassau Street in front of Maclean House and the Andlinger Center for the Humanities. Some are programmatic, ranging from community auditing to Communiversity, from athletic venues to cultural events, from the children's library to the Art Museum. Some mobilize the volunteer energies of hundreds of students each year; others involve University investments in helping to meet a broad range of community needs. And some involve the simple act of outreach: inviting members of the community to an open house on campus planning, or improving wayfinding so our neighbors will feel more welcome to explore the beauty of the campus and enjoy both its liveliness and its serenity.

Brent Henry
Chair, Trustee Committee
on Public Affairs

November 2006 Plans in Progress event

December 2007 Princeton Regional Planning Board meeting

November 2006 Plans in Progress event

CAMPUS PLAN PRESENTATIONS TO THE PUBLIC AND THE UNIVERSITY COMMUNITY

2005

2006

December
Undergraduate Student Life Committee, University Student Government, and Graduate Student Government

February
Undergraduate Class Officers

March
Princeton Regional Planning Board

April
Princeton Borough Council and Princeton Township Committee

June
Academic and Administrative Managers Group

July
Alexander Street/ University Place Open House

September
Council of the Princeton Universit[y] Community

As a result of the "Plans in Progress" open house and other opportunities for public input, the planning team was able to collect feedback from diverse groups of people both within and outside the University. While input was wide-ranging in its subject matter, a number of recurring themes became clear.

Dinky station

Many people had questions or expressed concerns about the proposal to relocate the Dinky railroad station approximately 460 feet to the south in conjunction with the development of the planned Peter B. Lewis Center for the Arts. The critical importance of the Dinky to the life of the community (and to the University) was underscored by a wide range of people. At the same time, many expressed support for the creation of additional services at the station that are not currently available, including an open and accessible waiting room, additional retail offerings, more convenient parking, better accommodations for bikes, and links to the University shuttle system and a community jitney service. Many also supported the idea of an arts-related development adjacent to McCarter and Berlind theaters. The idea of introducing retail establishments such as restaurants and cafés to support the arts development and Dinky riders was generally popular, although tempered by a concern that they complement, not compete with, Nassau Street businesses.

Pedestrian safety

Pedestrian safety was a common concern for both the University population and neighbors, particularly where large numbers of students frequently cross major arterial roadways such as Washington Road and Alexander Street. Many students, faculty, and employees also noted that some campus pathways lacked adequate lighting, drainage, and accessibility for the disabled, creating unsafe or unwelcoming conditions.

Parking

Parking was a frequent issue both for employees of the University and its neighbors. While many in the community expressed support for the proposed new parking facility east of the stadium, some neighbors expressed concern about the appearance of the facility and sought assurance that the traffic patterns into and out of the facility would minimize impacts on neighboring streets.

Campus growth

University staff noted the impacts of campus growth in several ways. Some identified the need to adjust to different parking locations, and others expressed concern that their offices may be relocated off-campus to create additional space for academic development, although they welcomed some of the ameneties that could be provided at off-campus locations. Additionally, members of the staff responsible for maintenance, services, security, and other areas expressed concern that resources will be stretched by the increase in the number of campus buildings.

Sustainability

Broad support was expressed by all groups for the proposed initiatives in environmental sustainability, campus landscape, and restoration of natural ecological areas. Others expressed an interest in additional sustainability initiatives, in particular for the enhancement of facilities for bicycling.

Campus architecture

Strong opinions on the style of campus architecture were common, particularly from students but also from others. The recent construction of Whitman College in a collegiate gothic style spurred numerous calls for a return to gothic architecture for new campus buildings. Other voices, however, called for Princeton also to continue to be a place where some of the world's leading architects can make major contributions to defining a campus that is both anchored in a distinctive history and ever evolving to meet new needs and new challenges in a changing world.

> The townsfolk of Princeton won a competition to bring a fledgling college campus to their community in 1756, and both campus and community have drawn upon each other for sustenance ever since. The planning process invigorated an already lively dialogue between these two diverse, dynamic, and ever-evolving organisms.
>
> —ROBERT K. DURKEE,
> VICE PRESIDENT AND SECRETARY OF THE UNIVERSITY

2007

October Department Chairs	November Plans in Progress: Open Forum for Campus and Community	November Undergraduate Student Life Committee	December Princeton Regional Planning Board—joint meeting with Borough Council and Township Committee	February Alumni Day	April Princeton Regional Planning Board— Master Plan Subcommittee	June Academic and Administrative Managers Group

THE ISSUES: AREAS OF PARTICULAR COMMUNITY INTEREST IN THE PLANNING PROCESS

New Jersey requires all municipalities to update their master plans periodically. By coincidence, the Princeton Regional Planning Board (which oversees long-range planning for both Princeton Borough and Princeton Township) had a review scheduled for 2007, which allowed for considerable overlap with the campus planning process. During the two-year campus planning process, representatives of the planning board and the University met on several occasions, both informally and in public session, to discuss areas of common interest.

Since the community plan had previously anticipated that the University would expand in West Windsor, these discussions focused on the implications of the University's decision to grow instead as a more compact, pedestrian-oriented campus on the Princeton side of Lake Carnegie. In general, the goals of the master plan and the campus plan were well aligned and local officials expressed support for the University's guiding principles.

CAMPUS AND COMMUNITY EDGES

While the community takes an interest in all growth on campus, in part because any growth has an impact on traffic, parking, the environment, and public services, it takes particular interest in growth near the edges of the campus. Much of the University's growth over the next ten years will be along its southern edge where it owns all of the land between the campus and the lake. The community has an interest in the University's sustained commitment to Faculty Road (which it owns and maintains) as a distributor of traffic that can enter and leave the campus without traveling through community neighborhoods, and it has a strong interest in maintaining community access to Lake Carnegie as a highly valued amenity. However, the principal issues raised by the Campus Plan focused on the northern, eastern, and western edges.

The North Edge Nassau Street is the historic dividing line between campus and town, forming one of the most distinctive and archetypal "college town" images in America, although there have long been exceptions to the rule. For example, the building known as Lower Pyne that still stands at the northeast corner of Nassau and Witherspoon streets was originally constructed in 1896 as a University dormitory. It was converted to University office use in 1950 and continued to serve that purpose until it was sold in 1984. The University also has owned Palmer House, at the corner of Nassau Street and Bayard Lane, since 1969, and uses it to provide overnight accommodations for University guests. Some administrative offices are located in tax-paying office buildings north of Nassau Street, and while it is the University's policy not to cross Nassau Street except in unusual circumstances, a number of exceptions have been made in recent years, especially when the purpose is to help sustain the vitality of the downtown business district. This

is one of the reasons that the University made a significant investment in the rehabilitation and restoration of the Garden (movie) Theater in 2001 and played an instrumental role in bringing one of the nation's leading independent bookstores, Labyrinth Books, to Nassau Street, along with a satellite of the Princeton University Store, an independent entity that sells Princeton apparel and other insignia items. Both stores reinforce the retail presence on Nassau Street and provide ratable properties for the borough.

The East Edge Unlike the well-defined boundary of Nassau Street, the east and west edges of campus have grown gradually over time. To the east, campus expansion in the 1960s and 1970s brought buildings, primarily in the Engineering Quadrangle, close to residential neighborhoods that consist largely of small single-family homes. In 2005, after thorough discussion with neighbors and public officials, a revised "E3 zone" ordinance was adopted for the area abutting these neighborhoods that carefully defines the parameters for future expansion in the E-Quad and in the area roughly bordered by Prospect Avenue, Olden Street, William Street, and Washington Road. The ordinance strengthens the buffer behind the homes on the west side of Murray Place, defining an eastern edge of the campus north of Prospect Avenue. This plan extends the concept of a defined eastern edge to the south by identifying FitzRandolph Road as a boundary beyond which the University proposes not to locate academic buildings. There are plans for housing and support uses such as additional capacity for daycare and some athletic fields east of FitzRandolph, but those are all uses compatible with the residential character of this neighborhood. A proposed new parking facility is intended to meet current and future parking needs in a way that minimizes the likelihood that growth in this area will have an impact on traffic or parking on neighboring streets.

The West Edge This edge of campus is well defined along University Place and College Road but is in a period of transition along Alexander Street south of University Place. This area historically has been defined by the transportation and service uses that followed the canal and later the railroad line into campus and town, and it continues to be a major gateway into the Princeton community from Route 1 by both car and train (and in the future potentially by bus rapid transit as well). The Alexander Street corridor south of the Arts and Transit Neighborhood is one of the few areas of Princeton zoned and used for service activities, such as gas stations and light industrial uses. Many of those establishments have moved or gone out of business in recent decades, and the University has obtained many of these properties for eventual development. This plan assumes that a gas station will continue to be located here, but leaves flexibility for future discussion of potential uses for the rest of the area. While no immediate development is proposed, the overall strategy is to promote mixed-use development that takes advantage of access to transit, while maintaining service uses that benefit the community.

THE ARTS AND TRANSIT
NEIGHBORHOOD AND THE DINKY

Significant discussions have focused on proposed changes to the terminus of the Dinky train that New Jersey Transit operates between Princeton and Princeton Junction. The level of interest in this proposal illustrates the importance that many attach to this service, which connects travelers to the Northeast Corridor and thus New York City, Philadelphia, Newark Liberty International Airport, and many other destinations. The Dinky is an important link for University students, faculty, staff, and visitors, which is why the University historically has provided significant financial support for the rail service and taken responsibility for maintaining the station buildings and providing parking spaces for commuters. After extensive study and consultation with New Jersey Transit, it was deemed necessary to move the station as part of an integrated development anchored by the proposed Peter B. Lewis Center for the Arts, while meeting neighborhood parking needs and accommodating the potential addition of bus rapid transit service. The plan minimizes the distance of this move, while creating a vastly improved transportation facility for all users.

A new Transit Plaza would enable multi-modal connections to the train, including a proposed community jitney service, campus shuttles, taxis, bike storage, and future bus rapid transit service, which would extend beyond the station into the community. The design of the plaza and surrounding roadways would optimize the movement of all of these systems, reducing the current congestion resulting from a roadway layout that was not originally intended for the volumes and types of traffic now in the area. Relocating the rail terminus would also permit direct access to the University's west garage from Alexander Street, providing convenient parking for patrons of new and existing arts activities including McCarter and Berlind theaters, and reducing travel distance, thus reducing congestion and pollution, for many University employees who park in the garage.

The Transit Plaza would also include a new station building with an indoor waiting room, café, and newsstand, a relocated Wawa store closer to the station, and convenient parking replacing all current spaces. The adjacent arts complex and plaza would offer riders opportunities to enjoy outdoor cultural activities, visit exhibitions and performances, and patronize new retail establishments. While the new station location would require a slightly longer walk for pedestrians, they will have new public transit options for getting to and from the Dinky, as well as a more pleasant walk and an improved waiting experience at the station.

Nassau Street

LOCAL AND REGIONAL TRAFFIC

Several proposed projects affect existing traffic patterns and roadway configurations. The plan leverages the opportunity of campus redevelopment to improve the roadway network, mitigate congestion points, and optimize the flow of traffic in the regional system.

The University generates traffic in the form of daily commuters and visitors. The majority of vehicles that arrive on campus approach from Route 206 south, or from Route 1 via Alexander Street and Washington Road. While the plan redistributes and expands parking facilities across the campus to meet the needs of the next ten years, it maintains the current balance of traffic volumes on these approach roads by utilizing University-owned Faculty Road as a "collector-distributor," shifting commuters from their road of approach to their assigned parking location. This strategy gets cars off the regional network as early as possible, and reduces impacts on neighborhood streets.

At the proposed Arts and Transit Neighborhood, one planning strategy is to relocate administrative office spaces out of the congested Alexander Street corridor, thus reducing the University's contribution to peak hour commuters in the area. These commuters would be replaced with visitors to arts and cultural activities, making maximum use of less congested off-peak times such as afternoons and evenings. A proposed roundabout at the intersection of Alexander Street and University Place, together with a relocation of the Wawa store and a major pedestrian crossing, would greatly improve this seriously congested intersection, with local and regional benefits.

Other traffic planning strategies are described in later pages. Working from this conceptual framework, the University will continue an ongoing dialogue and partnership with the township and borough of Princeton and other agencies to more fully develop the details of traffic planning initiatives.

AFFORDABLE HOUSING

By state mandate, municipalities in New Jersey must ensure that development within their borders includes provision for affordable housing. This means that as the University plans additional housing for its faculty, staff, and graduate students and adds new space to meet its academic and other needs, it also must help provide additional non-University affordable housing in the community. The University has a long history of supporting such housing in Princeton Borough and Princeton Township, with annual contributions to both municipalities for this purpose as well as the contribution of property near the Lawrence Apartments. Recently, the University has agreed to purchase land in the community for affordable housing; to construct affordable units on a borough street adjacent to its Stanworth apartments; and to expand the number of units available in the township through Princeton Community Housing, an organization that the University helped establish 40 years ago. While the state formula for determining the number of affordable units associated with university construction remains under review, the University is prepared to meet the resulting obligations, while continuing to provide substantial housing for its faculty, staff, and graduate students, who therefore do not have to compete for lower-cost housing in the broader community.

CHAPTER 3
THE EVOLUTION OF
A CAMPUS (1756-2006)

Princeton University has always been a dynamic institution, evolving from a two-building college in a rural town to a thriving University at the heart of a busy multifaceted community. The campus changed dramatically in the last century with the introduction of iconic "collegiate gothic" architecture and significant postwar expansion. Although the campus exudes a sense of permanence and timelessness, it supports a living institution that must always grow in pace with new academic disciplines and changing student expectations. The Campus Plan anticipates an expansion of 2.1 million additional square feet over ten years, and proposes to achieve this growth while applying the Five Guiding Principles.

1906 view of Princeton University by Richard Rummel. In this view, the original train station can be seen below Blair Hall, whose archway formed a ceremonial entrance to the campus for rail travelers. The station was moved to its current location in the 1920s.

Campus History

Starting as a small academic enclave in a pastoral setting, the campus has grown in its 250 years to span almost 400 acres.

In 1753, after competing with New Brunswick, the community of "Prince-Town" persuaded the trustees of the College of New Jersey to select it as the new site for the growing institution, based in part on what were seen as the pedagogic benefits of a sheltered location far from the corrupting influence of cities. Land was donated by the FitzRandolph family for the relocation of the college from Newark, where it had moved a few years before from its original home in Elizabeth. The relocation was completed in 1756.

The unique terrain of the chosen site resulted from its situation "...on the first high land which separates the alluvial plain of South Jersey from the mountainous and hilly country of the north. There is a gentle depression between it and the mountain, and a gradual decent on every other side of it towards the streams that nearly encircle it." [1] Understanding this underlying geology does much to explain the experience of Princeton's campus as a stepping hillside whose wide-open southern vistas are today obscured by the growth of trees and construction of buildings. The woodlands and fields below the campus would permit the growing University to expand far beyond its original 4.5-acre tract—a boundary line still visible today, traced by the path of McCosh Walk across the upper campus.

The shape of the land influenced architects and landscape architects, particularly between 1900 and 1940, who made use of its hills and escarpments to create the dramatic compositions and sense of spaciousness which define the unique character of the campus. Despite its modern density of development, the campus still maintains a character of open views and lack of enclosure that contrasts with that of many other universities defined by quadrangles. The terrain also has a newfound importance in this Campus Plan—which seeks to recover the symbiotic relationship between campus design and natural systems, and to restore the environmental health of the woodlands and watersheds on which the campus is built.

The design of Nassau Hall, which once housed the entire college, was adapted from the College of William and Mary, and its collegiate symbolism would in turn influence university buildings around the country including those of Harvard, Brown, Dartmouth, Georgetown, and Rutgers.[2] A unique feature of the design was the decision to locate the building 300 feet back from Nassau Street, Princeton's

In this 1875 view, with Nassau Street in the foreground, Princeton's campus can be seen occupying high ground overlooking the Stony Brook, now Lake Carnegie, and a sweeping vista of farms and open land which has now become the Route 1 corridor of shopping malls and office parks. In this period the campus still occupied its original 4.5-acre land grant, which has now expanded to almost 400 acres.

The basic pattern of the campus layout, with rows of buildings following east-west walks which step down the hillside, is already clear in this view. Although many buildings shown here were demolished over time to accommodate growth and changing architectural tastes, and many new buildings were added, the fundamental relationship of the campus to the natural terrain is still intact.

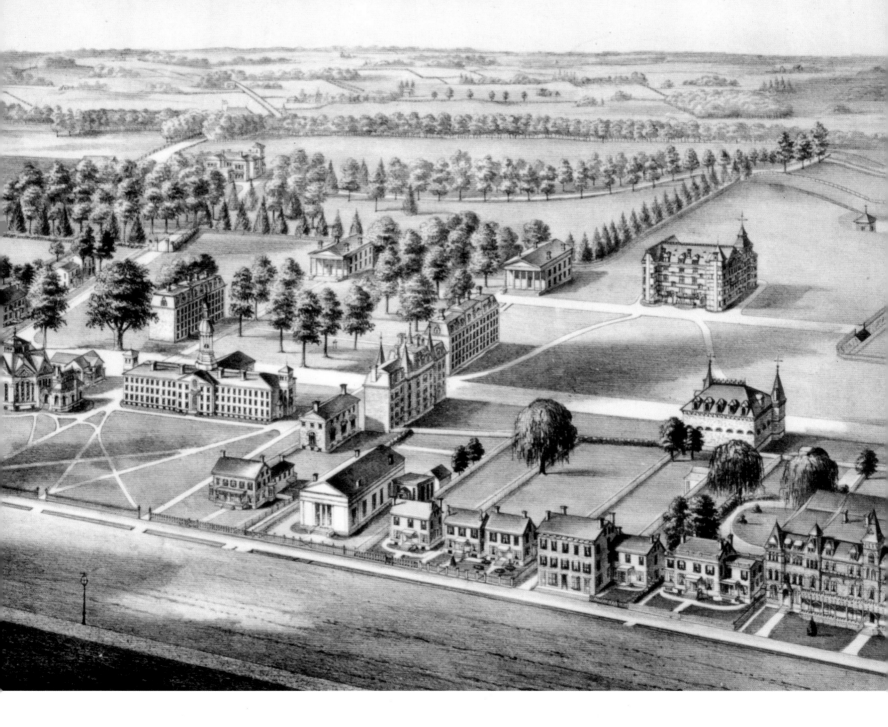

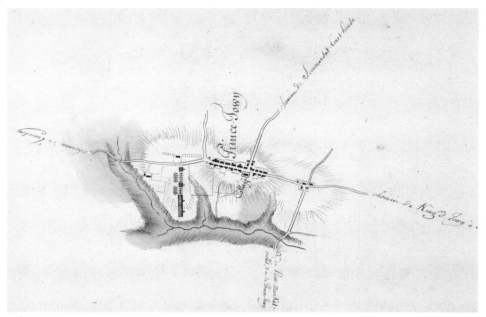

Topographic map of Princeton University by Louis-Alexandre Berthier, 1781
Depicting an encampment of the Continental Army during the Revolutionary War, this map also clearly shows Nassau Hall located on a hill above three streams leading to the Stony Brook valley below. Though altered by development, these streams are still important natural features of the campus.

Plan for the Architectural and Topographical Development of Princeton University, Ralph Adams Cram, 1911
This plan reveals a subtle combination of axial symmetry with informal building arrangements following the terrain. New buildings define courtyards and create walls around the edge of campus, separating it from the surrounding town. A notable feature of the plan is its "upside down" orientation—with north pointing downwards—so that Nassau Hall is clearly identified as the front of campus.

main street. This pairing of a broad open green space with a building inspired the first known American use of the word "campus" to describe the grounds of a university or college, in 1774, supplanting the earlier term "yard" still used today to refer to the historic grounds of Harvard and other universities.[3] At Princeton, this marriage of architecture and landscape began with Nassau Hall would become a defining quality over the University's long development.

Today the very idea of campus is synonymous with American education. As described by John Turner, the author of the most comprehensive history of American campus planning, "The word campus, more than any other term, sums up the unique physical character of the American college and university...[B]eyond these purely physical meanings, the word has taken on other connotations, suggesting the pervasive spirit of a school, or its *genius loci*, as embodied in its architecture and grounds. Campus sums up the distinctive physical qualities of the American college, but also its integrity as a self-contained community and its architectural expression of educational and social ideals." [4]

Princeton's campus design evolved with changing tastes and planning trends, and while each generation sought to define the look of the campus, many of the traces and monuments of previous eras persisted. In the late 1800s, President McCosh deliberately commissioned buildings in an eclectic range of architectural styles, but insisted on a robust landscape and park-like character for the overall space. Later, attempts to create a sense of greater order were interspersed with counteracting efforts to create picturesque and varied spaces and buildings. The resulting mix, with some areas more unified and some more varied, is one of the reasons the campus is so appealing today. In the words of architects Robert Venturi and Denise Scott Brown, who designed five major buildings on campus between 1983 and 1999, this syncopation has "made the Campus Plan incomplete and yet ironically whole at any one time." [5]

In 1906, ten years after the College of New Jersey renamed itself Princeton University, the trustees appointed Ralph Adams Cram to the newly established position of supervising architect, which he held until 1929. Although many of America's greatest architects would work on the campus over its history, with varying success, Cram remains the central figure who understood Princeton's nature as an institution, and the uniqueness of its site, better than any other. He was inspired by the vision of University President Woodrow Wilson to emulate the collegiate model of Oxford and Cambridge: "a place full of quiet chambers, secluded ancient courts, and gardens shut away from intrusion—a town full of coverts, for those who would learn and be with their own thoughts." [6] Cram's interpretation of this idea would transform the campus, breaking down the scale of the University into smaller architectural and social groupings centered on courtyards and sheltered from the surrounding town by walls and archways. The language of gothic architecture allowed Cram to design complex, picturesque spaces, creating for the observer "the revelation of the unexpected."

Cram's influence was seen not just in the design of individual buildings, but through a series of comprehensive master plans for the campus between 1908 and 1925, which would guide the work of numerous architects as late as the 1940s. According to Cram's biographer Douglass Shand-Tucci, "During that time and notwithstanding his other important collegiate gothic work...Cram created—not just in his firm's work but in that of others—what most would agree is the most resplendent gothic university campus in the New World." [7]

During the same period, Beatrix Farrand served as the supervising landscape architect, establishing the distinctive approach to landscape that together with the planning and architectural vision of Cram would create an enduring identity for the campus. Cram and Farrand often sharply disagreed over the design of the campus, but today it is clear that the University's buildings would not have the impact they do without the unifying power of the campus landscape—the simple and elegant greens, complementary plantings, tree canopy, and carefully choreographed views Farrand cultivated over three decades. Many of her landscapes survive today, including broad areas of campus, as well as numerous individual trees and her signature "wall plantings"—actual trees pruned to grow against the side of a building. Their endurance is a testament to her understanding of sustainable landscapes, a concept which this Campus Plan has reinvigorated.

The image of Princeton created in the first half of the 20th century is indelibly and lovingly held in the consciousness of anyone who has attended the University or visited the campus. Despite the rich variety of architectural styles on campus, the collegiate gothic period continues to be a defining characteristic of Princeton's campus identity. The power of this image is evidenced today by the immense popularity, especially among alumni and students, of the recently completed Whitman College dormitories, designed by Demitri Porphyrios in an interpretation of the University's gothic style, and constructed with a deep commitment to traditional methods of stoneworking and building.

After the Second World War, the University grew rapidly, increasing its square footage by over 150 percent by 1980. Campus growth was driven by the national emergence of the sciences as a major source of expansion for universities, reaching far beyond the traditional humanities that once defined the liberal arts college education. Princeton also saw the creation or expansion of its three professional schools: the School of Architecture, the School of Engineering and Applied Science, and the Woodrow Wilson School of Public and International Affairs.

In these postwar years, campus development occurred with a conscious shift away from the collegiate gothic vision of Ralph Adams Cram and his contemporaries. Buildings such as the Engineering Quadrangle, Jadwin and Fine halls, and the recently demolished Butler College dormitories contrasted with the historic campus not only because of their austere architecture, reflecting the modernist sensibilities of their designers, but also as a result of reduced attention to the landscapes and pathway connections that support and reinforce diverse architecture and unite it into a common campus setting. The size and bulk demanded by buildings for the sciences further departed from the intimate scale of the older campus; large introverted complexes with disconnected internal courtyards and blank exterior walls,

Wyman House Garden by Beatrix Farrand, 1941

New South by Edward Larrabee Barnes, 1971

Wu Hall by Venturi Scott Brown, 1983

such as Jadwin Physics and the E-Quad, worked against the planning of the campus, and continue to pose challenges today to the vitality of their surroundings.

In the 1980s and '90s, development on campus became more sensitive to context. The buildings of Robert Venturi and Denise Scott Brown exemplified a renewed interest in creating a modern identity for the campus that nonetheless made strong references to Princeton's historic architecture. Development during this period sought to impart a greater sense of coherent identity to an expanding space, and to create a sense of place in some of the less successful areas of the postwar campus.

Princeton as an institution has long ago been transformed from its English Protestant collegiate roots, which its gothic architecture aspired to symbolize, to a modern University of great diversity with myriad global influences, supporting the most advanced research and fields of

Icahn Laboratory by Rafael Viñoly, 2002

Both the public and the architectural community have tended to see the issue of tradition versus innovation in absolute terms: either the University turns its back on the past and commits to innovation, or it resists the new and stakes its claim for the continuity of tradition. This is clearly a false dilemma. Technology and society change continuously, and the most interesting architects working today are those who look for a synthesis of history with the demands of the present. The Campus Plan recognizes that it is above all the scale and texture of our outdoor spaces (both new and old) that make Princeton work so well. We need to honor the past through scale, materials, texture, and transition while still building innovative works of architecture that will effectively serve our teaching and research needs in the decades to come.

—STANLEY T. ALLEN,
  DEAN OF THE SCHOOL OF ARCHITECTURE

inquiry. Recent buildings on campus tell a story of the inherent tensions between the contemporary identity of the University, the integrated sense of the campus as a whole, and the individuality of the architect. Navigating these tensions can be a significant challenge for even the most skilled architects, especially in the storied context of Princeton's beloved campus. This Campus Plan advances the idea that diverse and open modern architecture, expressing the contemporary identity of the University, can successfully fit within the overall sense of campus established by enhanced attention to the landscape and careful planning of the campus layout.

The Icahn Laboratory, designed by Rafael Viñoly Architects, is one of the best recent examples of a confident contemporary building with a strong identity that nonetheless fits elegantly within the context of the campus. It joins two other buildings in the gentle curve of the Ellipse, an open space conceived as part of the 1995 master plan by Machado and Silvetti Associates. A major campus pathway follows the building's external structure alongside a grand public atrium containing a popular café. These features successfully weave the building into the pattern of campus life and allow it to contribute to a larger idea of the campus beyond the specialized needs of the Lewis-Sigler Institute for Integrative Genomics, which it contains.

If anything can be learned from this vibrant history, which expresses through the development of the campus the history of American planning, architecture, and landscape architecture, it is that the Princeton campus is not a pristine artifact frozen in time. Despite indelible images which instill a sense of permanence, the campus has in fact been continuously evolving and changing. This is the nature of a living institution at the leading edge of new fields of knowledge, for which growth is a matter of survival and continued preeminence in the world of higher learning.

It is important to view this Campus Plan in its historical context; while it may appear that the next ten years will yield dramatic changes to the scale and density of the campus, they are actually very consistent with the history of campus evolution. Over the course of 250 years, the campus has constantly grown. It has roughly doubled in size three times since 1900, and has seen gradual but continuous aesthetic and structural transformations and refinements. Princeton's campus is simultaneously a site of historic significance and a constantly evolving space, a "work in progress" that is never truly completed. This Campus Plan continues the evolution of the campus into its next stage, for which a new set of challenges must be confronted and solved.

1 John F. Hageman, quoted in Breese, 4-5

2 Paul Venable Turner, *Campus: An American Planning Tradition* (Cambridge, The MIT Press, 1984), 47

3 Breese, xvi

4 Turner, 4

5 Rhinehart, ix

6 Turner, 227

7 Douglass Shand-Tucci, *Ralph Adams Cram: An Architect's Four Quests* (Amherst and Boston, University of Massachusetts Press, 2005), 50

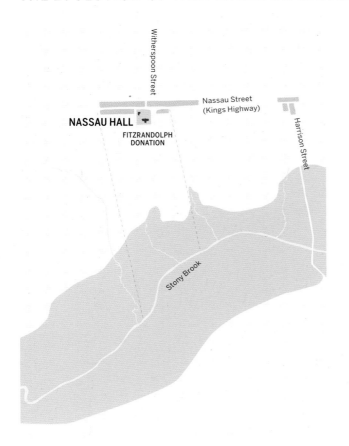

> "It [the campus] was as much a state of mind as an architectural style, charged with connotations of Athenian democracy, purity, wisdom, and independence."
> ....
> AS QUOTED IN "CAMPUS: AN AMERICAN PLANNING TRADITION," PAUL VENABLE TURNER, 1987

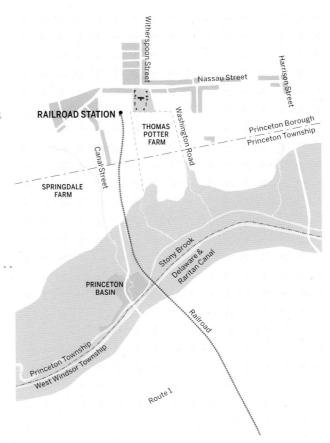

1756 A COLLEGE IN THE HEART OF NEW JERSEY

In the late 1600s, Nassau Street (then King's Highway) was a major traveling route between the Raritan River and the Delaware River. In the mid-1700s, located halfway along the route between New York and Philadelphia, the town of Prince-Town provided an overnight stay for travelers and began to grow along Nassau Street. In 1756, the College of New Jersey, as Princeton University was then known, was relocated from Newark, NJ, to Prince-Town, NJ, with approximately 70 students.

1852 THE CAMPUS' FIRST EXPANSION

Princeton developed into a village with relatively easy access to Philadelphia and New York. The campus was organized into an open quadrangle plan with a central axis and clear hierarchy, with Nassau Hall at the center. The new back campus quadrangle reflected the high value placed on the preservation of landscape openness by maintaining generous spaces between buildings.

The town of Princeton continued to expand outward from Nassau Street as well as in the Princeton Basin area with hotels, offices, loading basins, and factories dependent on the canal and railroad.

LEGEND

- Open/underdeveloped areas
- ● Campus buildings
- ● Developed areas
- ○ Forested areas
- ○ Main campus areas

1746
College of New Jersey founded in Elizabeth

1774
First recorded use of the term "campus," taken from Latin and used to describe college grounds, in reference to the front green of Nassau Hall

1813
Princeton Borough delineated

1834
D&R canal constructed, initially carrying freight as well as passengers

1839
Railroad in operation

1696
Town of Prince-Town settled

1756
Set on a protected topographic ridge, Nassau Hall was the largest academic building in the colonies and had an expansive panorama of farmland and forested valley to the south.

1801
Route 1 built

1830
Joseph Henry suggested a symmetrical back campus quadrangle with two new dormitories and new buildings for the debating societies, Whig and Clio.

1838
Mercer County and Princeton Township delineated

1852

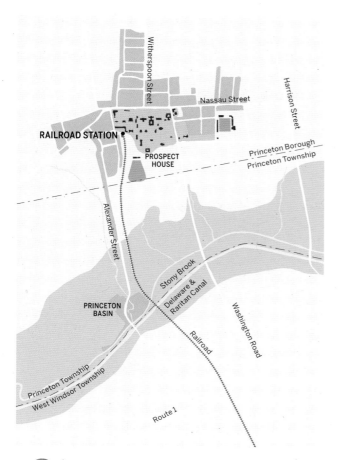

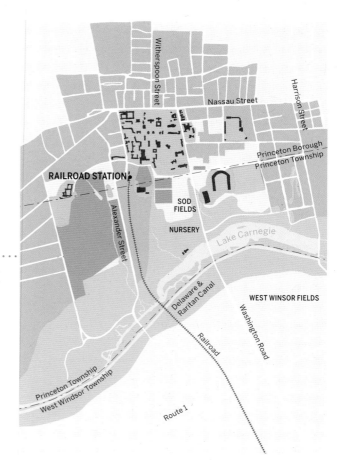

Collegiate gothic is a "return step by step to the old ideals and sound methods of English colleges... to those...eternally enduring principles in life and thought and aspiration..."

....

RALPH ADAMS CRAM, 1914

1897 A CAMPUS IN A PARK

During the second half of the 19th century, President James McCosh (1868-1888) and President Francis Patton (1888-1902) oversaw a period of rapid building expansion that favored a more park-like setting for buildings, placing less importance on axes and symmetry than previous styles. The Victorian style of architecture provided an organic approach that complemented this landscape philosophy. This change of style coincided with a pedagogic shift from the fixed curriculum of a small Protestant college to a more modern concept of a university.

The town of Princeton continued to expand, surrounding the campus on three sides. The railroad station, still in its original northern location near Blair Hall, provided the gateway to the town as well as the University.

LEGEND

- Open/underdeveloped areas
- Developed areas
- Main campus areas
- Campus buildings
- Athletic fields
- Forested areas

1927 THE CAMPUS LOOKS INWARD

A major building program in the early 20th century was initiated by President Woodrow Wilson (1901-1912) and overseen by Ralph Adams Cram, supervising architect. In addition to new buildings, Lake Carnegie was created and the railroad (Dinky) station was relocated to the south.

Princeton was one of the first universities to undertake a master plan for its future growth. Wilson and Cram shared a vision for the campus that shifted away from the McCosh era's outward-looking and expansive landscape to a more enclosed arrangement of buildings, influenced by the architecture and scholarly seclusion of Oxford and Cambridge and emphasizing academic discourse among faculty and students.

Princeton Borough and Township settlements continued to grow with new residential areas west of the golf course and east of FitzRandolph Road. As the Dinky station moved south, many residential properties along Alexander Street were transformed for industrial and warehouse uses dependent on rail transportation.

1896
Official name changed to "Princeton University." Collegiate gothic adopted as official architectural style

1907
Role of supervising architect created—first filled by Ralph Adams Cram

1913
Graduate college built on golf course site, rather than south of McCosh Walk as President Woodrow Wilson proposed

1879
Ivy Club, the first eating club, established

1897

1906
Lake Carnegie dedicated

1911
Ralph Adams Cram proposed a north-south axis from Nassau Hall to divide the campus into residential and academic zones. (Not completed)

1920s
Dinky station moved south

1927

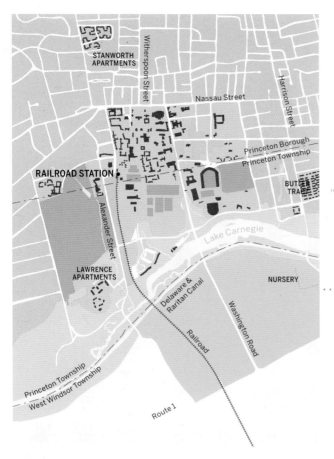

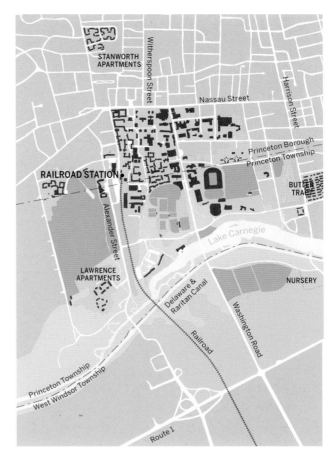

> "The University... is a growing organism whose form lies partly in the past, partly in the future..."
>
> JOSEPH HUDNUT, 1947

1975 THE RESULT OF RAPID GROWTH AND EXPANSION

The combined effects of the Great Depression and World War II resulted in a 14-year building hiatus at Princeton (1933-1947). Due largely to increased government funding for laboratory buildings, a major and rapid campus expansion occurred in the 1960s which pushed the campus boundary farther to the south and located major academic facilities east of Washington Road, including the engineering school. By 1951 collegiate gothic was no longer the official architectural style "due to cost and other factors" and Princeton University, like Oxford, Cambridge, and other American universities, intended to build in a "contemporary" style.

The township and borough of Princeton also experienced a building boom after World War II. In the decade from 1950 to 1960, the population of the township doubled. By the 1970s the area was heavily populated and many new streets were created.

2006 GROWING AND GREENING THE CAMPUS

Since the 1970s the campus has continued to grow, infilling to maintain walkability, bringing innovative architecture to complement the historic buildings, and sustaining its landscapes and natural resources. Still recognized around the world for its impressive, eclectic mix of architecture and beautiful gardens, greens, and natural areas, the campus of tomorrow will have to meet the needs of the evolving institution while maintaining the historic beauty of the campus.

The township and borough of Princeton have a population of just over 30,000 people. In addition the University, the area is home to the Institute for Advanced Study, the Princeton Theological Seminary, and the Westminster Choir College. Its equidistant location from Philadelphia and New York City, coupled with historic charm and cultural and educational amenities, has made it a very desirable place to live and work.

1962
The construction of the Engineering Quadrangle buildings solidified the campus' presence east of Washington Road.

1970s
The expansion of the campus toward the south and east marked a shift in its scale and character.

1982
System of residential colleges established

1969
Trustees vote to admit women undergraduates

1975

2006

Campus Growth
by 2016

The line graph below charts the growth of Princeton University in terms of building square footage and student population from 1900 to the start of the Campus Plan in 2006. The graph also projects the same data from 2006 to 2016 based on planned projects and future recommendations.

As the graph shows, the sizes of the physical plant and student population have increased steadily over the past century, but there are two periods of more rapid growth. The first period occurred in the 1960s with the boom in Cold War scientific research and funding. During this time, the construction of new and larger research facilities was accompanied by an increase in the graduate and undergraduate student populations. The second period of rapid growth began in the 1990s and continues to 2016. Though not as steep as it was mid-century, the last two decades of growth have expanded the size of the institution by almost 40 percent.

The early part of the 20th century saw building area and student population growing at similar rates, but that no longer holds true after 1960. Whereas the ratio of building area to population in 1940 was about 1,000 square feet per student, in 2016 it will approach 1,600 square feet per student.

Why is building area growing at a significantly higher rate than the student population? It is partly because modern academic and research buildings are larger than their historic counterparts. Furthermore, a modern campus requires more than just academic and residential buildings; it must provide its population with a variety of infrastructural and support facilities that contribute to campus life and the efficient operation of a large institution.

In the ten years from 2006 to 2016 the campus is projected to expand by an additional 2.1 million square feet—not as much as the record-setting decade of the 1960s, but very likely the second most intensive decade

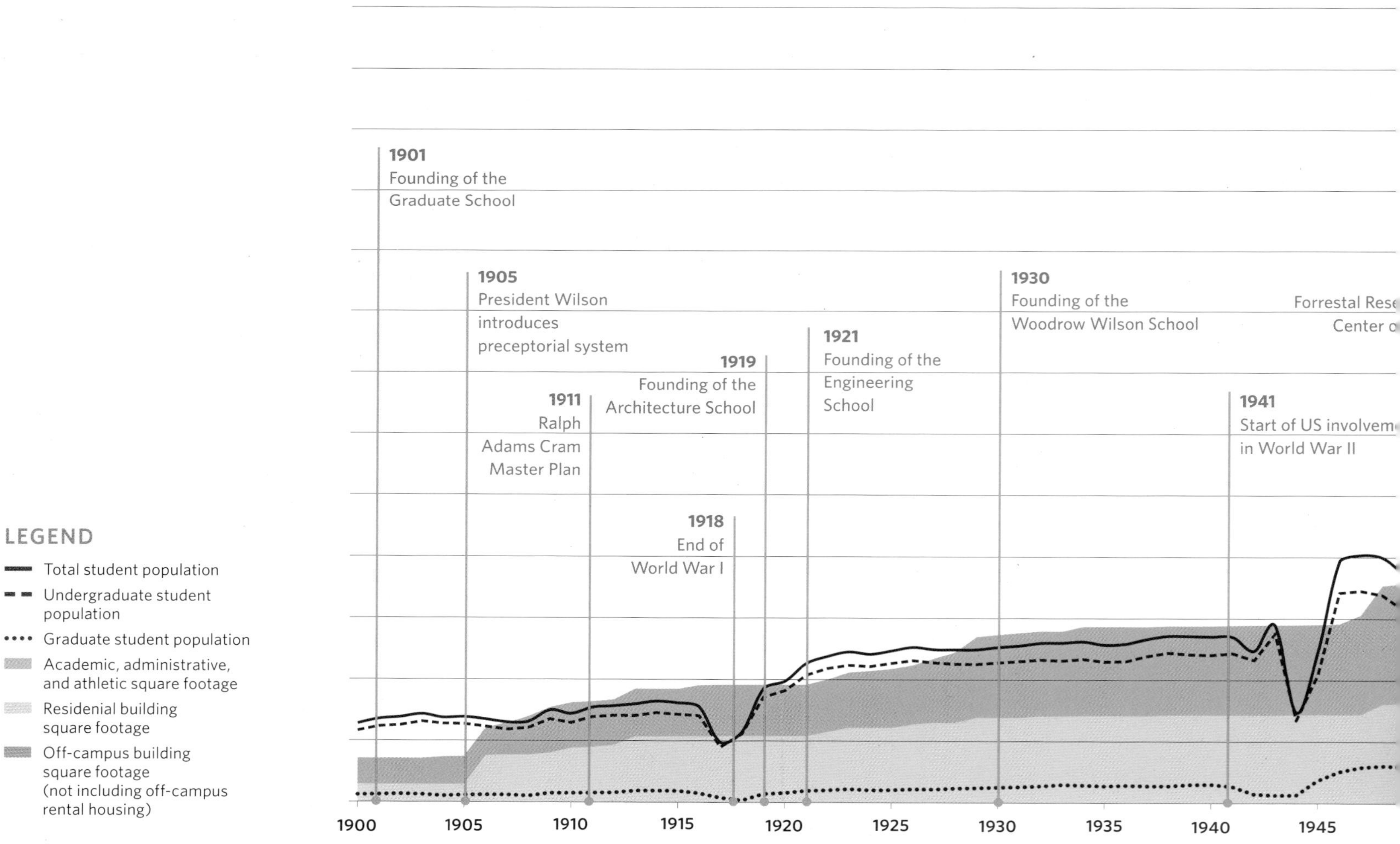

1901
Founding of the
Graduate School

1905
President Wilson
introduces
preceptorial system

1911
Ralph
Adams Cram
Master Plan

1919
Founding of the
Architecture School

1918
End of
World War I

1921
Founding of the
Engineering
School

1930
Founding of the
Woodrow Wilson School

Forrestal Rese
Center o

1941
Start of US involvem
in World War II

LEGEND

— Total student population
– – Undergraduate student population
•••• Graduate student population
▨ Academic, administrative, and athletic square footage
▨ Residenial building square footage
▨ Off-campus building square footage (not including off-campus rental housing)

1900   1905   1910   1915   1920   1925   1930   1935   1940   1945

of growth in the history of the institution. The lesson of the 1960s for today is that periods of substantial growth need careful planning to ensure that the additions enhance the campus setting rather than detract from it, and that the impacts on the environment and the surrounding community are well understood and thoughtfully addressed.

Balancing our desire to preserve the intimate yet majestic nature of Princeton's campus while meeting the needs of what is actually a very large and growing university was one of the most interesting challenges presented by the campus planning process. I believe that our neighborhood approach, and our landscape plan, were key factors in our ability to address this challenge successfully.

—KAREN MAGEE,
CHAIR OF THE TRUSTEE COMMITTEE ON GROUNDS AND BUILDINGS

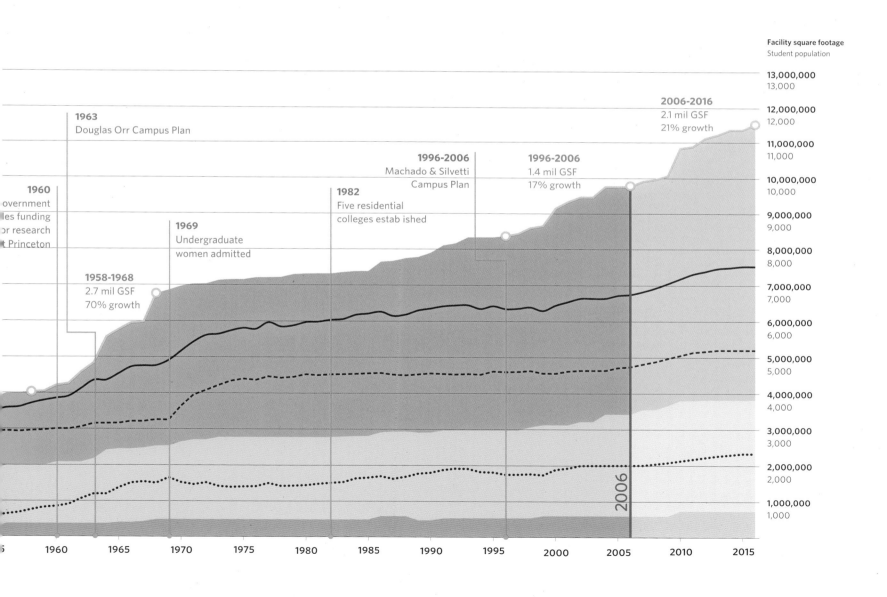

Facility square footage
Student population

13,000,000
13,000

2006-2016
2.1 mil GSF
21% growth

1963
Douglas Orr Campus Plan

12,000,000
12,000

1996-2006
Machado & Silvetti
Campus Plan

1996-2006
1.4 mil GSF
17% growth

11,000,000
11,000

1960
government
les funding
or research
Princeton

1982
Five residential
colleges estab ished

10,000,000
10,000

1969
Undergraduate
women admitted

9,000,000
9,000

8,000,000
8,000

1958-1968
2.7 mil GSF
70% growth

7,000,000
7,000

6,000,000
6,000

5,000,000
5,000

4,000,000
4,000

3,000,000
3,000

2006

2,000,000
2,000

1,000,000
1,000

1960   1965   1970   1975   1980   1985   1990   1995   2000   2005   2010   2015

Planning is so difficult because—at least in the early years of an institution's life—it seems so easy. We take the first steps naively, not quite realizing that each of them is full of consequence and will make every following move much more complicated. If the institution is lucky and alert, it may be able to turn future complexities into imaginative possibilities and perhaps even realities. But every successive intervention makes the design of the whole—if there still is one—more intricate. If we began, long ago, walking on air, we will almost certainly discover that, much later, we are pressed to invent new and surprising high-wire acts time after time.

The most difficult planning problem for an institution is to decide what its visible architectural and natural universe should "look like." If there is to be an incarnation, one must first of all seek its character and meaning, and then try to express its significance in tangible shapes and forms that might possibly suffice.

Princeton was the first college or university to have had the term "campus" associated with it. And once the term was there, it began—inevitably—to impose itself on the college and to demand a response and definition. It obviously implied that Princeton would be a separate place with its own boundaries and distinct identity—rather than an institution whose buildings were interspersed with the town and its residential neighborhoods. It would be an enclave; but "campus"—literally a field—also indicated something more open (and different from) the closed, walled and protected place of (for instance) an Oxford college.

When we press further, however, we are still left to discover what might be meant when the words campus, college, and university are brought together in conjunction. Which images—of architecture, landscape, textures, space, and sky—would satisfy so hopeful a vision and ideal? Scott Fitzgerald's "dreaming towers"? Auden's "careless beauty" in "a green county"? Zuleika's "multitudinous quadrangles" that were "venerable, magical, and enduring"? Waugh's "unwearied sinews, sequestered mind" inhabiting an idyllic collegiate world designed for youth's "zest, generous affections, illusions, and despair"?

Once Nassau Hall—then the largest academic building in the colonies—had been placed parallel to the town's main thoroughfare, but rather set back—with a modest "campus" or field in front—then some hint of a design, certainly not a plan, was already in place. The fact that the new hall stretched itself longitudinally, suggested that Princeton's buildings might traverse its grounds in lengths and lines, as much as they would cluster in quads and cloisters.

Nassau Hall also seemed to declare that we would construct our buildings, not in colonial wood, but in variegated, home-grown, somewhat rusticated stone. We would be sturdy and impressive. We would invite perambulation. We would also care about landscape and space as much as about structures; indeed, the patterning and dynamics of their continuous interplay would, perhaps, matter most of all.

We know what happened afterward. The campus eventually became one of the most potent American images of what a college or university seeks to embody and express. It represents, of course, only one possible set of meanings among many, but it is a particularly powerful set, reaching back—as it does—to medieval gothic emblems of spiritual aspiration, intellectual intensity, and a sufficient separation from the world of affairs to create a cosmos with its own conceptions of time, labor, ease, and achievement.

If that image is now more complicated than it was—with an admixture of modern buildings and textures, new fields and modes of knowledge, and a greater range of activities and complex services—that is simply because our own lives, our world, and our realities have necessarily altered in so many ways. But to Princeton's credit and honor, its aspirations and convictions concerning the fundamental nature and purposes of a university have admitted no impediments or alterations at all.

Princeton has just completed the most comprehensive, rigorous, and successful planning process in its entire history. For those of us who were involved in such ventures 20 (and even 30 or 35) years ago, the current effort has (with no hint of invidiousness) adroitly ex-posed the cheerful amateurism of all our earlier youthful tinkering and fiddling.

Did we really once build Spelman Halls, a new indoor Olympic-size swimming pool, a molecular biology building, Wu Hall, and any number of other structures without much concern about anything except the "program," the architecture, the site, and the cost?

Now, given the very substantial growth—over recent decades—of the population in the entire Princeton region, we know that the general lack of access roads, the traffic congestion, the pressure on community green space—and countless other considerations—can make any new construction (or analogous event) the trigger for an immediate chain reaction of innumerable problems and perplexities.

Shall we add a modest new wing to an equally modest academic building? But even the two or three dozen additional people in the new wing will need parking spaces—and the building will require electricity and heat (and air-conditioning) which will in turn strain the central steam plant slightly more. There will also be a slightly larger crowd in the lunchroom, the physical-fitness room, and the restroom. One can certainly manage for now—but later?

If we build, not a modest wing, but new high-intensity buildings for chemistry and neuroscience, with dozens and dozens more people, then there will be a far greater impact on the community, the campus, the energy supply, waste disposal, the ozone layer, the stream beds leading to Lake Carnegie, the storm-water catch basins, the shuttle service, parking lots, the cicadas, and the possible need for more traffic lights or pedestrian bridges on Washington Road. All these (and other) mundane items are—in effect—the atomic and sub-atomic particles that constitute the deep structure of our campus, and each has enough velocity and charge to affect even the least obvious of its neighbors, jostling and jolting them, unless we prove to be sufficiently astute in our planning to provide enough room for each, with comfortable cushions to serve as shock absorbers.

The trick in planning has been to pay the greatest possible attention to what we call our (and everyone else's) infrastructure, so that all the new outer structures and superstructures which the University may build in the future can shine forth in ways that enhance our sustaining vision of the campus and its meaning. Fortunately, the recent comprehensive process, led by President Tilghman and the University's exceptional consultants, has done precisely that. As a result, when the next round of buildings and pathways and plantings has been completed, everything will seem composed, enduring, and also animated by youth and zest once again. All our streams will continue to run brightly down their stream beds toward the brimful waters of Lake Carnegie, beneath all those dreaming—and also wakeful—towers.

Neil Rudenstine
Former provost and former chair of the
Trustee Committee on Grounds and Buildings

NEW CHALLENGES

The particular physical characteristics of the Princeton campus create unique challenges that distinguish this planning effort from those of other universities. The topography and ecology of the campus setting, its historic patterns of growth, and the evolution of the campus and community edge have created problematic conditions today that can either be exacerbated or repaired by new development. Each of these challenges is intensified by the increasing size of the functional area of the campus— the setting for the daily life of students, faculty, and staff.

CREATING A MORE WELCOMING CAMPUS

Princeton University receives more than 700,000 visitors each year. While Nassau Street is the University's traditional front, most visitors today arrive by car at what is clearly the back of campus, and find themselves in a distant and disorienting location with few directions. Once within the historic core, the intricate character that makes the campus beautiful also makes it confusing and difficult to navigate.

An unmarked and uninviting campus entrance at Lot 7 garage

CONNECTING THE WHOLE OF CAMPUS, FROM THE CORE TO THE EDGES

Although the historic core is highly walkable, more modern campus neighborhoods have fewer pathways and are more isolated from the center and from each other. Faculty in the E-Quad, for example, are disconnected from their colleagues in the natural sciences. To be truly pedestrian-oriented, the dense pathway network of the core must be extended across gaps and into outlying areas of campus.

A lack of campus character around Hoyt Lab

A paved and isolated "open space" in Jadwin Courtyard

INCREASING DENSITY WITHOUT LOSING OPEN SPACE

Princeton's "park-like" character is one of the most highly valued qualities of the campus by both the University community and the residents of the surrounding town. New buildings of increasing scale, parking garages, and infrastructure must be added while minimizing impacts on open space, natural features, and vistas of greenery.

The different architectural styles of Spelman Halls and Whitman College

UNIFYING DISPARATE CAMPUS AREAS

Over 250 years, campus neighborhoods have developed with widely varying styles of architecture, some of which lack coherent relationships between buildings. Recently completed buildings continue to express a wide range of architectural styles, a trend which will continue in the next ten years. This aesthetic diversity must nonetheless be integrated into a coherent whole.

Elm Drive stream erosion

GROWING SUSTAINABLY

The plan to concentrate growth in a limited space has significant environmental benefits, from the protection of surrounding open land to the reduction of driving between destinations on campus. At the same time, the local impacts of buildings on the natural features and underlying watersheds of campus are greater, and the ever-increasing energy demands of new buildings for the sciences and other uses make environmentally sustainable development a significant challenge.

Traffic backed up at a nexus of campus and community

ADDRESSING IMPACTS OF GROWTH AT THE EDGES

In the next ten years and beyond, campus growth will move increasingly to the edges of the campus, as this is the location of much of the remaining available campus land, and some of this growth will occur at points where the University meets the surrounding community. This means that the success of the plan will rely on a productive and sustained dialogue between campus and community.

CHAPTER 4
A VISION FOR
THE CAMPUS OF 2016

The Campus Plan consists of a vision for the campus of 2016, as well as a detailed framework and set of recommendations for how to get there. The following pages describe the vision, highlighting the areas of greatest transformation. This vision will come into focus over the course of time, as the plan is interpreted through the process of implementation, and as architects, landscape architects, and engineers develop specific designs for each individual project. The vision describes how each of these parts contributes to a complete portrait of the Princeton campus.

Production of Boris Godunov, spring 2007

Campus Plan
Key Initiatives

A plan cannot be merely a collection of accommodations for needed facilities and infrastructure; all of these elements must coalesce into a coherent, beautiful, and inspiring vision for the future campus.

. . . .

The vision for the complete campus of 2016 is shown in the following pages in "soft focus." The images give an overall impression of the campus neighborhoods of the future, but do not seek to describe exactly how future buildings and landscapes may look, as many of them have yet to be designed. Instead, they describe how together the numerous projects will add up to a larger idea of the campus.

The exact details of this vision will come into focus over time, as specific needs and constraints are understood, and as individual architects, landscape architects, and engineers develop their designs, drawing inspiration and guidance from the Campus Plan. A balanced interplay between the whole and the parts is key to successful campus design: this plan, therefore, provides a framework and creative stimulus to build upon. Designers and others charged with implementing its components must have clear objectives to follow in order that each discrete intervention, whether large or small, contributes to the overall integrity of the entire campus.

THE BIG IDEAS

A comparison of the maps on pages 50–53 highlights the areas of most significant change as proposed by the Campus Plan.

The first map shows the campus during the early stages of the planning process in 2006. At that time, two major projects had begun construction: Whitman College and the Lewis Library. While both of these facilities were designed before this plan was developed (notably in very different architectural idioms), much attention has been paid in the Campus Plan to their integration into the new vision for the campus, particularly by introducing appropriate landscape settings and vistas.

The second map shows the campus as it would appear in 2016 according to the recommendations of the Campus Plan. By this time, Whitman College and the Lewis Library will have long been complete and new landscaping and infrastructure will weave them into the fabric of the campus. At the Lewis Library, for example, the Sciences Green will create a spacious and elegantly landscaped open space setting for this Frank Gehry-designed landmark, previously hemmed in on all sides by roads and service areas.

A series of new building projects proposed by the Campus Plan are also shown. New buildings will be generally clustered in new or expanded academic districts to the south, east, and west of the core campus. These "campus neighborhoods" form a core element of the vision: the concentration of academic facilities with strong departmental and collaborative ties in these neighborhoods will nurture a sense of local community within the larger connected community of the University as a whole.

The campus neighborhood developments encompass President Tilghman's most significant academic initiatives, including the Peter B. Lewis Center for the Arts, the Neuroscience Institute, the expansion of operations research and financial engineering, a major addition to the School of Engineering and Applied Science, and new, state-of-the-art facilities for chemistry and psychology. Several other projects and renovations of existing buildings will create room for expanded programs in the humanities, social sciences, and other areas, new housing initiatives, and improved spaces for campus life and athletics.

In addition to academic, housing, and campus life developments, the plan recommends critical infrastructure projects to support campus growth, including a new central Data Center, a Transit Plaza, a reconstructed New Jersey Transit Dinky rail station with expanded amenities and inter-modal transportation connections, and a major new parking facility east of the stadium.

The Campus Plan also proposes an extensive network of improved or new green spaces. This scale of landscape improvement has not been undertaken by the University since the early part of the 20th century, and it will be essential to ensure the successful integration of so many new buildings. The landscape proposals take two major forms: the extension and restoration of campus landscapes —greens, pathways, and formal plantings—from the historic core to new campus neighborhoods; and the extension and restoration of natural features—woodlands, ravines, and stream watersheds—from the lake valley up into the campus.

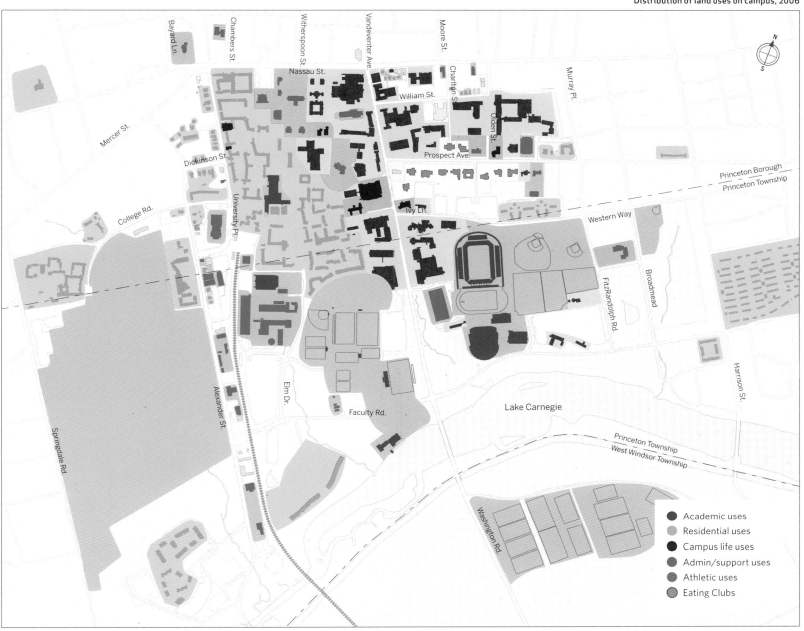

Bayard Ln.
Chambers St.
Witherspoon St.
Vandeventer Ave.
Moore St.
Charlton St.
Murray Pl.
Nassau St.
William St.
Olden St.
Mercer St.
Dickinson St.
Prospect Ave.
Princeton Borough
Princeton Township
College Rd.
University Pl.
Ivy Ln.
Western Way
Broadmead
FitzRandolph Rd.
Harrison St.
Springdale Rd.
Alexander St.
Elm Dr.
Faculty Rd.
Lake Carnegie
Princeton Township
West Windsor Township
Washington Rd.

- ● Academic uses
- ● Residential uses
- ● Campus life uses
- ● Admin/support uses
- ● Athletic uses
- ● Eating Clubs

CAMPUS FACTS

	2006	2016
Land Area (approximate acres)		
Main Campus	380	380
Springdale Golf Course	144	144
Butler Tract and Gray Farm	113	113
West Windsor Fields	375	375
Building Area (approximate square feet)		
Academic	3.8 million	4.7 million
Administrative and Support	1.6 million	2.1 million
Athletics	0.9 million	0.9 million
Undergraduate Housing	1.7 million	1.9 million
Graduate Student Housing	0.9 million	1.1 million

	2006	2016
Population (full-time)		
Undergraduate	4,800	5,200
Graduate	2,328	Approx. 1%*
Faculty	1,139	Approx. 1%*
Staff	4,260	Approx. 1%*
Academics and Campus Life		
Academic Departments	34	34
Residential Colleges	5	6
Eating Clubs	10	11
Varsity Teams	38	n/a
Club Sports	40	n/a
Intramural Teams	300	n/a
Student Organizations	230	n/a

* annual growth

LOWRIE
HOUSE

Stockton Street

Bank Street

Chambers Street

22
CHAMBERS

Witherspoon Street

Vandeventer Avenue

Nassau Street

LOT 9

MADISON

MACLEAN
HOUSE

HENRY
HOUSE

SCHEIDE
CALDWELL
HOUSE

AARON
BURR

HAMILTON   HOLDER

Elm Drive

STANHOPE

CHANCELLOR
GREEN

FIRESTONE
LIBRARY

GREEN

LOT 10

JOLINE   CAMPBELL

ALEXANDER

NASSAU
HALL

William

HOYT

Mercer Street

LOT 8

WEST
COLLEGE

EAST PYNE

CHAPEL

DICKINSON

FRICK

BLAIR

CORWIN

U-STORE

WITHERSPOON

BUYERS

CLIO   WHIG

MURRAY-DODGE

MCCOSH

BENORE

ROBERTSON

FISHER

Edwards Place

Alexander Street

University Place

LOCKHART

48

EDWARDS

MCCORMICK

ARCHITECTURE
SCHOOL

MARK

FOULKE

LITTLE

ART
MUSEUM

Dickinson Street

LAUGHLIN

DOD

PRINCETON
THEOLOGICAL
SEMINARY

HENRY

PROSPECT

WOOLWORTH

1879

CAMPUS
CLUB

1901

DILLON
GYM

BROWN

COLLEGE ROAD
APARTMENTS

PYNE

CUYLER

JONES

FRIST
CAMPUS
CENTER

CENTER FOR
JEWISH LIFE

WRIGHT

1903

1937

College Road

FEINBERG

MCCOSH
HEALTH CENTER

WALKER

5

SPRINGDALE
CLUBHOUSE

MCCARTER
THEATRE
CENTER

SPELMAN FALLS

PATTON

LOT 18   1939

1915

GAUSS

DODGE-
OSBORNE

GUYOT

LEWIS
(UNDER

1927 CLAPP   ENO
ROCK

MOFFET

WU   WILCOX

1938

SCHULTZ

WHITMAN COLLEGE
(UNDER CONSTRUCTION)

LOURIE-LOVE

1922

THOMAS

MCDONN

DINKY
STATION

NEW
SOUTH

1942

1941

NEW GRADUATE
COLLEGE

1940

SCULLY

ICAHN

LOT 6

BAKER
RINK

BLOOMBERG

POE/PARDEE
FIELD

OLD GRADUATE
COLLEGE

FORBES
COLLEGE

DINKY
COMMUTER
LOT

LOT 12

200 ELM
DRIVE

WYMAN HOUSE

MACMILLAN

CLASS OF
1895 FIELD

LOURIE
LOVE
FIELD

GULICK
FIELD

LOT 20

LOT 7
PARKING
GARAGE

CHILLED WATER PLANT

Springdale Road

COGEN PLANT

LOT 19

COOLING TOWERS

LENZ
TENNIS
COURTS

LOT 28

SPRINGDALE GOLF COURSE

TENNIS
COURTS

LOT 16

LOT 17

BEDFORD
FIELD

CLASS OF
1952 STADIUM

Elm Drive

LOT 23

Walnut

Alexander Street

SHEA ROWING
CENTER

LOT 23A

HELM

HIBBEN AND MAGIE
APARTMENTS

Princeton Township

West Windsor Township

LAWRENCE
APARTMENTS

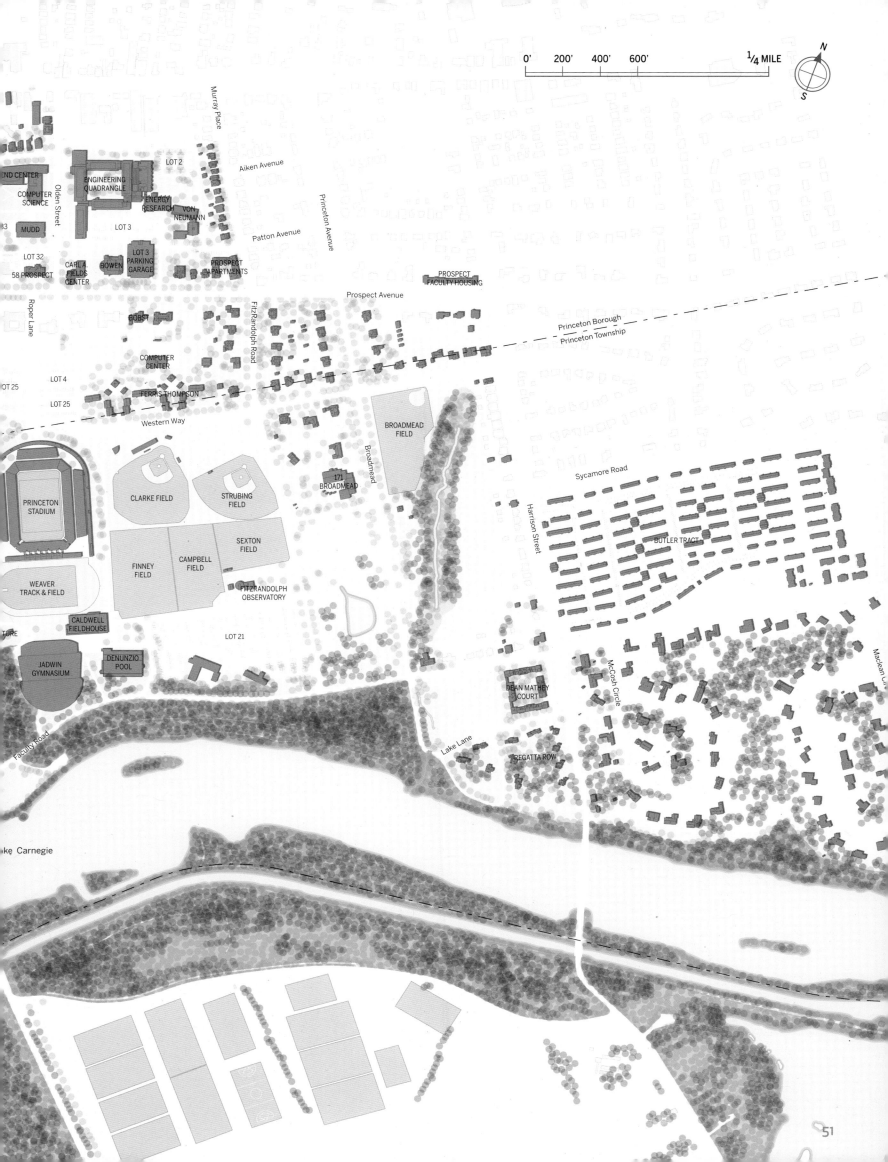

0' 200' 400' 600' 1/4 MILE

N S

END CENTER

COMPUTER SCIENCE

Olden Street

#3

MUDD

LOT 32

58 PROSPECT

Roper Lane

OT 25

LOT 25

LOT 4

Murray Place

ENGINEERING QUADRANGLE

LOT 2

ENERGY RESEARCH

VON NEUMANN

LOT 3

CARL A. FIELDS CENTER

BOWEN

LOT 3 PARKING GARAGE

PROSPECT APARTMENTS

BOBST

COMPUTER CENTER

FERRIS THOMPSON

Western Way

Aiken Avenue

Patton Avenue

Princeton Avenue

FitzRandolph Road

Prospect Avenue

PROSPECT FACULTY HOUSING

Princeton Borough
Princeton Township

PRINCETON STADIUM

WEAVER TRACK & FIELD

CLARKE FIELD

STRUBING FIELD

FINNEY FIELD

CAMPBELL FIELD

SEXTON FIELD

FITZRANDOLPH OBSERVATORY

171 BROADMEAD

Broadmead

BROADMEAD FIELD

Sycamore Road

BUTLER TRACT

Harrison Street

TURE

CALDWELL FIELDHOUSE

LOT 21

JADWIN GYMNASIUM

DENUNZIO POOL

Faculty Road

DEAN MATHEY COURT

McCosh Circle

Maclean Circle

ke Carnegie

Lake Lane

REGATTA ROW

51

THE CAMPUS PLAN

Core Campus

No major new development is planned. Extensive restoration of the campus landscape will revitalize historic spaces while meeting modern functional needs. Projects include reconstruction of campus greens and pathways and a tree-planting program across the entire area: **Holder Court restoration** (completed in fall 2007); **McCosh Walk restoration**; **Blair Walk restoration**.

Arts and Transit Neighborhood

Redevelopment of a large area at the campus edge will create a dramatic new gateway, with public plazas, cultural and retail spaces, and reconfigured roads and transportation systems to improve traffic flow and transit connectivity: **The Arts Plaza**, framed by the **Peter B. Lewis Center for the Arts**, a restaurant and café, and located across from the McCarter and Berlind theaters; **The Transit Plaza**, connection point for the NJ Transit Dinky rail service, commuter and campus parking, regional and local buses, a community jitney, campus shuttles, a bike station, the Wawa convenience store, and a new Dinky station building.

Natural Sciences Neighborhood

Supporting interdisciplinary collaboration and research in existing and new natural sciences programs, this neighborhood will be linked by a pedestrian footbridge over Washington Road. New construction will enable the natural woodlands and streams of the area to be restored and enhanced, and will create a major new campus green space: **Neuroscience and Psychology buildings**; **Chemistry building**; **Streicker Bridge**; **Restoration of Washington Road ravine, woodlands, and stream**; **Lewis Library** (opening in 2008); **Sciences Green**.

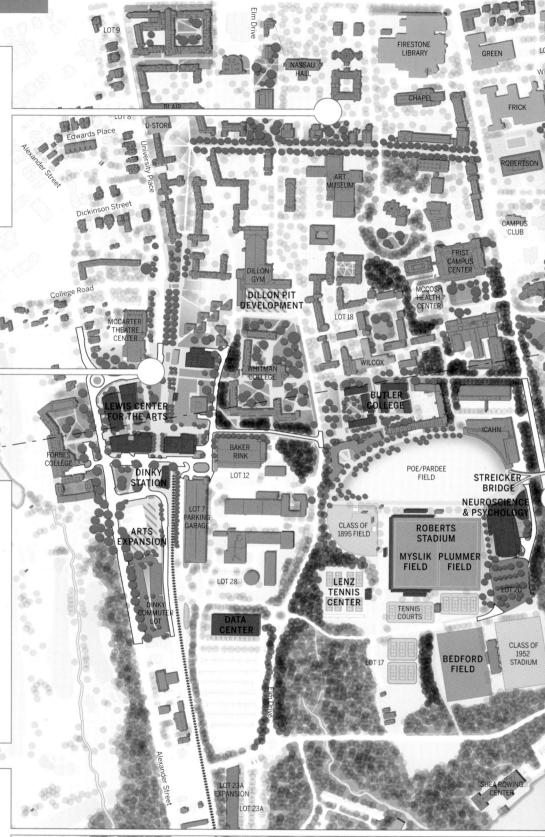

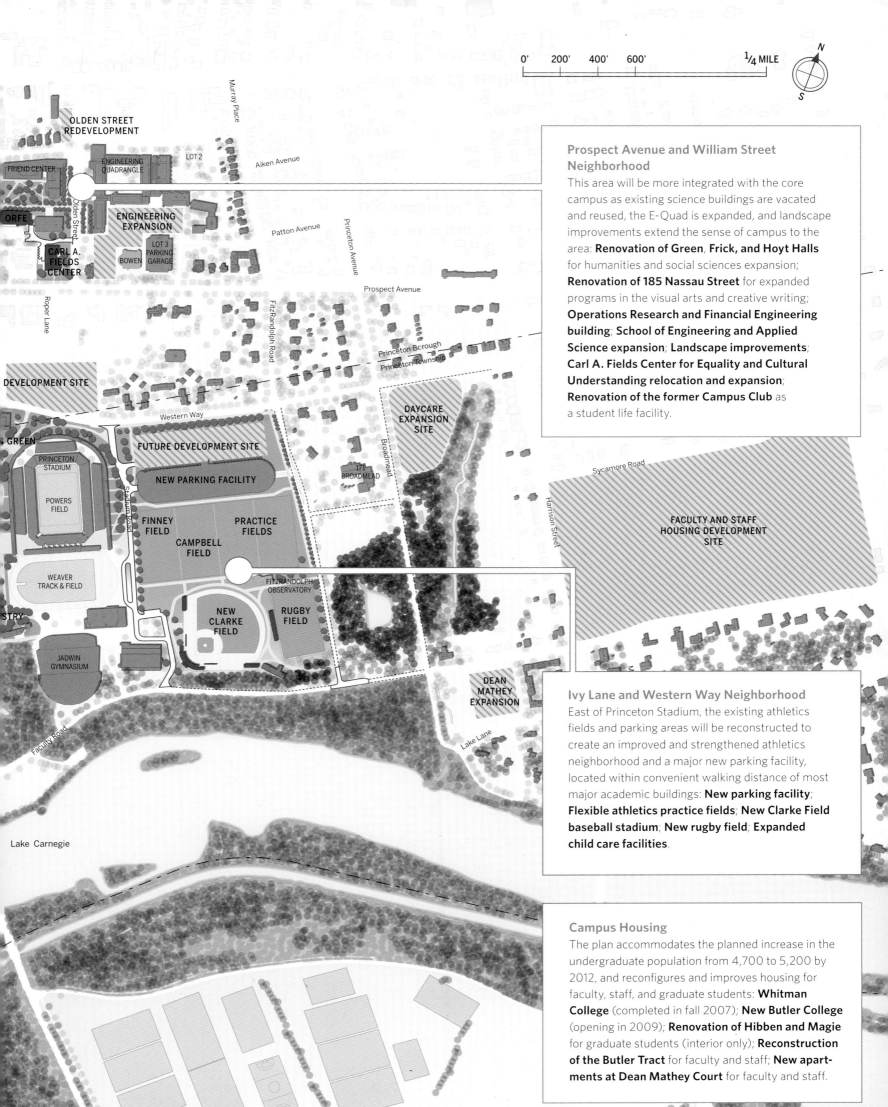

Prospect Avenue and William Street Neighborhood

This area will be more integrated with the core campus as existing science buildings are vacated and reused, the E-Quad is expanded, and landscape improvements extend the sense of campus to the area: **Renovation of Green, Frick, and Hoyt Halls** for humanities and social sciences expansion; **Renovation of 185 Nassau Street** for expanded programs in the visual arts and creative writing; **Operations Research and Financial Engineering building**; **School of Engineering and Applied Science expansion**; **Landscape improvements**; **Carl A. Fields Center for Equality and Cultural Understanding relocation and expansion**; **Renovation of the former Campus Club** as a student life facility.

Ivy Lane and Western Way Neighborhood

East of Princeton Stadium, the existing athletics fields and parking areas will be reconstructed to create an improved and strengthened athletics neighborhood and a major new parking facility, located within convenient walking distance of most major academic buildings: **New parking facility**; **Flexible athletics practice fields**; **New Clarke Field baseball stadium**; **New rugby field**; **Expanded child care facilities.**

Campus Housing

The plan accommodates the planned increase in the undergraduate population from 4,700 to 5,200 by 2012, and reconfigures and improves housing for faculty, staff, and graduate students: **Whitman College** (completed in fall 2007); **New Butler College** (opening in 2009); **Renovation of Hibben and Magie** for graduate students (interior only); **Reconstruction of the Butler Tract** for faculty and staff; **New apartments at Dean Mathey Court** for faculty and staff.

Map labels:

OLDEN STREET REDEVELOPMENT
FRIEND CENTER
ENGINEERING QUADRANGLE
LOT 2
Aiken Avenue
Murray Place
ORFE
ENGINEERING EXPANSION
Patton Avenue
Princeton Avenue
CARL A. FIELDS CENTER
BOWEN
LOT 3 PARKING GARAGE
Prospect Avenue
Roper Lane
Olden Street
FitzRandolph Road
DEVELOPMENT SITE
Princeton Borough
Princeton Township
Western Way
DAYCARE EXPANSION SITE
Broadmead
171 BROADMEAD
Sycamore Road
Harrison Street
FACULTY AND STAFF HOUSING DEVELOPMENT SITE
GREEN
PRINCETON STADIUM
POWERS FIELD
FUTURE DEVELOPMENT SITE
NEW PARKING FACILITY
FINNEY FIELD
PRACTICE FIELDS
CAMPBELL FIELD
Student Road
WEAVER TRACK & FIELD
STRY
FITZRANDOLPH OBSERVATORY
NEW CLARKE FIELD
RUGBY FIELD
JADWIN GYMNASIUM
DEAN MATHEY EXPANSION
Faculty Road
Lake Lane
Lake Carnegie

Transit Plaza in the new Arts and Transit Neighborhood

Commuters arrive at the new NJ Transit Station on foot and by bus, bicycle, or car. The former Dinky station building, 460 feet to the north, is a short walk away along a broad landscaped path. The Transit Plaza will include the Wawa store and other retail facilities for commuters.

ARTS AND TRANSIT NEIGHBORHOOD P82

View looking north toward the new Arts Plaza

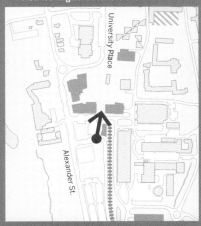

Arts Plaza in the new Arts and Transit Neighborhood

Enjoying the new Arts Plaza, patrons dine at a café in the former Dinky station building. Students and local residents walk along a generous shaded walkway connecting the historic campus and downtown with the new NJ Transit Station just beyond.

ARTS AND TRANSIT NEIGHBORHOOD P82

View looking south toward the new Dinky station

The redesigned New South Green

Students and visitors lie out on a newly landscaped lawn and enjoy a performance or open rehearsal at the Experimental Media Studio. The Whitman College archway in the distance is reframed as a campus gateway that is visible and accessible from the Arts Plaza. New South is visible to the right.

ARTS AND TRANSIT NEIGHBORHOOD P82

View looking east toward Whitman College

The Ellipse, new Neuroscience and Psychology buildings, and Streicker Bridge

A stroll along the sweeping arc of the Ellipse leads past Icahn Laboratory to the new Neuroscience and Psychology buildings. Streicker Bridge crosses over Washington Road, leading to the new Chemistry building and the athletics neighborhood.

NATURAL SCIENCES NEIGHBORHOOD P88

View looking east toward Icahn Laboratory

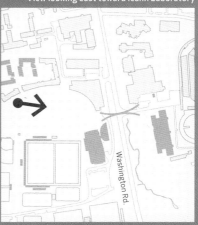

Nature pathway west of the new Chemistry building

People jog and stroll along the nature path leading to Streicker Bridge. Newly restored woodlands and planted stormwater treatment landscapes frame a pastoral setting around the Chemistry building and along Washington Road, where the Armory building and a parking lot were previously located.

NATURAL SCIENCES NEIGHBORHOOD P88

View looking north toward Jadwin Hall

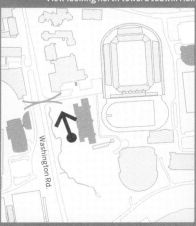

Redesigned Sciences Green

Students relax in the sun and shade of the Sciences Green outside Fine Hall, Princeton Stadium, and the new Lewis Library. With new pedestrian pathways, this major new outdoor space serves as the centerpiece of the Natural Sciences Neighborhood.

NATURAL SCIENCES NEIGHBORHOOD P88

View looking west toward Lewis Library and Fine Tower

New garage and athletic fields

Improved practice fields east of Princeton Stadium belong to a consolidated athletics neighborhood forming a green belt on the southern edge of campus. The new parking garage located along Western Way is convenient to the most heavily populated areas of campus.

IVY LANE AND WESTERN WAY NEIGHBORHOOD P96

View looking west across practice fields toward Princeton Stadium

New ORFE building and an improved Shapiro Walk

The new Operations Research and Financial Engineering building and surrounding campus landscapes enliven Shapiro Walk. Used by students, faculty, and staff, this major pathway runs through the heart of this academic neighborhood, connecting the E-Quad with Scudder Plaza and McCosh Walk in the historic campus.

PROSPECT AVENUE AND WILLIAM STREET NEIGHBORHOOD P100

View looking west toward Shapiro Walk

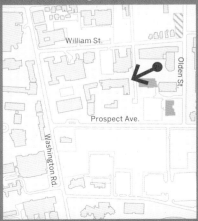

A restored and enhanced Blair Walk

With new paving and plantings, Blair Walk is restored to its historic character. In the tradition of Princeton's processional pathways, it extends southward along its axis to connect the Core Campus to the new Arts and Transit Neighborhood.

CORE CAMPUS P80

View looking north toward Blair Arch

CHAPTER 5
THE PLAN

Ten-Year Projects • A Campus of Neighborhoods
Improving a Sense of Campus Community • Connecting the Campus
Supporting the Campus

The Campus Plan provides a comprehensive framework for making decisions about capital investments and development initiatives. It introduces ambitious new projects and initiatives intended to integrate growth with minimal impact on neighbors and the environment while safeguarding the very qualities that make the Princeton campus so special. This chapter presents the plan from two viewpoints—geographically and thematically—making it possible to understand the campus holistically as a family of distinct but interrelated neighborhoods with unique and shared infrastructure.

A class meeting in front of 1879 Hall

Ten-Year Projects

The Princeton Campus Plan is unprecedented in the University's history for its comprehensiveness. It touches on nearly every facet of the physical space of the campus, from buildings to landscape, from signage to campus shuttles. The uniqueness of Princeton's campus is the way in which these elements are integrated in a complete space, a strength that this plan reinforces. In addition to the many projects and initiatives specifically shown, the Campus Plan provides an ongoing forum and a context for innumerable decisions that will affect the physical design and functioning of the campus over the next decade. A wide range of issues can now be framed and explored by asking the question, "How would this concept fit into the Campus Plan?"

THE TEN-YEAR PROJECTS MAP

The map that follows summarizes most of the capital projects proposed by the Campus Plan, or integrated with it, for the ten-year period from 2006 to 2016. While a large number of projects are included, some proposals cannot be shown on a map, or are not technically part of the Campus Plan. Projects not shown on the next page include:

- Wayfinding and signage program (pages 140 to 145).
- Transportation demand management and campus transit systems (pages 146 to 157).

- Campus sustainability initiatives (pages 160 to 165).
- Development programs for which a site has not yet been selected.
- Building projects of a very small scale, or interior renovations, which do not have a campus planning impact (in other words, which result in no fundamental change of land use or physical design of the campus).

THE SCOPE OF THE CAMPUS PLAN

The map shows the ambitious scale of the University's plans for the next decade.

One measure of this scale is quantity: 70 individual projects are indicated in seven major categories. Some of these, such as the Arts and Transit Neighborhood, include numerous sub-projects. By the time this book is published, many of these projects will already be in the process of implementation, and some will be complete.

New building construction over the ten-year planning period will total approximately 2.1 million square feet in eight major projects. Approximately 850,000 square feet of existing buildings will be renovated for new uses, and approximately 150,000 square feet of new administrative and support space will be provided off campus.

The Campus Plan is not only about buildings, however. Equally important are projects that support campus life and enhance the infrastructure, open spaces, and circulation that support and connect the campus. The map shows a wide range of landscape and environmental restoration projects, athletic field improvements, parking facilities, and infrastructure including data and power supply; road, rail, bus, and shuttle facilities; bike paths; and stormwater management improvements. These elements are fully coordinated and integrated in an overall vision for the campus.

Taking all of these projects together, the total affected area of the campus is significant. Adding up the colored areas on the map, 127 acres of land will be largely reconstructed, fully one-third of the approximately 380 acres of the contiguous main campus. Also shown are approximately 50 acres of landscapes and natural areas that will be restored.

Much of this area is concentrated in a broad southern "belt" of new development, stretching across the entire campus, from the Arts and Transit Neighborhood on Alexander Street to the Butler Tract on Harrison Street. This sweeping arc of new growth will transform the southern edge of campus, redefining its relationship to the lake valley, and creating new gateways to visitors arriving from Route 1.

PROJECTS SERVE TO IMPLEMENT THE PLAN

The many projects shown in the Ten-Year Projects Map, as well as initiatives not shown, such as wayfinding and sustainability, will collectively serve to realize the physical implementation of the Campus Plan.

Enhancing the existing campus

While there is no longer available space for major construction within the Core Campus, the plan includes numerous projects that continue the University's stewardship of this significant historic area, while ensuring that it can continue to meet the functional needs of a modern institution. The reconstruction of Holder Court (L2), Cannon Green, and other spaces will restore the historic splendor of these landscapes, while subtly accommodating the need for vehicular access, high pedestrian traffic, reunion tents, and other factors that have damaged these original spaces over time.

Other projects are intended to enhance areas of postwar development, extending the sense of the campus, and better connecting these areas to the core. Along Shapiro Walk in the Prospect Avenue and William Street Neighborhood, for example, a landscape program (L13) will add pathways and create a richer palette of plantings, creating more attractive and walkable outdoor spaces for this part of campus.

Building to meet present needs

Most of the Campus Plan projects create spaces for the University's most critical new academic initiatives and other current and planned programs, and needed supporting infrastructure.

Examples of projects to meet current needs include the Arts and Transit Neighborhood (B1-3), where the Peter B. Lewis Center for the Arts will be located, Whitman College and the reconstructed Butler College (B5) to support a planned increase in the undergraduate population, and new playing fields such as the planned Roberts Stadium (A2).

Numerous supporting infrastructure projects are needed to enable the realization of these planned programs. The new parking facility (P5) will both support new growth and replace parking displaced by development. Streicker Bridge (F4) is a planned footbridge across Washington Road that will allow for crucial interdepartmental connections between several existing and new buildings in the Natural Sciences Neighborhood, as well as pedestrian crossing between the Ellipse and athletics areas.

Preparing for the future

Other projects are more strategic in nature. While they may address a current need, they have been planned in such a way as to prepare the campus to better support long-term strategic objectives of growth, sustainability, and management of its demands on infrastructure. These forward-thinking initiatives will ensure that the University has flexibility in the future without compromising the needs of the present.

For example, the stormwater management plan includes the creation of an infiltration and retention bed below the planned east athletic fields (S5) that will provide additional capacity for future growth while protecting the health of the natural watershed and reducing the impacts of runoff on streams and valleys. The relocation of the Data Center (B4) will allow for the expansion of this mission-critical facility at a new site, making use of proximity to the power plant for backup power and cooling, while removing an incompatible land use from the Prospect Avenue neighborhood, thus allowing for future uses more in keeping with the character of that area. The renovation of Frick, Hoyt, and Green halls (R6-8) will create space for the long-term growth of the humanities and social sciences, which would otherwise have few expansion options.

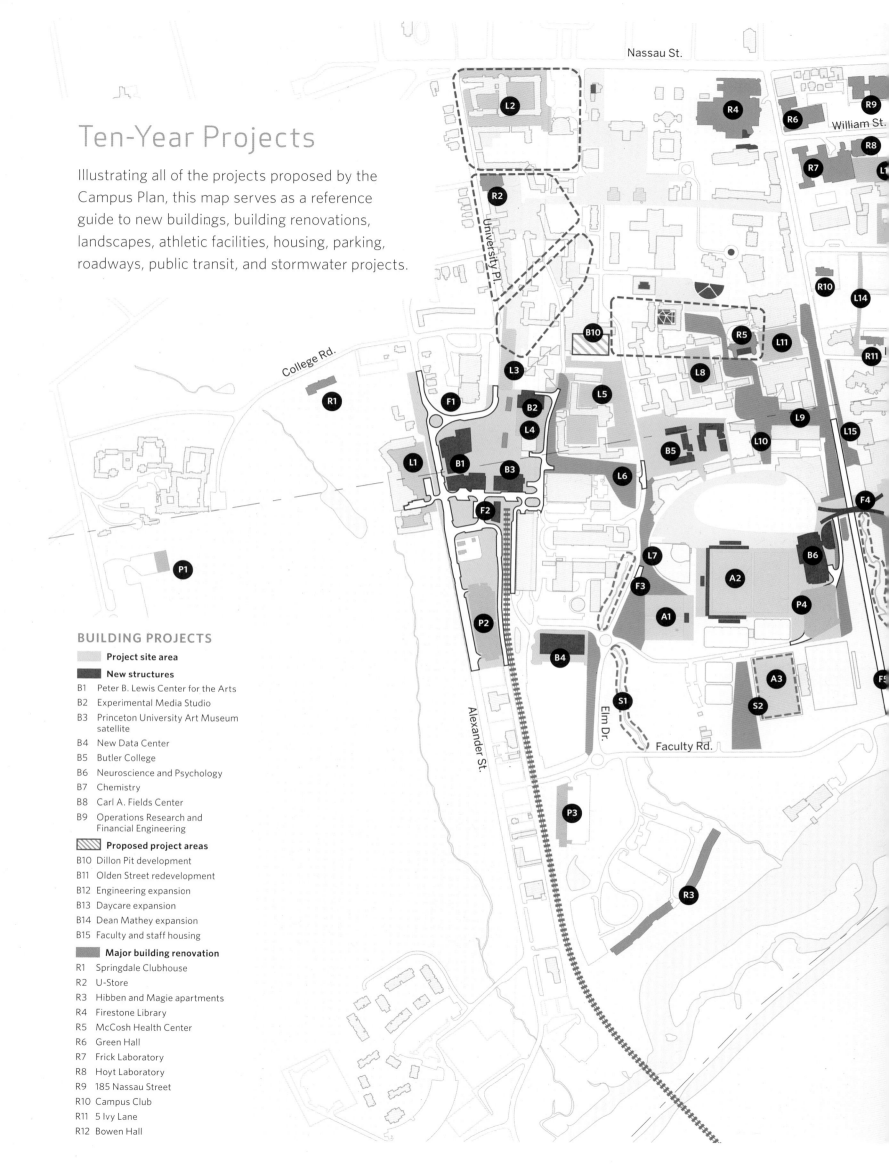

Ten-Year Projects

Illustrating all of the projects proposed by the Campus Plan, this map serves as a reference guide to new buildings, building renovations, landscapes, athletic facilities, housing, parking, roadways, public transit, and stormwater projects.

BUILDING PROJECTS

Project site area

New structures

B1 Peter B. Lewis Center for the Arts
B2 Experimental Media Studio
B3 Princeton University Art Museum satellite
B4 New Data Center
B5 Butler College
B6 Neuroscience and Psychology
B7 Chemistry
B8 Carl A. Fields Center
B9 Operations Research and Financial Engineering

Proposed project areas

B10 Dillon Pit development
B11 Olden Street redevelopment
B12 Engineering expansion
B13 Daycare expansion
B14 Dean Mathey expansion
B15 Faculty and staff housing

Major building renovation

R1 Springdale Clubhouse
R2 U-Store
R3 Hibben and Magie apartments
R4 Firestone Library
R5 McCosh Health Center
R6 Green Hall
R7 Frick Laboratory
R8 Hoyt Laboratory
R9 185 Nassau Street
R10 Campus Club
R11 5 Ivy Lane
R12 Bowen Hall

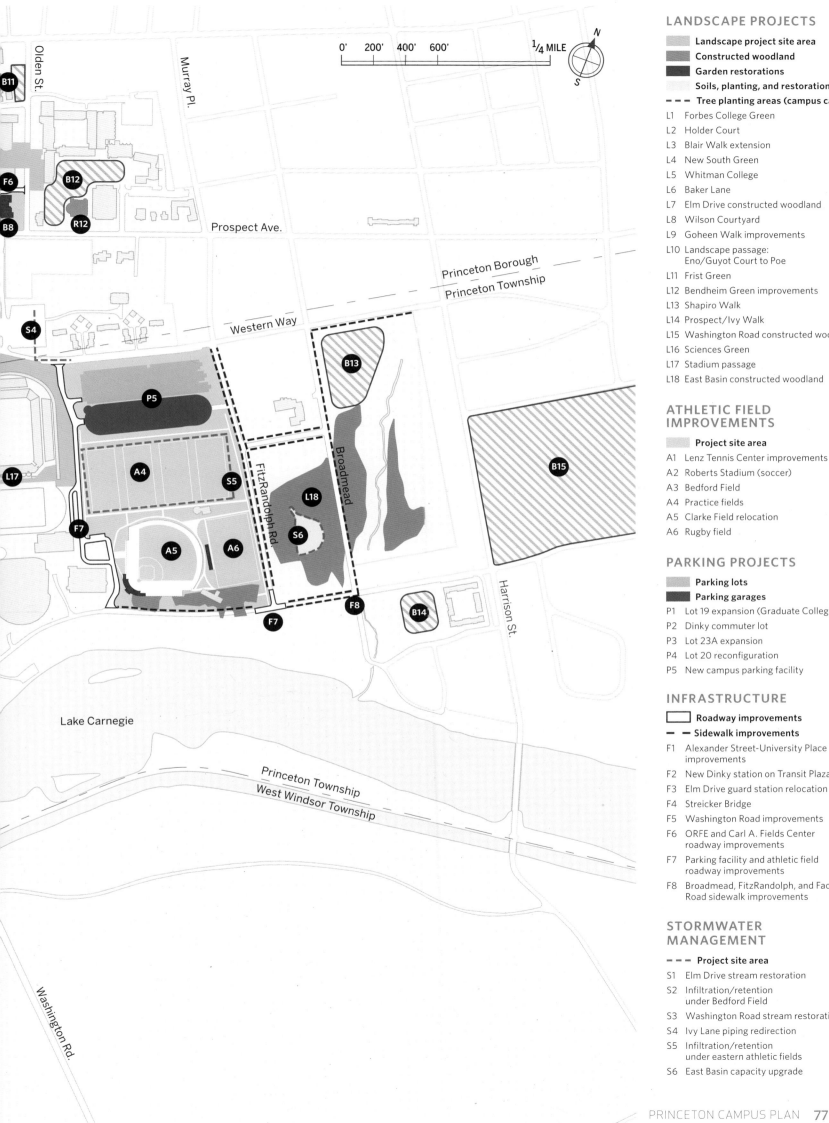

LANDSCAPE PROJECTS

| | Landscape project site area |
| Constructed woodland |
| Garden restorations |
| Soils, planting, and restoration |
- - - Tree planting areas (campus canopy)

L1   Forbes College Green
L2   Holder Court
L3   Blair Walk extension
L4   New South Green
L5   Whitman College
L6   Baker Lane
L7   Elm Drive constructed woodland
L8   Wilson Courtyard
L9   Goheen Walk improvements
L10 Landscape passage:
      Eno/Guyot Court to Poe
L11 Frist Green
L12 Bendheim Green improvements
L13 Shapiro Walk
L14 Prospect/Ivy Walk
L15 Washington Road constructed woodland
L16 Sciences Green
L17 Stadium passage
L18 East Basin constructed woodland

ATHLETIC FIELD IMPROVEMENTS

| | Project site area |

A1 Lenz Tennis Center improvements
A2 Roberts Stadium (soccer)
A3 Bedford Field
A4 Practice fields
A5 Clarke Field relocation
A6 Rugby field

PARKING PROJECTS

| | Parking lots |
| Parking garages |

P1 Lot 19 expansion (Graduate College)
P2 Dinky commuter lot
P3 Lot 23A expansion
P4 Lot 20 reconfiguration
P5 New campus parking facility

INFRASTRUCTURE

| | Roadway improvements |
- - Sidewalk improvements

F1 Alexander Street-University Place
    improvements
F2 New Dinky station on Transit Plaza
F3 Elm Drive guard station relocation
F4 Streicker Bridge
F5 Washington Road improvements
F6 ORFE and Carl A. Fields Center
    roadway improvements
F7 Parking facility and athletic field
    roadway improvements
F8 Broadmead, FitzRandolph, and Faculty
    Road sidewalk improvements

STORMWATER MANAGEMENT

- - - Project site area

S1 Elm Drive stream restoration
S2 Infiltration/retention
    under Bedford Field
S3 Washington Road stream restoration
S4 Ivy Lane piping redirection
S5 Infiltration/retention
    under eastern athletic fields
S6 East Basin capacity upgrade

PROSPECT AVENUE A
WILLIAM STREET
NEIGHBORHOOD

CORE CAMPUS
NEIGHBORHOOD

ARTS AND TRANSIT
NEIGHBORHOOD

NATURAL SCIENCES
NEIGHBORHOOD

View of the Campus Plan model

IVY LANE AND
WESTERN WAY
NEIGHBORHOOD

A CAMPUS OF NEIGHBORHOODS

- Core Campus

- Arts and Transit

- Natural Sciences

- Ivy Lane and Western Way

- Prospect Avenue and William Street

Princeton's main campus is large in scale and characterized by an intricate layout across hilly terrain. While the Core Campus has a strong historic character, newer areas have a varying sense of identity. These outlying areas include academic and other spaces that support the daily activities of a large portion of the University community. They are also the locations for much of the growth proposed in the Campus Plan. To reinforce these developing areas, the plan adopts the concept of "campus neighborhoods" as a guiding principle.

Campus neighborhoods are geographic areas defined by commonalities of character, use, or activity, such as the arts or the natural sciences. They break down the scale of Princeton's large campus into comprehensible districts, often in support of interdisciplinary collaboration between departments. The word "neighborhood" as it is used here connotes a sense of social and academic community organized within a distinct physical space.

Princeton's singular campus cannot be segregated into isolated parts, however. Campus neighborhoods therefore are not the exclusive locations for certain activities, but rather for a concentration of intensity in a particular realm. For example, the Arts and Transit Neighborhood will be a hub for the visual and performing arts, but many other arts activities will continue to be distributed widely across the campus. Neither will the physical design of neighborhoods create divisions between parts of campus. Instead, they allow for subtle shifts in architecture and landscape within a larger coherent whole.

The idea of campus neighborhoods is also a tool for planning, so that new buildings do not become individual monuments, but instead are woven into the landscape and infrastructure of their surroundings, avoiding a series of "projects" that feel disconnected from each other and from the campus.

In addition to the Core Campus, four emerging campus neighborhoods make up the heart of the Campus Plan—these are the areas which will undergo the greatest transformation over the next ten years.

Core Campus Neighborhood

Balancing preservation and modern needs

Most observers will immediately associate the physical presence of the Core Campus with the very identity of Princeton University. This cherished space is distinguished by its vast and diverse collection of historically significant architecture, including three national historic landmarks (Nassau Hall, Maclean House, and Prospect House) and many important works by some of the most notable American architects of the 19th and early 20th centuries, including Benjamin Latrobe, John Notman, McKim Mead & White, Ralph Adams Cram, and Richard Morris Hunt. Although many architectural styles are represented, the Core Campus has a coherence resulting from a history of judicious campus planning, most notably by Ralph Adams Cram in the early 20th century, and from the great attention given to creating a park-like landscape, first by President McCosh and later by pioneering landscape architect Beatrix Farrand. The collegiate gothic architecture added to the campus during the presidency of Woodrow Wilson further defined the enduring sense of place that makes the campus such a profound aspect of the University's character.

The Campus Plan recognizes that within the Core Campus, very little space remains for significant new development. This densely built area, which nonetheless maintains a park-like character as a result of the careful integration of buildings and landscape, has reached a point of substantial completion. As a result, emerging campus neighborhoods surrounding the core are the principal areas of focus of the Campus Plan. The four other neighborhoods discussed in this chapter will absorb most of the projected new growth on campus in the next ten years and beyond and thus require significant attention to planning and design.

There are nonetheless a range of issues within the Core Campus that are addressed by the Campus Plan. Most of the initiatives of the plan in this neighborhood support the University's role as the ongoing steward of its historic legacy, while at the same time ensuring that the Core Campus continues to serve as the vibrant and active home for some of the most central functions of the institution, including academics, administration, and undergraduate life. The plan reinforces and builds upon Princeton's long experience in striking an appropriate balance between preservation and the operation of a modern institution.

As the Campus Plan took shape, the new Whitman College and Butler College dormitories were under construction. Designed to accommodate an expansion of the undergraduate class by 500 students, these structures will likely be the last major construction projects in the Core Campus. They complete a sweeping arc of undergraduate housing first envisioned as a campus planning concept by Ralph Adams Cram in 1908. Other building projects in the Core Campus include the planned expansion of health and recreation facilities, for which several potential locations are under consideration, including the "Dillon Pit"—a sunken terrace south of the Dillon Gymnasium—and the possible reconfiguration of the McCosh Health Center.

A significant focus of the plan is placed on the enhancement of the historic landscapes of the Core Campus. A comprehensive landscape strategy includes the revitalization of historic gardens, such as Prospect Garden; the improvement of processional walks, such as McCosh Walk; the restoration of historic yet actively used campus greens, such as Holder Court; a tree planting and maintenance program; and soil restoration throughout the neighborhood. The landscape approach will not only enhance the historic beauty and park-like character of the Core Campus, but is also necessary to adapt the landscape to the intensive pressures placed on it by modern functional needs.

The original campus landscape was not designed to accommodate the high traffic and heavy use that occurs today, including vehicular traffic for maintenance, moving days, deliveries, and other purposes; heavy pedestrian activity, including recreational sports such as volleyball; and the large crowds and construction of tents, platforms, and other structures that occur regularly for commencement, reunions, and other events. Like Farrand's early plan for the campus, the plan creates resilient landscapes that are more resistant to damage from these factors, while also requiring less maintenance and improving environmental sustainability through measures such as the passive reuse of rainwater instead of irrigation. New standards for soils, planting, and paving will support these goals and buttress the health of historic trees. The introduction of young trees in the Core Campus will create a successive generation of tree canopy and mitigate the potential loss of distinctive older trees.

Together these initiatives will ensure the preservation and sustainability of the qualities that make Princeton's Core Campus one of the nation's most significant academic settings—the very place where the word "campus" was first used to refer to the grounds and buildings of a university.

Rendering of Blair Walk restoration

Rendering of Holder Court restoration

Arts and Transit Neighborhood

Creating a cultural and transportation hub that is both a campus and community destination

Unlike the historical development of cloistered enclosures separating the University from its surroundings, the new Arts and Transit Neighborhood at the western edge of campus will form a public space that is a nexus of both campus and community life. New public plazas will complement Princeton's existing public spaces—Palmer Square, the Scudder Plaza fountain, and Hinds Plaza at the public library—with a focal point for cultural life. New activities in the area will build upon and strengthen the longstanding presence of two anchors of the Princeton community: the McCarter Theatre Center and the New Jersey Transit Dinky railroad station.

The neighborhood will be the home of the new Peter B. Lewis Center for the Arts. According to President Tilghman, the center will enable the University "not only to expand its programs in the creative and performing arts, but to establish itself as a global leader in the quality of its offerings and in their integration into a broader liberal arts education." The neighborhood will support academic programs in theater, dance, and music (which will also maintain its presence in Woolworth Hall) with new teaching, rehearsal, and administrative spaces. Shared performance venues will include a black box theater, a film theater, an experimental media studio, and a performance hall with a fly loft and orchestra pit. A new building for the Princeton University Art Museum will complement the existing museum with galleries for contemporary and rotating exhibits, teaching spaces, and a museum lounge/café and shop.

In addition to their teaching function, the new performance venues will host University-produced performances and other activities that will be open to the public. Combined with the art museum and the existing McCarter and Berlind theaters, the neighborhood will become a vibrant cultural destination for the region. Restaurants, cafés, and other public amenities will support the needs of visitors, while also appealing to faculty, staff, and students, as well as to the many riders of the Dinky and other transit services in the area.

These spaces will not all be housed in a single large structure but in a "village" of smaller buildings, compatible with the scale and texture of the surroundings, and interspersed with plazas and landscaped open spaces following traditions of campus and town planning in Princeton. The buildings will be designed by a variety of architects, establishing a diversity of architectural expression within a coherent whole created by the neighborhood planning framework.

Before this vision for a mixed-use arts neighborhood can be implemented, many layers of transportation infrastructure in the area must be reconfigured into a coherent and functional system. The project itself will not generate new traffic—in fact it will reduce peak-hour traffic by replacing administrative offices with cultural uses. However, the roads and transit facilities in the area were not originally designed to handle the volume of regional and commuter traffic they now support. Changing regional traffic patterns, growth of town and campus, and the increasing appeal of the Dinky to daily commuters and other users have all led to significant traffic congestion. Any revitalization must improve traffic and transit facilities to create a more functional and attractive site.

A comprehensive upgrade of this regional transportation center will include the reconfiguration of the roadway network with a roundabout to reduce traffic congestion, and the creation of a multi-modal transportation hub. This proposed "Transit Plaza" will serve rail commuters and provide connections for cars, taxis, buses, a community jitney, campus shuttles, and bicycles, as well as the future bus rapid transit service proposed by New Jersey Transit. A new Dinky station building, with improved amenities for commuters including retail space, as well as the relocated 24-hour Wawa store, will face the pedestrian-oriented plaza.

Public parking for Dinky commuters and other users will be replaced, while parking for visitors to the new arts facilities and McCarter and Berlind theaters can be provided in the University's existing Lot 7 garage, utilizing capacity created by the reassignment of some University employees to the proposed new parking facility east of Washington Road. As a result of road and track realignments, the Lot 7 garage will be accessible directly from Alexander Street.

Taken together, the proposed transportation improvements, retail, public spaces, and buildings for the arts will create a lively and attractive gateway to the township and borough of Princeton as well as to the University.

MCCARTER
THEATRE

University Place

BERLIND
THEATRE

EXPERIMENTAL
MEDIA STUDIO

WHITMAN
COLLEGE

ARTS
PLAZA

NEW
SOUTH

LEWIS CENTER FOR
THE ARTS

PRINCETON
UNIVERSITY
ART MUSEUM
SATELLITE

Alexander St

FORBES
COLLEGE

DINKY
STATION

LOT 7
GARAGE

TRANSIT
PLAZA

CONNECTIONS TO THE CAMPUS

Arts on campus

The Peter B. Lewis Center for the Arts and the Princeton University Art Museum satellite will create a new focal point for arts instruction, exhibition, and performance alongside the McCarter and Berlind theaters. The program will include retail and public amenities to enliven the new mixed-use district. At the same time, the new buildings will complement existing arts facilities across the campus. Existing destinations such as Richardson Auditorium, the Princeton University Art Museum, 185 Nassau Street, and myriad theater, rehearsal, gallery, and studio spaces will continue to serve the arts communities on campus and throughout the region. This strategy supports the "edge-to-edge deployment" of the arts on campus recommended by President Tilghman's 2006 Creative and Performing Arts Initiative.

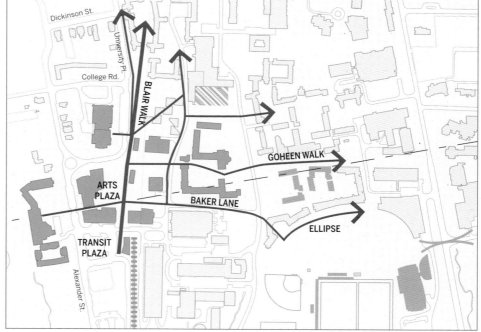

● Proposed facilities

1	Rocky/Mathey Theatre	7	Princeton University Art Museum	12	McAlpin Auditorium Woolworth Center of Musical Studies
2	McCarter Theatre Center	8	Wilson Dance Studio	13	Frist Campus Center
3	Richardson Auditorium	9	Wilcox Theatre	14	185 Nassau Street
4	Dillon Gym Dance Studio	10	Butler College Memorial Court	15	Bernstein Gallery
5	Class of 1970 Theatre Whitman College	11	Peter B. Lewis Rehearsal Space (Bloomberg)	16	Taplin Auditorium
6	Theatre Intime			17	New Carl A. Fields Center

Pedestrian connections

The Arts and Transit Neighborhood will create a gateway to both the campus and the surrounding community for visitors arriving by car, bus, train, and bike, with a new pathway network radiating into the campus and connecting the Dinky station to Nassau Street. The historic Blair Walk, designed by Beatrix Farrand in the 1920s as a pedestrian promenade into the Core Campus, will be extended to the new station. New public plazas, animated by retail and arts activities, will form a crossroads for campus and town walking routes in both east-west and north-south directions.

Pedestrian pathways

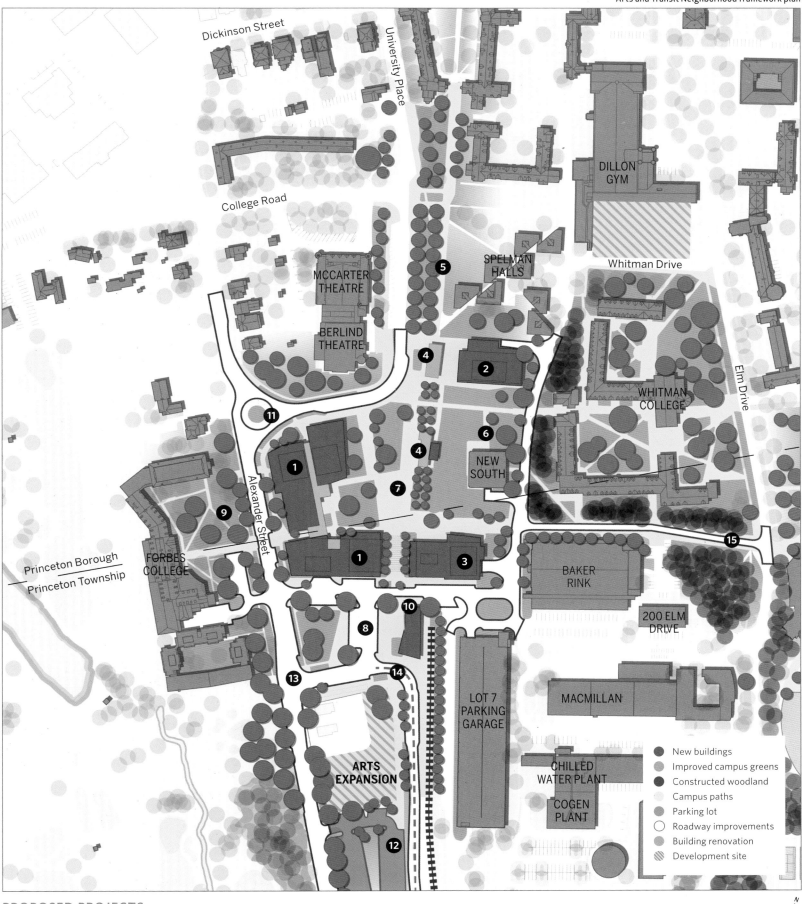

Dickinson Street

University Place

College Road

DILLON GYM

MCCARTER THEATRE

SPELMAN HALLS

Whitman Drive

BERLIND THEATRE

5

4

2

WHITMAN COLLEGE

Elm Drive

11

6

1

4

NEW SOUTH

7

9

Alexander Street

15

FORBES COLLEGE

1

3

BAKER RINK

Princeton Borough
Princeton Township

200 ELM DRIVE

10

8

13

14

MACMILLAN

LOT 7 PARKING GARAGE

CHILLED WATER PLANT

ARTS EXPANSION

COGEN PLANT

12

New buildings
Improved campus greens
Constructed woodland
Campus paths
Parking lot
Roadway improvements
Building renovation
Development site

PROPOSED PROJECTS

Arts and Retail Facilities

1   Peter B. Lewis Center for the Arts
2   Experimental Media Studio
3   Princeton University Art Museum satellite
4   Repurposed Dinky buildings for retail

Public Spaces and Amenities

5   Blair Walk extension
6   New South Green
7   Arts Plaza
8   Transit Plaza
9   Forbes Green

Infrastructure

10   New Dinky station
11   New roundabout
12   New Dinky commuter parking lot
13   Improved roadways

14   Potential bus rapid transit
15   Baker Lane

0'   100'   200'

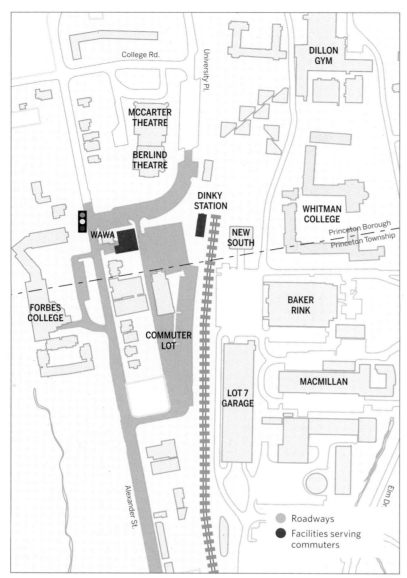

Transportation infrastructure, 2006

Transportation infrastructure, 2016

Legend (2016 map):
- Improved roadways
- Facilities serving commuters
- New buildings
- Bus rapid transit line
- Community jitney route
- Bike route

Legend (2006 map):
- Roadways
- Facilities serving commuters

The proposed design reconfigures roadways, the Dinky rail line, and parking areas to improve traffic flows and create a multi-modal transportation hub at the new station, which can also accommodate potential bus rapid transit service.

TRAFFIC AND TRANSIT

The redesign of the roadway network at the Arts and Transit Neighborhood will alleviate existing congestion by reducing peak-hour traffic-generating land uses and by eliminating the concentration of conflicting traffic movements at the intersection of Alexander Street and University Place (see Traffic section, page 152). A new roundabout will remove a traffic light and nearby parking at the problematic intersection. It will encourage the natural flow of traffic toward University Place and provide an arrival point to both the campus and community when approaching from the south.

A new signalized pedestrian crossing at Forbes College will move pedestrians away from the vehicular intersection. Further to the south, the Transit Plaza will reduce traffic congestion by providing off-the-road access to the Wawa and the drops-offs for a community jitney, the Dinky, and the arts venues. By removing these functions from the intersection of Alexander Street and University Place, the proposed redesign will maintain a smoother flow and more controlled distribution of traffic. A road linking to Lot 7 garage will draw University employees, visitors, and patrons of the arts directly from Alexander Street.

The existing administrative uses and parking lots on the site contribute to peak-hour morning and afternoon traffic as employees travel to and from work. The replacement of these uses with cultural and retail uses will reduce peak hour volumes since the new uses will draw visitors to the neighborhood in the evenings, afternoons, or weekends when the roads are less congested. Although all the public and commuter parking spaces that are currently on the site will be replaced in kind, University-related parking will be reduced at the site.

The new Arts and Transit Neighborhood is carefully planned to provide a 21st century mixed-use transit hub. The incorporation of a new Transit Plaza into the plan is an important environmental first step. The Transit Plaza will provide an improved station for the Dinky, stops for a proposed community jitney, a stop for University shuttles, bike rental and storage, and dedicated space for a possible future bus rapid transit expansion. These amenities and services will promote the use of public transit as an alternative to single-passenger vehicles for commuters and visitors. Direct access to the Lot 7 garage will reduce the vehicle miles traveled by commuters who arrive from the north to park in the facility by three-quarters of a mile in each direction. This in turn reduces the associated carbon emissions. Through energy efficient design, new buildings in the neighborhood will perform significantly above the requirements set by ASHRAE Standard 90.1.

Model photo of Arts and Transit Neighborhood looking east toward the Natural Sciences Neighborhood

Princeton University Orchestra

ARTS IN SOCIETY

I am tempted to rely on that over-used, misapplied word "revolution" to describe the establishment of the University Center for the Creative and Performing Arts, because there is something so unique, so forward-looking, even daring about it. But the term is wholly inaccurate because, innovative as it is, the concept is not disruptive. In fact, it is just the opposite: the realization of the necessity of art as a full and integral part of first-rate, higher education combined with a recognition of how artists work. The notion of the solitary writer, painter, musician, is an attractive myth (but even van Gogh had Gauguin as a housemate for a while). The relationship between creative art and research/analysis/criticism is an inseparable one. I can't think of a single living artist who has not collaborated with someone in another genre (screenwriting, set design, or lyrics, narrative, music composition, video, photography, theater performances, architects, dance choreography, film). And I can't think of any who did not rely on or produce appropriate scholarship.

So innovative as it is, the center is also natural, organic, "… indispensable" as President Tilghman has said, "to Princeton University's special version of liberal arts education." While I am not certain, I don't believe there is another university in the country which has committed itself so concretely to the view of intellectual life as deficient without serious attention to the arts. Not just for the aspiring professional artist: not limited to an amiable pastime available in separate enclaves; but an assumption that art is an intellectual pursuit —struck, perhaps, by lightning bolts of inspiration; inoperable without the power of the imagination, but a pursuit deeper and much more profound than even the talent and genius of its purveyors. Princeton University is a natural habitat for such a pursuit.

Excerpts from remarks by

Toni Morrison
Goheen Professor in the Humanities, Emeritus
April 19, 2007

Natural Sciences Neighborhood

Fostering scientific collaboration in a natural setting

The natural sciences represent one of the most dynamic areas of growth and change at Princeton. Rapid advances in the sciences continue to generate new fields of inquiry, which require larger research buildings of ever-increasing technological sophistication. New interdisciplinary programs have been created, including the Lewis-Sigler Institute for Integrative Genomics and the Princeton Neuroscience Institute, and longstanding scientific disciplines such as chemistry can no longer accommodate modern laboratory-based research in the aging buildings that house them.

The Campus Plan proposes new buildings for chemistry, neuroscience, and psychology as part of a significant expansion and consolidation of science departments into a Natural Sciences Neighborhood at the south end of Washington Road. Such concentration has significant advantages. In the words of President Tilghman, speaking of the Neurosciences Institute, "To forge a true community of scholars, with shared facilities and instruments, we plan to construct a state-of-the-art neuroscience center in close proximity to other scientific disciplines, allowing faculty and students to move between the institute and their home departments with ease. The questions with which the institute will grapple are among the most exciting in the scientific world today, and the creative collaborations, serendipitous discoveries, and intellectual advances that lie ahead will shape the face of neuroscience in this country and beyond."

Streicker Bridge, a pedestrian footbridge across Washington Road designed by the distinguished Swiss engineer Christian Menn, will reinforce these connections by linking multiple buildings that have previously been separated by this major roadway. Outdoor pathways and basement-level passages will link buildings on either side of the road like a "ladder," with the bridge and the Goheen Walk crosswalk acting as the rungs.

One significant challenge of the Natural Sciences Neighborhood design is integrating the increasing size and bulk of modern research buildings into the human scale of the campus. The large mass of these buildings is due partly to their stringent requirements for high-technology systems and equipment, and partly to the fact that, at Princeton,

teaching continues to be emphasized in addition to research. As a result, the new Chemistry building will include more fume hoods and lab benches than would be required for a pure research space.

A structure like the Chemistry building would be vastly out of scale if it were located within the Core Campus. The planning strategy instead positions these buildings at the southern edge of campus, where the natural landscape of robust woodlands and ravines will provide an appropriate visual and experiential buffer to their size, as well as a pastoral view from offices and labs. A modern architectural vocabulary, emphasizing lightness and transparency, will characterize these structures, reducing their apparent size and relating them to the scenic surroundings in a very different way than the stone and brick buildings of the upper campus.

The design of this neighborhood will actually improve rather than degrade the natural ecology of the site. New buildings are located on existing parking lots, resulting in a net increase in green space over existing conditions today. The surrounding woodlands will be restored and expanded up to and between buildings, improving ecological balance by interconnecting fragmented natural areas. Stormwater runoff, currently directed to an overstressed and eroded streambed along Washington Road, will be recaptured for use as gray water within buildings, with the excess directed to "biofiltration" areas: landscapes that are both aesthetic and functional. These measures will allow the stream to be restored, further enhancing the natural balance of the entire Washington Road valley.

Combined with the advanced sustainability measures planned for the Chemistry, Neuroscience, and Psychology buildings, the Natural Sciences Neighborhood will be one of the most environmentally sustainable areas of campus. Appropriately, scientists and students in the natural sciences will be able to experience and appreciate the implementation of environmental principles in their daily surroundings.

GUYOT

MOFFET

SCHULTZ

THOMAS

ICAHN

LEWIS LIBRARY

FINE

PEYTON

SCIENCES GREEN

PRINCETON STADIUM

JADWIN PHYSICS

STREICKER BRIDGE

CHEMISTRY

Washington Rd.

NEUROSCIENCE & PSYCHOLOGY

CONNECTIONS TO THE CAMPUS

The planning framework for the Natural Sciences Neighborhood has been guided by a deliberate strategy to create new avenues for scientific collaboration and discovery by consolidating the natural sciences disciplines for the first time on campus. Its location at the foot of Washington Road will establish the neighborhood as one of the gateways to the campus, with Streicker Bridge as the iconic arrival point. The bridge will be part of a larger network of pedestrian connections to tie the neighborhood to the rest of the campus.

Consolidation of academic departments

While the majority of natural sciences buildings are located south of Ivy Lane and the Frist Campus Center, some natural sciences departments have been historically housed in buildings along the northern portion of Washington Road. With the construction of the new Chemistry, Neuroscience, and Psychology buildings, all natural sciences departments will be consolidated into one neighborhood. Frick Laboratory, Hoyt Laboratory, and Green Hall will no longer house the natural sciences. Instead, they will be made available for humanities and social sciences departments, thus alleviating overcrowding in other academic buildings. This shift in building uses creates distinct interdisciplinary precincts on campus, with a natural sciences concentration in the south and humanities and social sciences in the north.

A ladder of pathways along Washington Road

Historically, pedestrian walks have played an important role in preserving the connections between the eastern and western portions of campus. These connections will become especially important for the Natural Science Neighborhood as new buildings straddle the main thoroughfare of Washington Road. The new Streicker Bridge will complete a critical southern link on campus, providing a safe and scenic pedestrian passage from the Ellipse to Princeton Stadium. This new east-west link will be a rung in a "ladder" of east-west links on campus. The ladder is composed of a combination of existing and proposed north-south pathways that parallel Washington Road. Apart from Streicker Bridge, the rungs of the ladder are made up of established crossings at McCosh Walk, Prospect Avenue, Ivy Lane, and Goheen Walk.

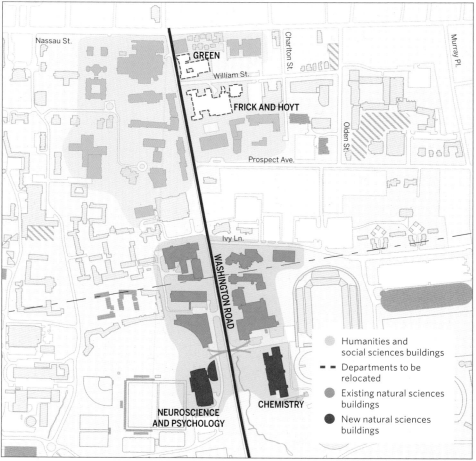

Consolidation of the natural sciences

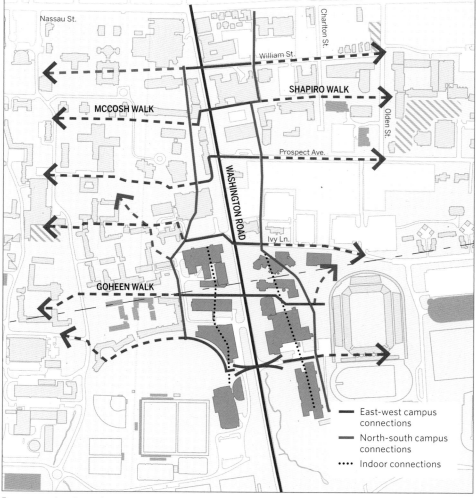

East-west pedestrian pathways

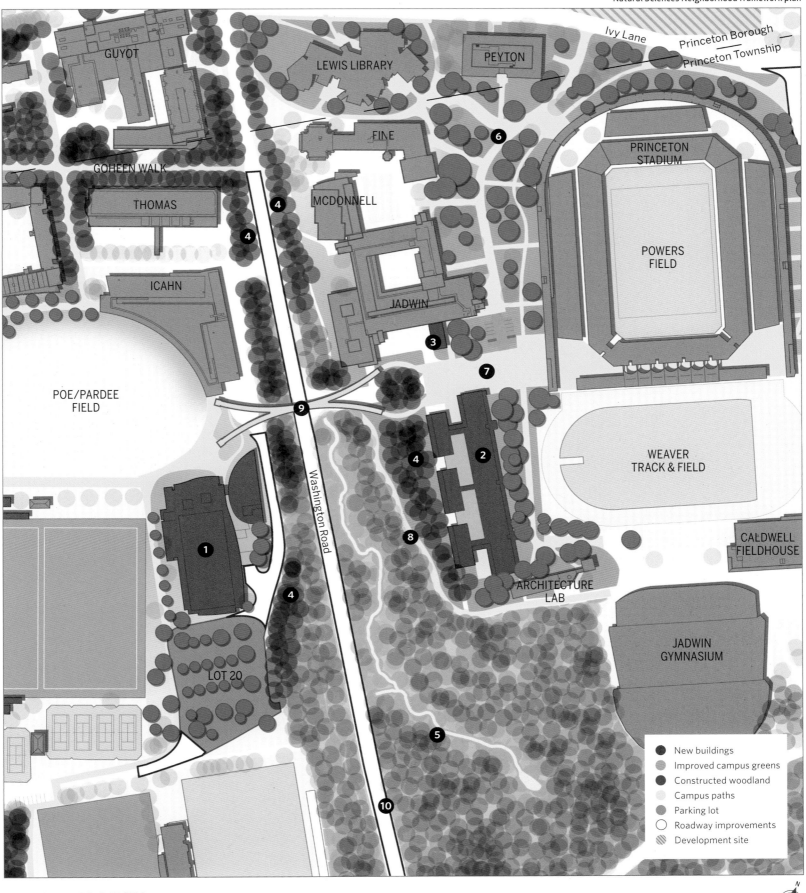

GUYOT

LEWIS LIBRARY

PEYTON

Ivy Lane

Princeton Borough
Princeton Township

FINE

6

PRINCETON
STADIUM

GOHEEN WALK

THOMAS

MCDONNELL

4

4

POWERS
FIELD

ICAHN

JADWIN

3

POE/PARDEE
FIELD

7

9

4

2

WEAVER
TRACK & FIELD

Washington Road

8

CALDWELL
FIELDHOUSE

1

ARCHITECTURE
LAB

4

JADWIN
GYMNASIUM

LOT 20

5

10

- ● New buildings
- Improved campus greens
- ● Constructed woodland
- Campus paths
- Parking lot
- ○ Roadway improvements
- Development site

PROPOSED PROJECTS

Academic Buildings

1   Neuroscience and
    Psychology

2   Chemistry

3   Jadwin Physics loading
    dock improvement

Landscapes and Stormwater Management

4   Constructed woodland

5   Stream restoration

6   Sciences Green

7   Chemistry Plaza

Pedestrian Safety

8   Woodland path

9   Streicker Bridge

10 Washington Road improvements

0'   100'   200'

N
S

Chemistry

Architect: Hopkins Architects of London in collaboration with Payette Associates of Boston, MA
Landscape Architect: Michael Van Valkenburgh Associates
Size: 240,000 – 250,000 square feet
Scheduled completion: Fall 2010

Key features The Chemistry building will be clad primarily in glass and stone panels set in a structural framework. It will feature state-of-the-art laboratory and teaching spaces on the east side of the building with offices on the west side of the building facing Washington Road. The two wings of the buildings will be joined by a skylit atrium that will feature pedestrian connectors at three levels and public meeting spaces. A new multi-modal pedestrian plaza is being designed at the entrance of the building. In addition to being located at the eastern terminus of the Streicker pedestrian bridge, this plaza will serve as an active gathering and circulation space creating an animated focal point for the Natural Sciences Neighborhood. The building's design incorporates several "green" features which are discussed in the Green Princeton section of this chapter.

Landscape The landscape design for the Chemistry building takes into account its location adjacent to a sensitive stream and existing woodlands, both of which will be enhanced and restored. A nature walk is proposed to run along the building's western edge, paralleling the stream channel. In addition to providing an opportunity for recreation, this new nature walk will improve pedestrian circulation within this neighborhood. The area on the east side of the new Chemistry building will be landscaped to remove the existing parking lot and strengthen the pedestrian connections to the athletics facilities to the east and south and the other science buildings to the north. The overall experience of the sciences neighborhood will be further improved by providing a green corridor that connects all the science buildings along Princeton Stadium's west façade.

Neuroscience and Psychology

Architect: Rafael Moneo Arquitecto of Madrid, Spain in collaboration with Davis Brody Bond of New York City
Landscape Architect: Michael Van Valkenburgh Associates
Size: 200,000 square feet

Key features The Neuroscience and Psychology buildings will take an innovative approach to studying the brain and nervous system by housing two disciplines in separate wings of a shared space. The Department of Psychology and a new Neuroscience Institute will be located in two new buildings that will incorporate classrooms, laboratories, offices, meeting rooms, and some specialty spaces, such as a place to house the University's functional magnetic resonance imaging (fMRI) scanner.

The buildings will also frame the southeast corner of Poe Field, just west of Washington Road. The northern entrance will have a physical and aesthetic relationship to the new Streicker Bridge, which will connect the buildings to other parts of the Natural Sciences Neighborhood on the eastern side of Washington Road.

Streicker Bridge

Designer: Engineer Christian Menn of Switzerland in collaboration with U.S.-based HNTB
Scheduled completion: 2010

Key features The design for Streicker Bridge is a curved x-shaped superstructure supported by a single arch. The new bridge will span 300 feet and rise about 23 feet above street level at its highest point, serving as a gateway to the campus and the community for vehicles traveling north on Washington Road. The bridge will connect the athletics and science buildings on the east side of campus with new and existing buildings on the west side of campus, completing a critical missing link in the pedestrian route along the southern edge of campus. The approach to the bridge on the west side of campus will be framed by the Ellipse, Icahn Laboratory, and the new Neuroscience and Psychology buildings. The eastern terminus of the bridge will land in a new multi-modal pedestrian plaza that provides entry to Jadwin Hall and the proposed Chemistry building, as well as access to Princeton Stadium and other destinations to the east such as athletic fields and the proposed new parking facility.

Holder Court

Jadwin and Fine halls

Scale of buildings and open space

While the south end of Washington Road has been an appropriate location for science buildings, the scale and bulk of these facilities have made it difficult to create the intimate pedestrian-oriented scale that is characteristic of the historic area of campus. Open spaces such as the Jadwin courtyard and the perimeter of the stadium are uninviting and disjointed from the active interior life of the buildings—in contrast to the variety of social outdoor spaces of historic courtyards such as the one in Holder. While the Holder Court maintains a human-scaled ratio of buildings to open space, the post-war landscapes on the southern part of campus lack the same proportions and relationships between interior and exterior. As part of the proposed landscape and building designs in the Natural Sciences Neighborhood, dynamic pedestrian plazas and redesigned open spaces will bring new life to the outdoor spaces. Tree plantings, view corridors, and active façades will enhance the pedestrian qualities of the greens.

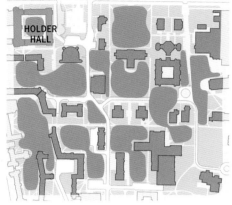

Historic campus landscapes

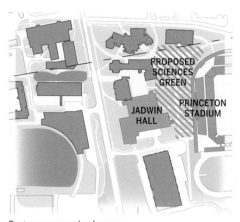

Post-war campus landscapes

Rendering of proposed Sciences Green

Sciences Green

The Sciences Green is an open space that lies between Princeton Stadium to the east and the natural sciences buildings to the west. It has the potential to be a defining central green for the Natural Sciences Neighborhood that frames the bold new architecture of Frank Gehry's Lewis Library and Michael Hopkins' Chemistry building. At present this area has a barren underutilized landscape that is further weakened by the vehicular ring-road around the stadium. While considering utilitarian issues such as the impact of new loading requirements for Peyton Hall, the new design for this area will open up key views through selective tree removal and re-orient pathways for deep views and north-south connectivity. Additionally, the Sciences Green will provide a foundation for the development of a new "East Diagonal" that will link this neighborhood to future development along Ivy Lane and Western Way.

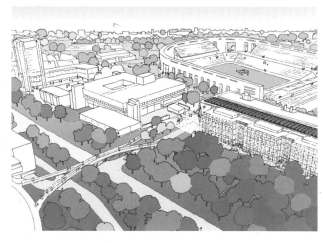

A bird's eye view of the new Chemistry building showing the solar photovoltaic panels highlighted in blue

CHEMISTRY BUILDING

In addition to landscape and stormwater strategies that will restore, enhance, and expand the natural areas, the new Chemistry building will incorporate sustainable building technologies. A series of proposed features will reduce energy demand and conserve water. As the highest utility user on campus, this building provides an opportunity to implement aggressive energy efficiency measures.

Extensive high-performance glazing will provide ambient daylighting of interior spaces, linked with sensors for control of dimmable electric lighting systems. Architectural shading elements will decrease solar heat gain in summer. One such element will be a roof canopy over the atrium interior, with solar photovoltaic panels designed to generate electricity. Integrated mechanical systems will enable optimal transfer of cooled and heated air from offices through the atrium and incorporate displacement heating and cooling in the auditorium. High-efficiency laboratory fume hoods with automatic sash closers will reduce both air supply and exhaust requirements, and heat recovery systems will capture energy from lab exhaust. A gray water system will collect and recycle stormwater for non-potable uses. Landscaped rain gardens and biofiltration areas will retain and filter additional building and site stormwater.

ENVIRONMENTAL RESTORATION

The experience of a naturalistic woodland setting as a feature of daily life has been a central theme of campus development at Princeton for the last 250 years. In this tradition, early 20th century designer Beatrix Farrand devised a series of pathways that drew people southward to Lake Carnegie across a lush stretch of natural woodland terrain. However, as vehicular traffic proliferated, the connection between the campus greens to the north and the woodlands to the south gradually fragmented, surrendering much of Farrand's original path network to parking lots, service areas, and roadways.

New developments in the sciences neighborhood offer an opportunity to restore the integrity of Farrand's vision by reuniting the woodlands with the rest of campus through the introduction of an expanded green belt that will extend northward up Washington Road to Lewis Library. The construction of the woodland threshold and the nature paths east and west of the Chemistry building will provide a lush natural setting for existing and new buildings from Lake Carnegie to the Frist Campus Center. It will reinforce the University's proximity to the natural valley of Lake Carnegie while providing an integrated stormwater system and restored natural habitats.

Contemporary scientific research is a study in contrasts: larger and larger scale effort to study more and more complex and, typically, ever-smaller scale phenomena. The challenge is to incorporate these large and complicated pursuits into the exquisite setting at Princeton, the paradigm set by the design, diversity, and execution of the buildings, and landscape of the Core Campus. The challenge is to architecturally control the massing of these new structures and integrate them into our campus in a cost-effective and environmentally sustainable way. This preservation, and in some ways augmentation, of the natural and historic beauty of our campus, while meeting the goals of our expanding scientific portfolio, is both demanding and exciting.

—PAUL LAMARCHE,
VICE PROVOST

Princeton stands unique among the world's "top ten" research universities with its small scale, its singular faculty committed to teaching undergraduate and graduate students, and its emphasis on high-quality research across all departments and divisions. As do their peers at other crucibles of leading research, scholars here pose and answer profound questions that could not even have been asked a few years ago. They generate ideas, scientific discoveries, and associated technologies that redefine society itself, often within a generation, let alone a lifetime. This relentless progress also spawns risks, side effects, and policy issues of great research interest themselves.

Today's research increasingly transcends traditional disciplinary boundaries, transforming the modes in which scholars operate. Princeton thrives in this new environment, as interdepartmental relationships have always been close, making it easy and natural to create institutes to address new initiatives and provide homes for shared facilities. Among these, the Princeton Environmental Institute and the Princeton Institute for the Science and Technology of Materials link researchers in engineering and the sciences as well as in other fields. Princeton researchers also benefit greatly from the presence of intellectual connections with the Princeton Plasma Physics Laboratory and the Geophysical Fluid Dynamics Laboratory at Forrestal, and the neighboring Institute for Advanced Study.

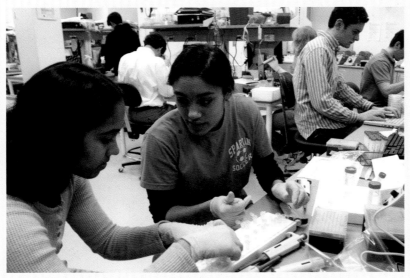

Undergraduate research in the Lewis-Sigler Institute's Integrated Science Program

Nevertheless we face a daunting challenge to keep up with all this, and to stay at the top! Research is expensive and space intensive: new laboratory buildings with sophisticated facilities, high startup costs for new faculty, and the constant need to renew all facets of our existing infrastructure can break any budget. The reason is simple—to make progress one must go where no one has gone before. As Princeton Nobelist Val Fitch once said, "You can't buy a world's-best department, but you have to pay for it!" In 2007, Princeton research sponsored by external funding totaled $240 million—22 percent of Princeton's operating budget. Almost 90 percent of this research funding was provided by agencies of the federal government. It is of great concern, therefore, that competition for government support has greatly intensified, and institutions are expected to share an increasing fraction of the costs.

The new Campus Plan strongly and optimally enhances Princeton's interdisciplinary connections among the sciences, and hence its competitiveness and attractiveness to outstanding scholars. As a prime example, the Lewis-Sigler Institute for Integrative Genomics brings biologists, chemists, physicists, neuroscientists, engineers, and computer scientists together to perform experiments, simulations, and theoretical research to produce a fundamental understanding of the genome. Connections among molecular biology, physics, and mathematics were firmly cemented by the arrival of the Carl Icahn Laboratory across the street from Jadwin Hall. By contrast, the current locations of chemistry, neuroscience, and psychology inhibit interactions and sharing of facilities with their natural partners. Fortunately these problems will soon disappear with magnificent new buildings and state-of-the-art facilities for chemistry, psychology, and neuroscience to be located in the same neighborhood as physics and genomics.

With the beautiful Streicker Bridge across Washington Road and the preservation of the natural landscape, a spectacular new Science Neighborhood will be complete. Princeton's research future is bright indeed!

A.J. Stewart Smith
Dean for Research

Ivy Lane and Western Way Neighborhood

Integrating a once-remote area into the life of the campus and strengthening athletics

Ivy Lane and Western Way are two names for one continuous road that crosses the borough and township border as it extends east of campus. Encompassing lands on both sides of the road, the neighborhood forms the southeast edge of campus, and is home to Princeton Stadium, Clarke baseball field, and other athletics facilities.

The neighborhood seems farther away from the center of campus than it really is, a quality amplified by limited pathways and relatively low activity levels. Despite its seeming remoteness, this area is gradually becoming more connected to the center of campus. The Frist Campus Center, located at the geographic center of campus, is in fact as close to this neighborhood as to the traditional campus core to the west. The new Lewis Library, designed by Frank Gehry, is also bringing increased activity to this area.

The Campus Plan anticipates the continuation into the future of the easterly direction of growth begun by the library. While the ten-year plan includes no specific plans for new academic buildings in this area, it is a crucial location for future academic development. The plan establishes the principles and conditions needed to support long-term growth so that, over time, the neighborhood will become a fully integrated part of the future campus. Future development will need to provide new open spaces and pathways, strengthen the athletics district, and create an appropriate transition between the larger scale of academic buildings and the smaller scale of the residential community to the east. The plan proposes that FitzRandolph Road be the limit of future academic development in this neighborhood, although support uses that are compatible with the residential context, such as daycare, may be located east of FitzRandolph.

Several projects planned within ten years will begin integrating more of the Ivy Lane and Western Way Neighborhood into the daily life of the campus.

A parking facility to be located south of Western Way will meet the critical demand for new spaces and the loss of other parking areas to development. The facility will combine a low-profile garage set into the hillside with a landscaped surface parking lot. This concept was developed after an extensive study of alternative sites and strategies, which determined that of all possible locations for new parking, this site was within the closest walking distance of the majority of academic and administrative buildings where Princeton's commuting employees work.

With adequate and convenient parking, employees will be encouraged to walk from their parking spots to work using improved pathways connecting north and west to the E-Quad, Natural Sciences Neighborhood, and Core Campus. As a result, the new facility will reduce dependence on shuttle buses and avoid the risk that people will seek more convenient parking on neighborhood streets. Traffic access will be from Faculty Road, which with small modifications will have the capacity to collect commuter traffic and thus reduce impacts on surrounding neighborhoods. Finally, some employees will be reassigned from the Lot 7 garage near the Arts and Transit Neighborhood, thus freeing up space in that facility and avoiding a costly new garage in the western part of campus.

At the same time, the current practice fields and Clarke baseball field will be rebuilt and improved, defining a newly strengthened athletics neighborhood centered on the Caldwell Fieldhouse and replacing the existing parking Lot 21. A new rugby field will be added, lighting will be improved, and some fields will be surfaced with artificial turf, vastly increasing their utilization.

The Data Center currently located at 87 Prospect Avenue will be relocated out of the area, since its planned expansion, including a significant backup power and cooling plant, was deemed not only incompatible with the residential context but also a poor use of space in this increasingly campus-like area. It will either be moved to the Lot 16 site on the west side of campus or to an off-campus site. The existing building will be used as administrative space and is likely to be demolished eventually.

Campus daycare facilities, located at 171 Broadmead, will be expanded to a site known as the "Broadmead Fields," convenient for employees using the new parking facility as well as for faculty and staff who live nearby. Eventually, daycare facilities may be expanded in this location, creating a daycare "village" designed as a set of small-scale buildings compatible with the residential surroundings.

Each of these projects will contribute to the increased vitality of the Ivy Lane and Western Way Neighborhood, making it an increasingly significant part of the campus and setting the stage for future academic expansion in the area.

LEWIS LIBRARY

Ivy Lane

PRINCETON STADIUM

Western Way

WEAVER TRACK & FIELD

NEW PARKING FACILITY

CALDWELL FIELD HOUSE

ATHLETIC PRACTICE FIELDS

DENUNZIO POOL

FITZRANDOLPH OBSERVATORY

CLARKE FIELD

RUGBY FIELD

Faculty Rd

Fitz-Randolph Rd.

ATHLETICS AND OPEN SPACE

As part of the Campus Planning strategy to achieve greater integration of landscapes and uses east of Princeton Stadium, the athletic fields will move to the south and parking will shift to the north. Flipping the athletic fields and the parking on the east side of campus will fortify both the athletics neighborhood and the Lake Carnegie valley. A segmented assortment of open spaces will be consolidated into a contiguous band of green between woodlands and developed areas. The proposed realignment of playing fields will maintain the existing acreage of open space while increasing the efficiency and utilization of the fields with more resilient playing surfaces.

PARKING

By shifting the parking from its former location at Lot 21 to its new location off Western Way, it will be within a ten-minute walk to major faculty, staff, and graduate student destinations. Furthermore, its proximity to athletics venues such as Jadwin Gymnasium and Princeton Stadium provides ample parking for large evening and weekend events when the parking facility is not used by commuters.

STORMWATER MANAGEMENT

The parking facility and realigned fields will be designed with an integrated stormwater management system. Runoff from the terraced surface lot will be captured in wide landscape strips that separate the parking bays. Runoff from the parking garage will be directed to a bioswale buffer that separates the structure from the athletic fields to the south. All storm water on the site will be treated and stored in underground retention basins below the athletic fields.

In order to reduce the runoff rates and volumes in the area, and in order to take full advantage of the detention areas under the athletic fields, some of the storm water will be shifted from adjacent watersheds to the new detention areas. This will help protect the Washington Road stream from further deterioration by redirecting runoff from the Ivy Lane parking lots away from the stream. It will also reduce the impact of future development on the East Basin.

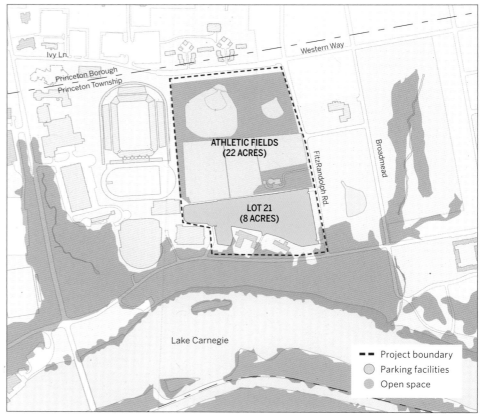

Predominantly developed areas and contiguous open space, 2006

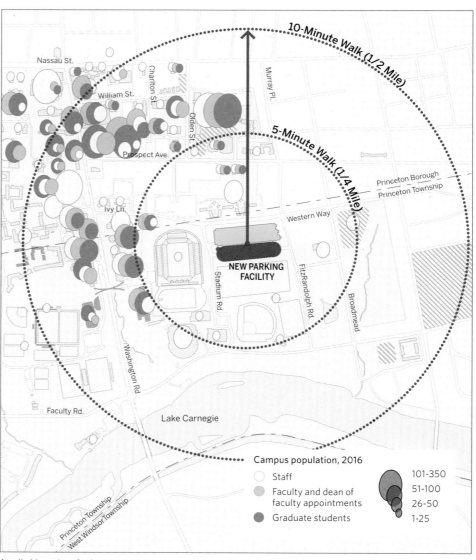

A walkable parking facility

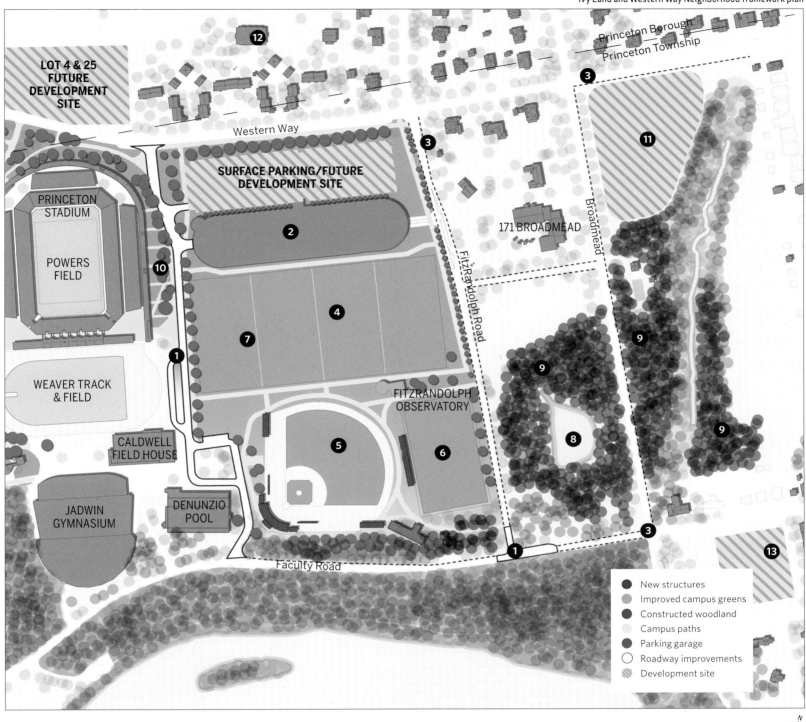

LOT 4 & 25 FUTURE DEVELOPMENT SITE

Western Way

SURFACE PARKING/FUTURE DEVELOPMENT SITE

PRINCETON STADIUM

POWERS FIELD

WEAVER TRACK & FIELD

CALDWELL FIELD HOUSE

JADWIN GYMNASIUM

DENUNZIO POOL

FITZRANDOLPH OBSERVATORY

171 BROADMEAD

Princeton Borough
Princeton Township

Broadmead

FitzRandolph Road

Faculty Road

Legend:
- ● New structures
- ● Improved campus greens
- ● Constructed woodland
- ○ Campus paths
- ● Parking garage
- ○ Roadway improvements
- ▨ Development site

0'   150'   300'

N
S

PROPOSED PROJECTS

Infrastructure Projects
1 Roadway improvements
2 New parking facility
3 Sidewalk improvements

Athletic Facilities
4 Realigned athletic practice fields
5 New Clarke baseball field
6 Rugby field

Landscape and Stormwater Management
7 Regional stormwater infiltration and retention (below playing fields)
8 East Basin improvements
9 Constructed woodland
10 Stadium landscaping and ADA access

Support Facilities
11 Daycare expansion
12 Data Center to be relocated

Housing
13 Expansion of Dean Mathey Court

Prospect Avenue and William Street Neighborhood

Extending the sense of campus
to a mixed area

The area east of Washington Road and south of Nassau Street is one of the first expansions of the campus beyond the original historic core. Development there began with the University's first two science buildings, Frick and Green halls, with the intent of extending the gothic character of the campus across Washington Road. Further implementation of this plan was interrupted by the Great Depression.

Growth eventually continued in the area, but largely without an organizing plan or unified approach to architecture and landscape, resulting in a haphazard neighborhood interspersed with streets, parking lots, and utilities such as an electrical transformer station. According to the Princeton University Campus Guide, "With the exception of the Eating Clubs on Prospect Avenue, the buildings in this precinct seldom communicate with one another. Nor does there appear to be an overall plan or design—whether it might be symmetrical, picturesque, or Beaux-Arts—which would provide a focus to pull it all together."[1] In recent years, this neighborhood's identification as part of the campus has been strengthened by improvements to Shapiro Walk, the organizing spine of pedestrian movement, and by new buildings that better define quadrangles.

In 1990, the University and Princeton Borough agreed on the details of a new E3 zoning district, establishing limits on the amount of new development and providing for expanded buffers, especially behind the neighboring homes on its eastern edge. In 2005, the University, the borough, and a group of neighbors approved amendments to the ordinance increasing the amount of development permitted in the Engineering Quadrangle, but also establishing more detailed requirements within the overall zone. These emphasize the importance of an effective shuttle system, provide greater protections for neighboring residents, and call for the "overall site design" of the district to include "courtyards and walkways similar to those that exist elsewhere on the University campus." It also requires the development and implementation of "a comprehensive landscape plan" for the E3 zone.

The Campus Plan strategy is consistent with this mandate to extend the sense of campus into the neighborhood. New buildings must define and revitalize open spaces, with their entrances and activities focused on landscaped greens and pathways. The new Operations Research and Financial Engineering (ORFE) building is an example of a design that fills a gap and creates activity, strengthening the adjacent quadrangle. Planned landscape improvements include robust new plantings to enhance the processional character of Shapiro Walk, a modern interpretation of the classic walks of the Core Campus designed by Beatrix Farrand. New trees and ground treatments, as well as additional pathways, will encourage greater pedestrian activity throughout the area.

Frick, Green, and the newer Hoyt Hall, having outlived their usefulness as science buildings, will be vacated as chemistry and psychology relocate to the Natural Sciences Neighborhood. They are well-configured, with renovations, to serve as expansion space for the adjacent divisions of the humanities and social sciences, consolidating and strengthening these activities around the Scudder Plaza fountain, an iconic and popular open space. 185 Nassau Street, a former elementary school, will continue to serve as a center for the arts, with expanded visual arts and creative writing programs made possible by the relocation of theater and dance to the planned Peter B. Lewis Center for the Arts on the west side of campus.

The east end of the neighborhood is home to the E-Quad, a self-contained set of buildings for the School of Engineering and Applied Science, built in 1962 with little relation to the surroundings. The plan anticipates a large addition between the original buildings and the more recently constructed Bowen Hall, on the site of an existing parking lot. Still in the planning stages, the new building will conform to the E3 zoning requirements and will enable the engineering school to meet urgent needs for expansion and modernization.

Prospect Avenue, known colloquially as "the Street," is home to Princeton's independently owned and operated eating clubs that were originally created as an alternative to Greek letter fraternities, banned at Princeton in 1855. They are housed in an elegant row of villa-like buildings built between the 1890s and 1920s, facing the avenue and creating a dramatic gateway to the campus from the east. Prospect Avenue constitutes a mixed-use and vital corridor for this neighborhood which the Campus Plan proposes to enhance by reusing two previous club buildings in a way that further integrates the avenue into the fabric of the campus. The former Campus Club will become a gathering space for undergraduate and graduate students, located in proximity to the Frist Campus Center, while the former Elm Club will become the new location for the Carl A. Fields Center for Equality and Cultural Understanding.

1. Raymond P. Rhinehart, *The Campus Guide: Princeton University* (New York, Princeton University Press, 1999), 60

CAMPUS CLUB

ROBERTSON

SCUDDER PLAZA

Washington Rd.

FRICK

GREEN

HOYT

WALLACE

185 NASSAU

Prospect Ave.

ORFE

Shapiro Walk

FRIEND CENTER

William St.

CARL A. FIELDS CENTER

MUDD LIBRARY

OLDEN STREET REDEVELOPMENT

Olden St.

BOWEN HALL

ENGINEERING EXPANSION

ENGINEERING QUADRANGLE

Nassau St.

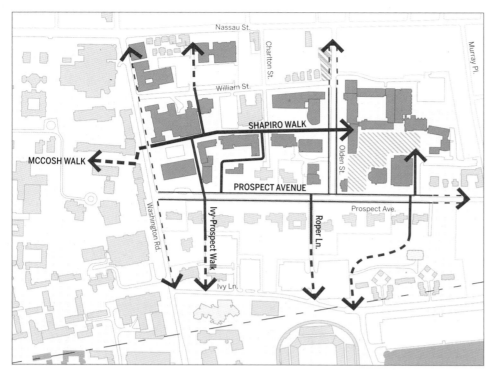

Pedestrian connections

CONNECTIONS TO THE CAMPUS

The Prospect Avenue and William Street Neighborhood is connected to the Core Campus along the spine of Shapiro Walk as it crosses Washington Road and becomes the historic McCosh Walk. Whereas Shapiro Walk is a broad and ceremonial east-west promenade, pathways to the south are more attenuated and dispersed as they take advantage of smaller opportunities to filter between the existing and former eating club buildings along Prospect Avenue. The existing walkway east of Bobst Hall links the Engineering Quadrangle to the Stadium, as does Roper Lane. Ivy-Prospect Walk creates a direct link between Scudder Plaza and Lewis Library. This plan aims to reinforce these pathways by clearly designating the existing walkways east of Bobst Hall and landscaping the Ivy-Prospect Walk east of Tower Club.

LANDSCAPE PROJECTS

Shapiro Walk

Pathways, landscaping, and green spaces will be improved along Shapiro Walk to create an attractive connection from Scudder Plaza to the engineering school. The landscape material will be selected for seasonal interest that can sustain the attractiveness of the walk during the winter months. The campus green along Shapiro Walk will be enhanced with the planting of additional shade trees and seating areas, making the lawn a pleasant space to spend time between classes or relax with friends, much like the greens of the historic campus.

Bendheim Center Green

A landscaped green in front of the Bendheim Center for Finance (the former Dial Lodge) will be made more accessible as a north-south pathway from Shapiro Walk to Prospect Avenue. This pathway is part of the larger strategy mentioned above to reinforce the connections to the Natural Sciences Neighborhood and the Ivy Lane and Western Way Neighborhood to the south.

Existing view of Shapiro Walk looking west

Proposed improvements to Shapiro Walk

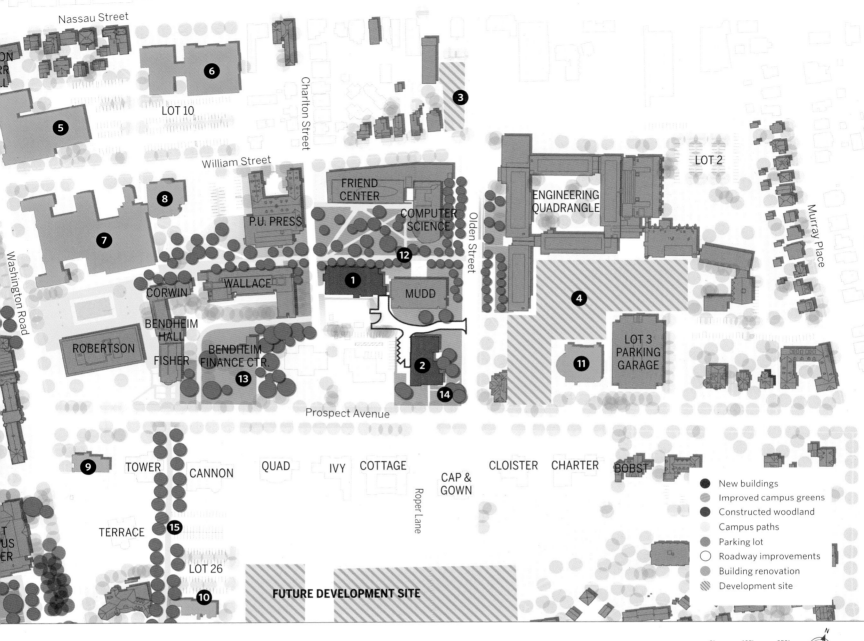

New buildings
Improved campus greens
Constructed woodland
Campus paths
Parking lot
Roadway improvements
Building renovation
Development site

0'   125'   250'

PROPOSED PROJECTS

New Buildings

1   Operations Research and
    Financial Engineering (ORFE)
2   Carl A. Fields Center
3   Mixed-use residential and
    office development
4   Engineering expansion

Building Renovations

5   Green Hall
6   185 Nassau
7   Frick Laboratory
8   Hoyt Laboratory
9   Campus Club
10 5 Ivy Lane
11 Bowen Hall

Landscape Projects

12 Shapiro Walk
13 Bendheim Center Green
14 Carl A. Fields Center landscape
15 Ivy-Prospect Walk

Operations Research and Financial Engineering Building

Architect: Frederick Fisher and Partners
Landscape Architect: Michael Van Valkenburgh Associates
Size: 45,000 square feet
Scheduled completion: Fall 2008

Key features Situated between engineering and the social sciences, the new ORFE building will exemplify the University's ability to bring together cross-disciplinary teams. It will be home to two academic programs, both of which seek to create a vibrant environment for teaching and research at the intersection of science and society.

The Department of Operations Research and Financial Engineering, founded in 1999, addresses problems related to decision-making and risk. It combines mathematics, engineering, and finance to help business leaders make critical decisions about financial markets, investments, or complex logistical operations. The Center for Information Technology Policy, founded in 2005, bridges a critical gap between policymakers and technologists in an age when computers are reshaping all aspects of life, from information privacy to national security to electronic voting.

The new glass structure will span four floors—one below ground and three above ground. It will house research studios and offices for faculty and graduate students. Conference rooms and a 65-seat lecture hall will grace the main floor, while a smaller classroom will be located in the basement. The building's entry is designed as a three-story atrium with a glass balcony that has a view of Shapiro Walk.

Sustainability aspects As designed, the building will incorporate energy saving techniques that make it 50 percent more efficient than the ASHRAE 90.1-2004 guidelines. As with other buildings on campus, ORFE's energy will be supplied by the University's central plant, thus taking advantage of the higher efficiency associated with cogeneration and thermal storage. An additional 5 percent in energy savings will come from daylighting control features. An extensive green roof, water efficient fixtures, and low-emitting materials will further reduce the building's environmental impacts.

Engineering Expansion

The proposed engineering expansion will create additional capacity for academic programs for the School of Engineering and Applied Science. The Campus Plan has shaped principles that will guide the selected architect in creating an expansion that enhances the functionality and aesthetics of the E-Quad while improving pedestrian circulation.

Planning principles In addition to the physical increase in building area (approximately 100,000 gross square feet), the new addition will create better access and exposure for the existing E-Quad courtyard and enliven the building's face on Olden Street. The addition will have a strong relationship to the redesigned Shapiro Walk. All new construction in the E-Quad will comply with the zoning requirements for this site that ensure buffers for the surrounding residential community.

Carl A. Fields Center for Equality and Cultural Understanding

Architect: Ann Beha Architects
Landscape Architect: Michael Van Valkenburgh Associates
Size: 21,000 square feet (includes renovated space)
Scheduled completion: 2009

Key features The Carl A. Fields Center will move from its current location on Olden Street to 58 Prospect Avenue, the former Elm Club. The new center will allow students greater access to cultural and social opportunities while providing more space for existing and expanded programming. An east and west addition that was added to 58 Prospect during a renovation in 1940 will be removed, and a new north addition will serve as the space for large social events. The landscape plan for the new center will relate to the landscape pattern established by other buildings on Prospect Avenue that features open front lawns framed by perimeter walls or hedges and space that provides room for outdoor gatherings under tents.

BUILDING RENOVATIONS

Frick, Hoyt, and Green renovations

With the completion of the new Chemistry, Neuroscience, and Psychology buildings, Frick, Hoyt, and Green will be vacated. The newly freed space in these buildings presents an opportunity to house programs in the humanities and social sciences that are currently overcrowded, thereby consolidating this area as an inter-disciplinary humanities and social sciences neighborhood. The southern façade of Frick Laboratory can be opened up to create a direct relationship to Scudder Plaza.

185 Nassau renovation

Currently, the Program in Theater and Dance, the Program in Visual Arts, the Program in Creative Writing, and the Princeton Atelier are located at 185 Nassau Street. Once the Program in Theater and Dance moves to a new facility planned in the Arts and Transit Neighborhood, the vacated space will allow expansion for the Program in Visual Arts. Creative Writing may also move from 185 Nassau Street, freeing up additional space.

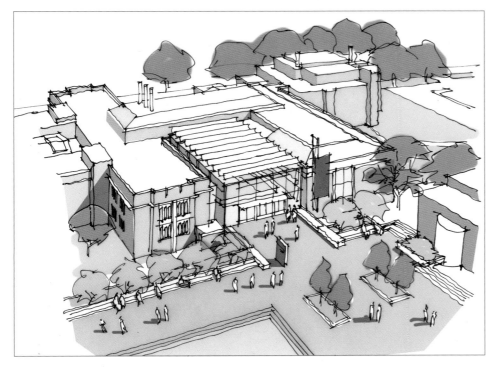

Potential Frick renovation
As the former Frick laboratory (shown left) is renovated for humanities and social science programs in the future, a new connection can be created to Scudder Plaza, an active gathering space that s currently isolated from the building. Such a connection would both enliven the plaza and better integrate the building and its future occupants with the campus, strengthening the interaction of the humanities and social science departments, with Scudder Plaza as a new focal point.

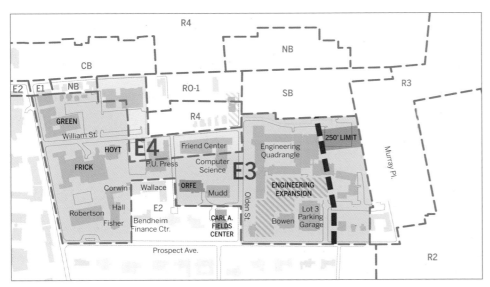

E3/E4 zoning districts
A 250-foot buffer behind the houses on Murray Place prohibits new buildings and imposes other restrictions. A landscape buffer behind the houses is also required.

BACKGROUND AND HISTORY OF THE E3 ZONING ORDINANCE

Princeton's E3 zone includes the Engineering Quadrangle east of Olden Street and an irregularly shaped parcel west of Olden that contains many but not all of the University's lands between Olden and Washington Road. Prior to 1990, the zoning for this area would have permitted an additional 950,000 square feet east of Olden and 634,000 square feet west of Olden. In 1990, the borough adopted an ordinance that reduced these capacities to an additional 200,000 square feet (plus a 140,000 square foot garage) east of Olden and an additional 200,000 square feet west of Olden.

In 2005 the borough adopted a revised ordinance that increased the square footage permitted east of Olden by 100,000 square feet. The ordinance allows the University to meet parking requirements at locations outside the zone "if those spaces are serviced by a certified shuttle system" and outlines requirements for such certification. It also contains provisions that govern building design and use, traffic circulation, landscaping, and other buffering behind the neighboring residences on Murray Place, and for the E3 district as a whole the ordinance calls for a comprehensive landscape plan and site designs that include "courtyards and walkways similar to those that exist elsewhere" on the campus.

Students eating at Wu Hall

IMPROVING A SENSE OF CAMPUS COMMUNITY

Housing

Campus Life

Athletics and Recreation

Robert K. Root, dean of the faculty in the early 20th century, remarked that Princeton evolved into a major university without ever losing "the character of a college." What makes a campus truly livable is not just the physical beauty of its landscape or superb academic and research facilities, but also more personal spaces and opportunities to make friendships and pursue interests of many kinds. Even with a population of several thousand and properties that now spread far beyond the original college core, Princeton can sustain a strong sense of community by providing quality housing and a lively calendar of events and activities for students, faculty, and staff alike, whether they live on campus or nearby.

Housing

New and renovated housing facilities will support the four-year undergraduate residential system and offer better living space options to graduate students, faculty, and staff.

The Campus Plan proposes a number of initiatives to address residential needs of undergraduate and graduate students, faculty, and staff. Almost all undergraduates live on campus, and Princeton prides itself on providing an environment in which learning and intellectual dialogue that begins in the classroom can continue in student residences located nearby. Princeton also houses an unusually high percentage of its graduate students. It provides both rental and for-purchase housing for faculty and staff, and offers assistance to faculty and staff who seek to rent or buy in local markets. The housing master plan focuses on the graduate student, faculty, and staff initiatives, while the undergraduate housing section addresses changes to the residential college system.

The need to upgrade housing led to a comprehensive planning approach both on campus and off campus. Housing types will be generally organized within concentric rings: undergraduate residential colleges will form the inner ring, graduate student housing will lie within the second ring, and faculty and staff housing will comprise the outer ring. Graduate student housing will be concentrated on the west side of campus in a loosely defined neighborhood with shared services. Faculty and staff housing will continue to be concentrated on the east side of campus.

HOUSING MASTER PLAN

Currently, over 70 percent of graduate students live in the areas immediately surrounding the campus. Improvements, renovations, and new construction are planned to convert the Hibben and Magie apartments to graduate student housing, while creating new staff and faculty housing on the current Butler Tract site and next to Dean Mathey Court.

Renovations of the Hibben and Magie apartments and their reassignment for graduate student use will create a mid-rise graduate student housing neighborhood in the western area of campus near the Graduate College and the Lawrence Apartments. Graduate students will benefit from this area's proximity to the campus and the new Arts and Transit Neighborhood, with its associated retail, including the Wawa; the Dinky and the campus shuttles; and the recreational pathways and woodlands along Lake Carnegie. In the future, there may be a bus rapid transit stop at the intersection of Faculty Road and Alexander Street near these apartments and there may be new retail and commercial developments along Alexander Street.

The clustering of faculty and staff housing just to the east of campus is part of the effort by the Campus Plan to use available land east of FitzRandolph Road for uses that are compatible with the existing character of this area (see also Chapter 5: Ivy Lane and Western Way Neighborhood and Chapter 7: Looking to the Future). The redevelopment of the Butler Tract site and construction of new apartments at Dean Mathey Court will create faculty and staff housing that is compatible with the area's residential scale and character, while simultaneously providing quick access to campus as well as to existing and new daycare facilities at Broadmead and Western Way.

In addition to creating a graduate student residential neighborhood on the west side of campus, the plan calls for a transition of most Stanworth apartments from faculty and staff to graduate student use. In time, the Merwick site adjacent to Stanworth is likely to be developed for faculty, staff, and potentially additional graduate student housing. The plan seeks to maintain the capacity to house approximately 70 percent of eligible graduate students in each of the next ten years. In addition to expanding the existing faculty and staff residential neighborhood east of campus, the housing master plan also recommends programs to help faculty and staff rent and purchase housing in the private housing market.

APPROACH AND ANALYSIS

To gather data for the planning process, surveys of faculty, staff, and graduate students were conducted. Graduate students also participated in facilitated discussion groups. In addition to contributing to the planning process, the survey data led the University to develop a web site and a services program to better inform students, faculty, and staff about housing options and to provide more assistance to those seeking housing in the private market.

Undergraduate housing

Graduate student housing

Faculty and staff housing

* hatched areas are new and
improved facilities

HOUSING INITIATIVES

1   Whitman College

2   Reconstructed Butler College

3   Hibben and Magie renovation

4   New apartments at
    Dean Mathey Court

5   Redevelopment of Butler Tract for
    new faculty and staff housing

6   Reallocation of Stanworth
    apartments for graduate
    student use

7   Development of Olden Street site
    for faculty and staff housing

Joline Hall, an undergraduate dormitory

HOUSING PROJECTS

Renovation and reconfiguration of the Hibben and Magie apartments

The Hibben and Magie apartments are adjacent mid-rise buildings that are currently occupied by graduate students, faculty, and staff. Spacious and solidly built, their popularity is understandable. However, they were constructed in the 1960s and have outmoded building systems and interior layouts. Given their close location to campus, the University will renovate the buildings and convert all units to graduate student housing. Residences in the Hibben building will be reconfigured as studio and one-bedroom apartments, since student demand for these apartment types consistently exceeds available supply. The Magie building will be fully rehabilitated, retaining its relatively large two-level apartments. Hibben and Magie will return to service with modernized infrastructure, refreshed ambience, and a unit mix that better serves the housing needs of the University's graduate students.

Reallocation of the Stanworth apartments to graduate students

Constructed in the late 1940s, the Stanworth apartments consist of 154 rental units in low-rise buildings. These are currently designated as faculty and staff housing, but many of these units will be gradually reallocated to graduate students over several years. Reusing these well-maintained apartments offers the opportunity to upgrade the graduate student apartment inventory in a cost-effective manner. Stanworth is adjacent to the Merwick Rehabilitation Hospital site that is being acquired by the University, offering a future opportunity to coordinate an expansion of the Stanworth site, as permitted under existing zoning, with the development of the Merwick site for faculty, staff, and possibly graduate student housing.

Redevelopment of the Butler Tract

The Butler Tract was constructed as temporary, barrack-style housing more than 60 years ago. This site has far exceeded its life expectancy, and it is now time to replace it. It will be developed with rental and purchase plan housing for faculty and staff. The buildings will be compatible in character and scale with the surrounding Riverside neighborhood (including the Gray Farm area that provides for-purchase housing for faculty and staff) and the Dean Mathey Court apartments. New street configurations will position homes facing outward along Hartley Avenue and Sycamore Street, better integrating the site into the fabric of the surrounding neighborhood. The community of graduate students living at Butler will move to the Hibben, Magie, and Stanworth apartments.

Hibben apartments

Stanworth apartments

Butler Tract

Development of new apartments at Dean Mathey Court

The townhouses and single level apartments at Dean Mathey Court are among the University's most sought after rental offerings. The vacant land on Faculty Road immediately west of Dean Mathey Court will be the site of new faculty and staff residences that will be configured to reflect the character, proportions, and outdoor open space that give the original Dean Mathey Court its character. Together with the new rental and purchase plan housing on the Butler Tract site, the new Dean Mathey apartments will replenish the faculty and staff housing inventory.

UNDERGRADUATE HOUSING AND THE RESIDENTIAL COLLEGE SYSTEM

A series of campus plans for the University created by Ralph Adams Cram between 1907 and 1925, initially under the leadership of University President Woodrow Wilson, defined the division between undergraduate residential and academic uses on campus that still exists today. Cram suggested that a grand north-south axis beginning at Nassau Hall be the dividing line of campus uses—with residential uses on the west and academic uses on the east. As a result, the undergraduate residential colleges have been located in an almost contiguous swath of land in the western area, creating a distinct and intimate undergraduate residential neighborhood. New undergraduate housing dormitories, including Whitman College and the reconstructed Butler College, extend this residential neighborhood southward, creating the challenge of integrating the new buildings into the campus fabric while still ensuring that they have a physical relationship to the historic residential core. In response to this challenge, the Campus Plan focuses on outdoor spaces, pedestrian connections, and landscape features to make these new facilities connect to and blend in with the surrounding campus.

In addition to new dormitories, the University introduced a new four-year residential college system in the fall of 2007. The four-year system builds on Princeton's existing residential college system that provides an immediate sense of community for new students, while serving as a vehicle for a rich and varied intellectual, cultural, social, and recreational life on campus. Under the new system, all freshmen and sophomores continue to live in residential colleges. In addition, three four-year colleges will be paired with three two-year colleges to give juniors and seniors the option to continue living in residential colleges. The new system sustains relationships for all juniors and seniors with their residential colleges, regardless of whether they live there beyond two years, by transferring academic advising from deans in West College to the residential college deans and directors of studies. Furthermore, all juniors and seniors have the opportunity to eat two meals a week at the residential colleges, and some juniors and seniors have dining contracts at both a college and an eating club. The newly completed Whitman College, the reconstructed Butler College, and the existing Mathey College will serve as four-year colleges.

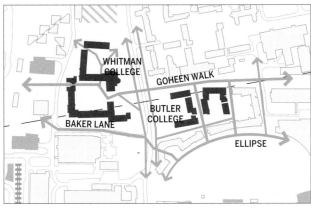

The construction of Whitman and Butler colleges will add new landscaped pathways

Community Action Group pre-orientation meeting

RESIDENTIAL COLLEGES AND STUDENT LIFE

I remember the first time I walked through the Princeton campus. It was pre-frosh weekend 2004 and I couldn't believe how large the campus was. Completely overwhelmed by the numerous impressive (and some strange-looking) buildings all over campus, I wondered how I would fit into this new environment. Everything was different from what I was used to. I shouldn't have worried. By the end of freshman year, I felt like I had always been a part of Princeton. Without a doubt, my residential college, Rocky, was instrumental in this. For the most part, residential colleges form a central part of a student's experience during the underclass years. It's hard to imagine what Princeton would be like without them. Residential colleges provide the first opportunities for new students to connect with the University. Through residential college trips, study breaks, and meals in the dining halls, these colleges foster a sense of community among students, a place to belong. In addition, the buildings, landscape, and facilities combine to create a campus environment that is aesthetically pleasing, yet very conducive to the pursuit of academic excellence. But perhaps the most interesting aspect of life at Princeton is how students from different backgrounds come together and, under the aegis of the residential college program and other extracurricular activities, build enduring relationships that enliven the college experience and promote a lifetime of association with Princeton.

When I've graduated from this place, I'll remember chatting with friends in various dorm rooms until three o'clock in the morning; walking down to the football stadium and watching the football team have an amazing season. I'll remember descending into the depths of Firestone (otherwise known as the C Floor) to find essential books for the numerous papers I had to write; toiling on the third floor of Frist during countless reading periods, amid all the other students working frantically beside me. I'll remember going into Richardson Auditorium or Theatre Intime and watching countless performances; walking by Dillon Gym, promising myself that tomorrow, I will go work out and never actually going. I'll remember walking through campus and feeling a sense of camaraderie with the people walking around me, knowing that we were all part of the same experience, which, in some ways, was also unique for each person. Most of all, I'll remember how, slowly but surely as I resided at Princeton, those large and strange buildings I encountered pre-frosh weekend began to signify one thing to me: home.

Misan Ikomi
Princeton Undergraduate,
Class of 2008

Whitman College

Architect: Demitri Porphyrios
Landscape architect: Michael Van Valkenburgh Associates
Size: 250,000 square feet
Completed: 2007

Key features The recently completed Whitman College is one of the University's first four-year residential colleges, and it is the first residential college at Princeton designed from inception for that purpose. In keeping with Princeton's collegiate gothic style, the complex is composed of courtyards, towers, and covered arcades and provides dormitory, social, dining, and recreation space for 500 undergraduates. Facilities at Whitman College include a library, digital photo lab, theater, and common rooms.

Landscape features The landscape plan for Whitman College carefully integrates the college's outdoor spaces into the campus landscape and pedestrian network. The grounds surrounding the college have been landscaped with 200 to 300 trees, including the installation of two 50-year-old, 55-foot-tall cedars in the north court. These large trees were planted at the outset in order to establish a strong landscape identity for the college that matches the scale and strength of the architecture. Much like the other iconic courtyards of the Core Campus, the north and south courts provide a shady and beautiful recreational place for Whitman College residents and the broader University community.

Butler College

Architect: Pei, Cobb, Freed and Partners
Landscape architect: Michael Van Valkenburgh Associates
Size: 112,000 square feet
Scheduled completion: 2009

Key features Many of the existing Butler College dormitories have been demolished, and the area will be rebuilt to serve as a four-year residential college. The complex will feature improved room configurations and house approximately 290 undergraduate students. The building's façade will be light red brick, with horizontal limestone strips accentuating design elements. Varying in height from two to four stories, the complex will house communal facilities in the lower level commons connecting all buildings. These facilities, which will have large windows opening onto courtyards, include a café, study areas, and seminar rooms. The arrangement of the new buildings will create an accessible complex and will provide a direct visual connection to the ellipse.

Landscape features The site features of the new Butler College will integrate the new building complex within the circulation and landscape of the University and create new internal landscapes that will give the college its own identity as a residential zone. New campus walks will traverse Butler College, and a new iconic landscape will create an amphitheater nestled within the residence halls. New pathway connections will allow easy pedestrian movement between the Core Campus and Natural Sciences neighborhoods.

Aerial rendering of Butler College showing new campus walks and green roofs

Wilcox-Wu renovation, Michael Graves and Associates

The new entrance pavilion
for Wilcox-Wu will reinforce
new pathway connections
through Butler College.

A GREEN PRINCETON

BUTLER COLLEGE

Like the new ORFE building, the newly constructed
Butler College complex will have green roofs, consist-
ing of vegetation and soil, or a growing medium, planted
over a waterproofing membrane. They will have several
functional and ecological benefits: the reduction of
stormwater runoff through rainwater collection, the
reduction of heating and cooling loads from higher insulation value, and the reduction of wear and tear on roof
structures. In addition to green roofs, the landscape
design for the complex will employ a sustainable stormwater harvesting and reuse system by reintroducing a
modernized version of the Farrand-era cistern system
that passively directs surface water to tree roots. Other
sustainability features incorporated into the project
include an energy efficient building envelope that is 30
percent greater than code requirements, natural light to
illuminate 90 percent of interior spaces, and the use of
low volatile organic compound (VOC) content materials
and water-efficient plumbing fixtures.

Campus Life

Expanded and improved facilities will
contribute to a rich and dynamic
environment for the campus community.

Princeton believes that a well-rounded education requires
not only excellent academic facilities, but also social,
cultural, athletic, and recreational facilities. Princeton also
strives to provide members of the faculty and staff with a
campus environment that allows them to do their best work.
The Campus Plan recommends improving several existing campus life facilities, while proposing new resources
that will benefit many members of the extended campus
community. Among the new facilities are expanded space
for child care and a new off-campus administrative office
neighborhood with a number of attractive features.

FRIST AS THE NEW "CENTER" OF CAMPUS

The most comprehensive campus life facility at Princeton is
the Frist Campus Center. Completed in 2000, Frist provides
dining, social, cultural, and recreational facilities and serves
as an interactive and vibrant hub for students, faculty, and
staff. The 185,000-square-foot facility is relatively new to
the historic campus, but in its short existence has become
the new "center" of the campus, providing a proverbial
bridge between historic buildings to the west and new buildings to the east. The location of Frist at a key nexus of the
east and west areas of campus has made it an important
benchmark for the Campus Plan. A key guiding principle
of the plan is that no main campus uses should be more
than a ten-minute walk from Frist (see the map in Chapter 1,
page 11).

The plan's strategy for campus life facilities is centered
on the premise that recreational, health, and social facilities are important contributors to a vibrant and dynamic
campus environment. These facilities are used by students,
faculty, and staff and are generators of indoor and outdoor
activity throughout the day.

Frist is undergoing a series of improvements that will
increase its usage and importance as a campus hub. Plans
include additional food service options, a renovated convenience store, mailboxes for all students, a package handling
area, and the relocation of several student group offices
to the building. In addition, the Frist south green is slated
to be improved and transformed into a central campus
gathering space.

HEALTH AND WELLNESS

McCosh Health Center has provided health services to
Princeton students since 1925. University Health Services
(UHS), located in McCosh Health Center, is a fully accre-
dited health care facility that provides comprehensive health
services to the University community.

The current location of UHS in a very central area of
the campus just south of the Frist Campus Center makes
it easily accessible for students and staff. The need for
additional services has caused UHS to outgrow its existing
facilities. Recognizing the desirability of maintaining its
central location, the planning team has identified opportunities for UHS to maintain the majority of its services at
McCosh Health Center and supplement them with satellite
facilities in other parts of campus—such as the Dillon Pit,
Frist Campus Center, or 5 Ivy Lane. Dillon Pit would have
the advantage of creating a natural relationship between
health services and the existing recreation facilities at
Dillon Gymnasium, whereas a facility on Ivy Lane has
greater vehicular access and development flexibility than a
site within the historic campus. Alternatively, the Campus
Plan has identified a potential future site for the full health
services program at the existing MacMillan building site.
Being close to residential, administrative, and recreational
facilities, this site provides convenient access to the campus
population while introducing a campus life destination to a
new neighborhood. In the event that the maintenance and
facilities offices in the MacMillan building are relocated,
the site would be highly desirable as an extension of the
surrounding Core Campus uses.

PROSPECT AVENUE

The location of eating clubs on Prospect Avenue east of
Washington Road dates back to the late 19th century.
Their presence makes Prospect a major location for
undergraduate social life. With the reopening of Cannon
Club, the development of the new Carl A. Fields Center,
and the renovation of Campus Club, there will be an
expansion of student life destinations on the avenue. The
new facilities proposed along this corridor will increase the
diversity of student life offerings and help create stronger
connections between this area and the campus west of
Washington Road.

Legend:
- Daycare
- Health care
- Retail
- Dining halls
- Café
- Mixed use

* hatched areas new or improved facilities

CAMPUS LIFE INITIATIVES

1   Improvements to Frist Campus Center
2   Campus Club renovation
3   Relocation and expansion of Carl A. Fields Center
4   University Health Services expansion options (location TBD)
5   Increased campus-oriented retail
6   Daycare expansion
7   Off-campus administrative neighborhood at Canal Pointe
8   Revitalized undergraduate dining options

Students grab a snack at Café Vivian in the Frist Campus Center

Campus Club, a former eating club that was donated to the University, will be renovated into a social and recreational space for Princeton undergraduate and graduate students. It will be a place where students can gather informally between classes as well as a place that they can reserve for dinners, receptions, musical and other cultural events, social events, meetings, precepts, and other uses. Its location on the corner of Prospect Avenue and Washington Road will provide a bridge of student-centered activity between Frist Campus Center and the eating clubs.

DAYCARE EXPANSION

Currently, daycare for the campus community is offered by two outside providers that are located in a former private day school facility at 171 Broadmead. In 2004, a University Task Force on Health and Well-Being determined that there is a need for additional daycare capacity. The Campus Plan studied several locations for a new third daycare facility, including sites on and off campus. All sites were thoroughly evaluated, taking into consideration issues such as access to parking and major transportation routes, proximity to campus, the surrounding community context, and opportunities for future expansion.

The corner of Broadmead and Western Way, across the street from 171 Broadmead, was determined to be the ideal location for a new daycare facility for several reasons. For parents commuting from off campus, the new facility will be located in close proximity to the proposed Western Way parking garage, making parking convenient. The facility would also be located close to the expanding faculty and staff residential neighborhoods east of Broadmead, where at least some parents using the daycare facility might live. The scale and use of the daycare facility would be compatible with the surrounding residential area and in keeping with the University's desire to locate only non-academic uses east of FitzRandolph Road. (See also Chapter 7: Looking to the Future.) The clustering of daycare facilities provides convenience for parents with more than one child in the system.

OFF-CAMPUS ADMINISTRATIVE NEIGHBORHOOD

Certain functions of the University, such as the Forrestal Research Center and a number of administrative uses, have been located in off-campus neighborhoods since the 1950s. As the University seeks to adhere to its guiding principles and locate new academic and residential buildings within a ten-minute walk of the Frist Campus Center, it has had to develop a more thoughtful strategy for increasing the use of offsite locations for administrative functions. The

Campus Plan recommends that these functions be clustered. It also recommends that these locations be made as attractive as possible to those who work there, and that easy access be provided between these locations and the campus.

The University is implementing this recommendation in an off-campus administrative neighborhood under creation in West Windsor on Canal Pointe Boulevard near its intersection with Alexander Road. Instead of being conceived as an isolated office building, this new facility is being designed as a complete neighborhood with amenities. Currently scattered at various locations across the main campus, the Office of Information Technology (OIT) will be consolidated at this new facility, although some OIT support functions will remain on the main campus. The Treasurer's Office will also move to this site, thereby freeing space in New South for academic use.

Canal Pointe Boulevard was chosen as the site of the new off-campus neighborhood for a variety of reasons. Proximity to the Route 1 interchange makes it convenient to commuters who arrive using this artery. The connection to Alexander Street keeps it within five minutes of the rest of the campus via a planned shuttle route and a proposed bicycle route. In the future, this location could also be a stop in a potential bus rapid transit system under study by New Jersey Transit for the Alexander Street corridor.

ON-CAMPUS RETAIL

As an amenity to both the University population and the community at large, new retail facilities will introduce a vibrant mixed-use quality to some campus neighborhoods and surrounding streets. The independently owned and operated Princeton University Store has already transferred its apparel and insignia business to Nassau Street next to the new Labyrinth bookstore. In its University Place location, the U-Store will continue to provide a broad range of products and services, including its convenience store, pharmacy, dorm furnishings, and school supplies. Career Services will move to the upper level of the existing U-Store building.

As part of the Arts and Transit Neighborhood plan, the Wawa convenience store will be maintained and relocated to be adjacent to the new Dinky station. Other potential retail uses—such as a restaurant, a café, and a bicycle center—will line the pedestrian plazas and pathways that connect the performance arts venues to the Dinky station. These retail amenities will serve the campus, the community, and arts visitors who may be arriving by train, by car, or on foot. They will also serve current and future residents along the Alexander Street corridor.

Athletics and Recreation

Existing and new athletic fields will be optimized through the introduction of modern surfaces and technologies.

Football game at Powers Field

Princeton is an NCAA Division I school that offers 38 varsity sports and nearly 40 club teams. Varsity and club sports play an important role in the undergraduate student experience, with nearly 1,200 students participating in these activities each year. In contrast to several peer institutions, the Princeton campus is unique in that most of its major athletic facilities are located on the main campus, in walking distance from academic and residential areas. This proximity assists students in balancing their academic pursuits with participation in athletic programs and reinforces Princeton's long-held belief that athletics should be integrated into, not separated from, the overall life of the campus.

The Campus Plan strategy for the athletics program is to augment its facilities by introducing improvements such as artificial turf and lighting to increase the utilization and efficiency of existing facilities. This approach allows varsity athletics programs to remain on sites north of Lake Carnegie at a time when demand for new land for academic and residential space is very high. The plan also includes enhancement of campus recreation.

ATHLETIC FIELDS

Bedford Field
On the west side of campus, Bedford Field will be converted to an artificial turf field. The area underneath the renovated field will serve as the stormwater retention basin for the Neuroscience and Psychology buildings.

Eastern athletic fields
As described in the Ivy Lane and Western Way Neighborhood plan, the Campus Plan includes a reconfiguration of the athletic facilities in the eastern areas of campus. The new complex, to be located south of the new parking facility, will consist of practice fields, a new baseball field, and club sports facilities.

Practice fields
The new practice fields in the eastern area of campus will have a flexible configuration and will be lit for night play, which will increase their year-round utilization. The fields will have a combination of natural and artificial surfaces, allowing athletes to practice for various competition settings. Additionally, the area underneath the fields will serve as a stormwater retention area.

Clarke Field relocation
The new baseball facility will take advantage of its location in the southern edge of the campus to provide attractive views of the lake valley. Grassy berms with paved footpaths will surround the playing field to recreate the informal seating that currently overlooks Clarke Field.

Rugby field
The new facility will bring club sports events from south of Lake Carnegie to the main campus. The artificial surface field will be the site for practice and competitions and will feature lighting and seating. The location of this new facility on the main campus will ease access for athletes and spectators.

West Windsor fields
Princeton maintains additional athletic fields in West Windsor, south of Lake Carnegie, for club and intramural sports. The Campus Plan recommends that lighting and restroom facilities be considered for the West Windsor fields.

Passive recreation space
In addition to formal athletic facilities, the Campus Plan recommends sustaining and creating open spaces for informal recreational use. For instance, the newly completed Whitman College has two large courtyards that are available for socializing or informal recreation, and the future New South Green, to be located in the Arts and Transit Neighborhood, is being designed to encourage informal recreation and outdoor socializing. Landscape improvements along the edge of the Ellipse will make that area a more attractive space for students to play sports informally or through the intramural sports program.

Roberts Stadium

Architect: Anderson Architects
Landscape architects: Quennell Rothschild and Partners LLP
Scheduled completion: Fall 2008

Key features An improved soccer facility, including the new Roberts Stadium for soccer, is planned for the area just south of the Ellipse. It will feature a three-sided stadium, a playing field with a natural grass surface, and an adjacent practice field with an artificial surface. Myslik Field will be a competition field, and the practice field, to be called Plummer Field, has been separately funded by an anonymous donor. Three free-standing pavilions will house a ticket office, press box, concession stand, team rooms, restrooms, and other facilities. The stadium will have a 3,000-person capacity, and the playing field will be lighted for night games.

Lenz Tennis Center

Architect: Dattner Architects
Landscape architect: Michael Van Valkenburgh Associates
Scheduled completion: 2010

Key features The existing Lenz Tennis Center, which was constructed about 30 years ago by Princeton's own maintenance shops, is to be replaced with a new 3,500-square-foot varsity tennis facility. The program under consideration for this new building includes separate varsity locker rooms for men and women, four coaches' offices, a large room for team meetings and other tennis functions, public restrooms, storage, and support spaces. The intent is to provide convenient access to the existing courts and grandstand and allow the varsity tennis coaches to observe practice and matches from the new structure.

FITNESS AND RECREATION

Built in the 1940s, Dillon Gymnasium and its subsequent addition, now the Stephens Fitness Center, are located in the western area of campus in close proximity to the undergraduate residential neighborhood. Even when the Stephens Center opened in 2000, it was unable to meet the full demand for its facilities, and the growth in the campus population creates further need for expansion. The Campus Plan has studied several sites for expanded fitness and recreation facilities, including options where health and fitness could be located in the same building.

Recognizing that fitness and recreation facilities are actively used throughout the day, the Campus Plan recommends that fitness facilities be easily accessible to undergraduates living on campus, while still being at a convenient location for graduate students, faculty, and staff. Dillon remains an ideal location, but in addition to proposing an expansion of the Stephens Center on-site at the Dillon Pit, the Campus Plan has also identified potential satellite sites for fitness and recreation.

One opportunity is to incorporate a fitness center in the vicinity of the new parking facility east of Washington Road. This location has the advantage of being near the arrival and departure point of commuters who are likely to use the fitness center either before or after work. The facility would be a natural extension of the athletics neighborhood and, at the same time, it would provide a social anchor for future development in the Ivy Lane and Western Way Neighborhood.

Another potential satellite location is within the Sciences Green. As a narrow multi-level structure along the western edge of Princeton Stadium, a fitness center would bring vitality to the Natural Sciences Neighborhood where many of the existing buildings, such as Jadwin Hall and Fine Hall, face inward and do not directly engage the adjacent open spaces. The fitness center would be easily accessible to the rest of campus via the new Streicker Bridge and a short walk away from the new parking facility.

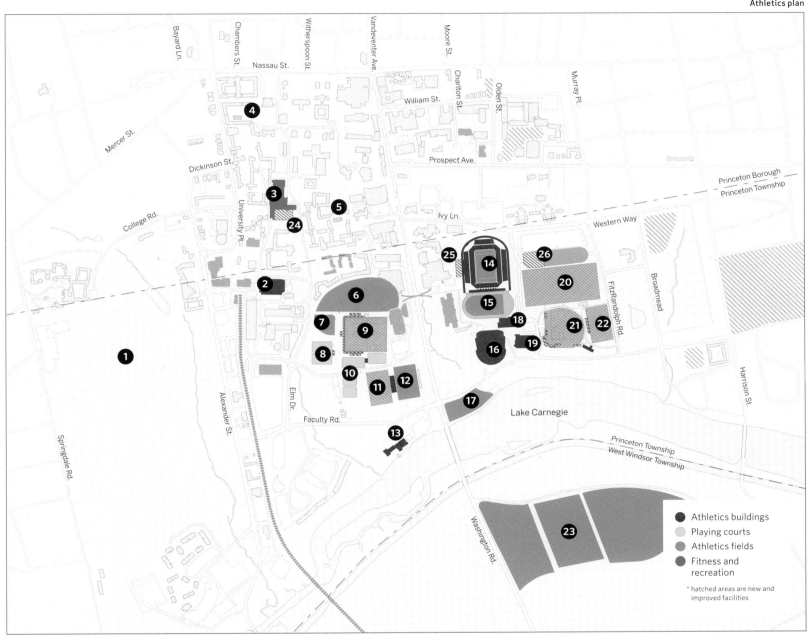

ATHLETICS FACILITIES

1   Springdale Golf Course
2   Baker Rink
3   Dillon Gymnasium and Stephens Fitness Center
4   Holder volleyball court
5   Wilson volleyball court
6   Poe-Pardee Field (Ellipse)
7   Class of 1895 Field
8   Lenz Tennis Center
9   Roberts Stadium
10 Tennis courts
11 Bedford Field

12 Class of 1952 Stadium
13 Shea Rowing Center
14 Princeton Stadium
15 Weaver Track and Field
16 Jadwin Gymnasium
17 Lake field
18 Caldwell Fieldhouse
19 DeNunzio Pool
20 New practice fields
21 Clarke Field
22 Rugby field
23 West Windsor fields

FITNESS EXPANSION OPTIONS

24 Dillon Pit
25 Princeton Stadium
26 New parking facility

A fall day in McCosh Courtyard

CONNECTING THE CAMPUS

Landscape

Stormwater Management

Wayfinding

The landscape of Princeton's campus has always been a defining element of its identity and experience. Beginning with the enclosure of the "front campus" between Nassau Hall and Nassau Street in 1756, the relationship between the architecture and the landscape has created a feeling of an intimate academy, unique to this setting. However, part of this campus experience is the myriad pathways and courtyards that, while beautiful to experience, can leave visitors feeling lost. Today, as the University grows, it is vital to maintain and restore the landscape quality of both the campus and natural areas as well as a sense of coherence and connectedness. This goal is achieved, as described in this chapter, through comprehensive strategies in both landscape and wayfinding.

Renewing the Campus Landscape

Affecting approximately half of the main campus area, the Campus Plan will further enhance, restore, and green the already verdant campus.

Princeton's campus is renowned for the superb quality of its physical environment and the way that its landscape legacy supports and reflects the continued excellence of the institution. During the era in which Beatrix Farrand was the University's consulting landscape architect and Ralph Adams Cram was the consulting architect, decisions were considered from both perspectives equally, and many of the University's most cherished spaces resulted from a vigorous exchange between the two disciplines. When Princeton discontinued the tradition of a campus landscape architect in the 1960s, however, there was no longer an individual or organization charged with promoting a vision for the continuity of the overall campus landscape.

The plan will restore a strong voice for the campus landscape and reframe new development within an understanding of the campus and its boundaries. Given Princeton's current diversity of building styles, scales, and programs; its ongoing commitment to architectural innovation; and the historic importance of its wooded setting, a planning process that prioritizes the continuity of the landscape will be needed to preserve the character of the campus experience while also allowing it to develop in new ways. There have been multiple master plans for the University campus, each providing a roadmap for future building sites and social spaces between buildings. The Campus Plan is distinguished by a landscape approach that fully engages the potential to unite the experience and function of the campus through an integration of its overlapping systems.

LANDSCAPE OBJECTIVES

As the University continues to grow, there are many obstacles to the continuity of open spaces in an already strained relationship between the historic core and the newer campus periphery. Elements of historic campus landscape traditions need to be balanced with and woven into the practice of expanding a modern campus. Four landscape principles provide the foundation for this complex undertaking:

- Invent within the traditional pattern of campus-making
- Translate topography into campus form
- Reassert the presence of the woodland threshold
- Anticipate the impact of increased land management and environmental pressures

In support of these objectives, the Campus Plan identifies strategic stand-alone landscape improvements, independent from building projects, each selected for its potential to connect new development and create value for the whole of the campus. Together with proposed architectural projects, the plan adopts a landscape-based approach to weaving disparate parts of campus, different scales of architecture, and different eras of construction into a cohesive campus with a consistently strong identity.

A COMPREHENSIVE LANDSCAPE PLAN

There is a high demand for quality open space at Princeton. Increasingly, University staff now dedicate much effort to accommodating requests to host activities on the campus greens, courtyards, and smaller campus spaces. Escalation in use exacerbates an already acknowledged demand for investment in the landscape.

This plan performs the traditional role of locating landscape areas for improvements, while also recognizing that the campus landscape is made of and relies on a collection of systems: stormwater, planting communities, programming, topography, and land management practices. Every new building, landscape, and infrastructure project at Princeton offers the opportunity to further integrate these systems into a fundamentally sustainable landscape network. The goal of this plan is to allow the function and experience of the landscape to improve even as the use of the campus expands.

Existing woodland

Constructed woodland

Existing campus greens

Proposed campus greens

Proposed connective landscape

Garden restorations

The Campus Plan recognizes the challenges of sustaining the overall experience of a campus that is now five times the size of its historic core.

University Chapel, 2007

INVENTING WITHIN THE TRADITIONAL PATTERN OF CAMPUS-MAKING

The Core Campus landscape experience at Princeton is defined by light-filled courts with open corners, high canopy trees, and stone walks. As the University has grown, the main campus has expanded to be over five times the area of the historic campus, which results in a landscape that feels stretched at the edges. Simultaneously, an increased campus population has put substantial strains on all areas of the landscape, but most particularly the well-loved historic core. In order to strengthen the overall campus experience as well as safeguard the historic core, a degree of inventiveness within Princeton's traditional patterns of campus-building is required.

The north and south edges of campus have each developed a distinctive feel that is missing from the middle ground between the two. To the north, the historic campus alongside Nassau Street is structured primarily by buildings while to the south, the campus areas adjacent to Lake Carnegie are structured primarily by the woodland landscape. These two themes are reinforced by the placement of buildings and landscapes. Toward Nassau Street the buildings are of a similar size and create configurations

that frame the campus open space, whereas buildings located toward Lake Carnegie exist as semi-independent objects anchored by their relation to wooded areas. These two different campus spaces exist harmoniously at Princeton, but the transition between these systems is problematic, especially as the two campus types have grow closer together.

During Beatrix Farrand's tenure as the consulting landscape architect at Princeton, the two campus types were developed as clearly separate zones for academic and recreational activities. Several nature trails created by Farrand established a delicate network of circulation between these two environments. As the campus progressed and expanded, however, recreational spaces and higher levels of activity were developed at the boundaries of the northern portion of the campus. Taken together, these athletic fields, parking lots, maintenance service areas, dumpsters, and infrastructure resulted in a "middle landscape" that offers, at best, a bland environment without any of the cohesiveness presented by the northern and southern campus types. It is the aspiration of the Campus Plan to diminish the conditions that characterize the middle landscape and to reinvigorate the rich juxtaposition of the two dominant landscape types on campus.

These recommendations suggest this juxtaposition as a way to reclaim a quality that has been largely absent from the Princeton landscape as it has expanded. This goal will establish a campus-wide framework around which several other needed improvements can be structured. These might include campus wayfinding, sustainable stormwater landscapes, ecological improvements to the campus woodland area, and the development of a new landscape language that can withstand contemporary levels of use and help mediate the escalation in building size and complexity that seems unavoidable as the campus continues to develop.

Through its implementation, the Campus Plan will open up new potential for the Princeton campus landscape to be sensitive, sustainable, and beautiful while simultaneously inviting greater use and creating improved functional performance. For instance, in the redesign of Butler College, the need to create a below-grade dining facility presented the opportunity to establish a new social landscape at the heart of the residential college. Providing space for quiet study and small gatherings, Butler College Memorial Court is a contemporary expression of the tradition of small-scale courtyards epitomized by the 1903 Garden, the McCosh Infirmary, Chancellor Green Courtyard, and Pyne Terrace. Similar in spirit to Beatrix Farrand's cisterns that collected rainwater for passive irrigation, originally in evidence at Holder Courtyard and Cuyler Terrace, Butler College Memorial Court uses 21st-century techniques to create a stormwater reservoir that can be tapped into during the drier months of the year.

NASSAU STREET

Campus

Woodland

LAKE CARNEGIE

Building as campus structure

Eliminate the middle landscape

Landscape as campus structure

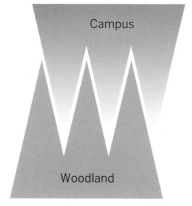

The ten-year landscape plan aims to increase the articulation of the campus in currently undefined areas, better marrying its building with its landscape context.

Diagram of forested areas and circulation network

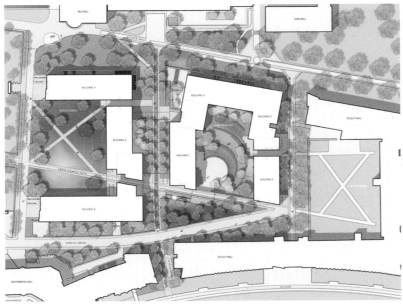

Butler College landscape plan

HISTORY OF CAMPUS LANDSCAPE ARCHITECTS

1870-1875 Donald G. Mitchell, essayist, novelist, and farmer who had published a treatise on landscape gardening, was appointed to make plans for the improvement of the entire campus. Under the leadership of President McCosh, the character of the campus landscape became that of an "English nobleman's park," that is, open lawns dotted with trees laid out in an informal, not geometric, pattern. Mitchell is credited with the design of the grounds around the first Dickinson Hall, and with the remaking of a front campus 760 feet wide by 270 feet deep.

1906 The creation of Lake Carnegie in 1906, by the construction of a dam at the confluence of the Stony Brook and the Millstone River, marks the moment of greatest landscape change on the campus, transforming hundreds of acres of marshland into a 3.5 mile-long body of water.

1912-1943 Beatrix Jones Farrand had the greatest influence on the unique character of the historic campus. Farrand clearly articulated the function of the campus landscape as a framework for development and its fundamental role in furthering the goals of a liberal education. She proposed a systematic approach to the campus landscape that would provide uninterrupted circulation and views, emphasize the architectural qualities of the buildings, and provide beauty as an essential part of the experience of a university. Farrand cleared the grounds of shrubs and low branching conifers that would prevent views and circulation, introduced the concept of "two-dimensional shrubs" espaliered against building walls to add color and texture to the primarily deciduous tree palette, and carefully orchestrated the terracing of the topography to provide a sense of quiet harmony. All of these would become hallmarks of the Princeton landscape.

1943-1957 Alfred Geiffert, Jr. a prominent landscape architect of the great estate era.

1958-1961 Markley Stevenson of Philadelphia, known for his design of the Normandy American Cemetery "Omaha Beach" in Colleville sur Mer, France.

1961-1973 Michael Rapuano, of the New York firm Clarke & Rapuano, nationally known for their work on public and private projects of great importance and scale, conducted the first comprehensive tree survey and report in 1964.

1974-1982 Robert L. Zion of the firm Zion and Breen, Cream Ridge, New Jersey. Zion was responsible for the design and construction of Firestone Plaza.

Early 1980s-2000 From the early 1980s until 2000, there was a shift in the campus planning approach to landscape. Rather than a consulting landscape architect being on-call, individual designers were hired in conjunction with each building project—linked to the architects of the buildings. These landscape architects have included:
• Louise Schiller (new stadium, many sites throughout the campus)
• Skip Burke (Machado Silvetti Architects)
• Carla Tiberi
• Michael Vergason (Shapiro Walk, Friend Center and surrounds)
• Andropogon Associates (Frist Campus Center)
• Barbara Paca
• Sasaki Partnership (Forrestal Campus)
• Henry Arnold (tree study in late 1980s)

2000-2005 Quennell-Rothschild of New York was commissioned to undertake several improvement projects, including the renewal of Scudder Plaza, Ellipse walk, and the landscaping around the Aridlinger Center for the Humanities.

2005-present Public garden designer Lynden B. Miller was hired to continue the Beatrix Farrand tradition. She has designed gardens for Wyman House, Maclean House, Lowrie House, and Prospect House.

2005-present Michael Van Valkenburgh Associates is in the process of planning and designing the landscape—its overall structure as well as specific spaces—which will knit the campus together as it evolves over the next ten years.

Blair Walk

TRANSLATE TOPOGRAPHY INTO CAMPUS FORM

The historic campus establishes open greens at the center of academic life by placing them on high, flat ground. As is often related, the early grounds at Princeton inspired the first use of the word campus, etymologically based on the Latin for "open field" or "expanse surrounded" in reference to the flat open terrain that separated Nassau Hall from Nassau Street.

As campus expansion increasingly encountered the topography of the land descending down to Lake Carnegie, however, the transitions between high ground and low ground became opportunities to develop a new relationship between architecture and landscape.

Throughout the history of campus expansion southward toward the lake, the University's existing topography has been transformed into landscape spaces that guide circulation and orientation. The campus is organized by two basic types of circulation that are an intuitive outgrowth of the campus topography:

- North-south tributary paths that maneuver around buildings and incorporate steps and transitions in grade through shifts in geometry and elevation
- East-west walks that collect the smaller tributary paths that are characterized by their consistent elevation and straightened geometry

The Campus Plan seeks to extend and perhaps expand this approach to developing campus circulation through the encounter of the underlying topography. For instance, the New Butler Walk will establish a connection between the Ellipse and Wilcox Hall, reinforcing the importance of the spaces at each end, while also supporting the integration of the residential college into the campus as a whole. Framed on either side by the buildings of Butler College, the New Butler Walk will be lined with upright beech trees that are not used elsewhere on campus, reinforcing its processional aspects and giving the space a specific horticultural

character. Inspired by campus paths adjacent to Nassau Hall, new bluestone pavements are introduced to meet the circulation needs of the growing population at the heart of campus. These are integrated into a system of new-generation rain cistern technologies which serve the dual purpose of reducing runoff and allowing for stormwater reuse.

This manner of negotiating place and elevation within the campus is a valuable system that should remain, as existing pathways extend from the campus core into new precincts. For instance, Shapiro Walk is being reconceived so that it might extend the strong landscape character of McCosh Walk across Washington Road all the way to the E-Quad. Similar to the role that Lourie-Love Walk plays in the west, a new public corridor between Prospect Avenue and Ivy Lane improves north-south connections in the eastern precincts of campus. East-west circulation will also be strengthened through improvements to McCosh Walk and Goheen Walk, retrofitting these pathways to better withstand the stresses of contemporary use.

Topographic form and circulation

The Blair Archway offers the iconic example of this topographic planning tradition. At the time of its completion, it served as the arrival gateway for the original Dinky train line that stopped at the base of the archway steps. The translation of topography into campus landscape was expanded upon in this location with the moving of the train arrival point to the south. The new procession to the train, developed in collaboration between Beatrix Farrand and Ralph Adams Cram, carefully blends the rising hillside into the architecture and the landscape and absorbs the Blair Archway within the interior of the campus. The further extension of the processional walkway from Blair Arch past Pyne Hall to the Arts and Transit Neighborhood is one of several projects that further translate topography into campus form and increase a sense of connectivity across seemingly disparate parts of campus.

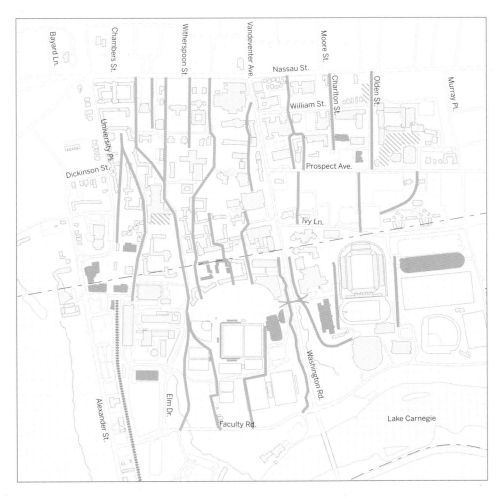

North-south pathways, such as this one at Cuyler and Walker halls, incorporate transitions in grade

North-south pathways travel the sloped topography to the lake and maneuver around varied building sizes and styles.

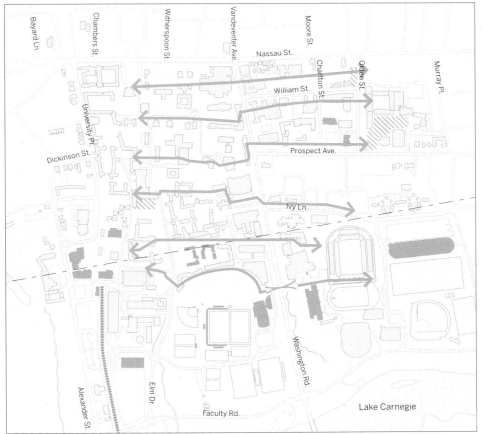

East-west pathways, such as Goheen Walk, are level and straight

East-west pathways provide level and straight terraces that form the major walks of the campus.

A new diagonal will reinforce
two critical circulation networks
for the expanded campus.

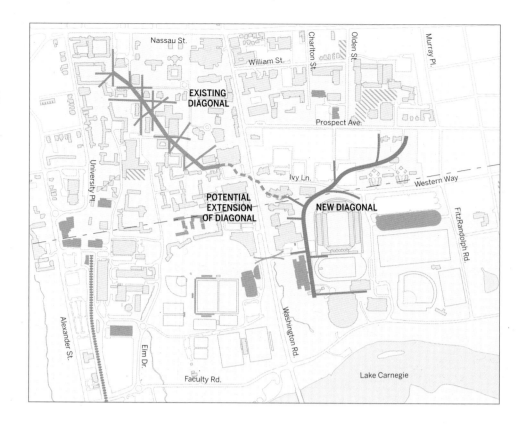

Extend the diagonal

As the campus grew, this system of east-west walks and
north-south pathways was not enough to fully connect
the campus. Over time, diagonal pathways developed that
linked the historic upper campus with areas of growth.
Diagonals achieved an effortless continuity of the campus
landscape and alleviated a significant elevational obstacle.
One key diagonal path passes a series of buildings and
landscapes from Alexander Hall to the Frist Campus Center.
Increasing the role of this corridor will be an
essential component in integrating the expanded lower
campus into existing walkways.

In effect, this plan proposes to clear the way for a
pedestrian path of least resistance that links the Core
Campus and campus lands to the east. Currently the
diagonal path ends abruptly at McCosh Health Center
and offers only a tenuous link to the Frist Campus Center.
The terminus of the diagonal in the area bounded by Frist,
McCosh Health Center, and Guyot is at the same elevation
as Washington Road, and thus presents the best opportunity to establish effective physical and programmatic
connections between the Core Campus and areas to the
east. The ease of the diagonal passage extended to this
area would provide a link to another collector of pedestrian
traffic occurring in the areas around Ivy Lane.

The new diagonal

The campus lands east of Washington Road and south
of Prospect Street are isolated from adjacent areas of
campus by virtue of the roads themselves and the kind
of architecture they support. As a result, this area has not
yet achieved cohesiveness with the image and tradition

of Princeton. Instead of supporting the outdoor social interactions and activities that characterize successful areas
of campus, its open spaces are generally residual and often
oriented toward vehicles and service uses.

In the Core Campus the architecture frames the
campus green spaces. By contrast, the eastern part of
campus has a collection of large structures floating within
undistinguished open spaces that aren't experienced as a
continuous campus landscape extending between buildings.
Given that Princeton's commitment to research will per-
petuate the need for large and programmatically complex
buildings, issues of scale will likely be ongoing for this area.

The development of the eastern campus landscape is
further complicated by the fact that the Princeton Stadium
complex occupies its geographical center. The mass and
location of the stadium allow few opportunities to cross
this area.

The largest unprogrammed and underutilized space on
campus is the perimeter of the stadium. Through improved
circulation and a complete transformation of its landscape,
the stadium's western edge presents a significant opportunity for the creation of a single unifying Sciences Green
at the heart of the Natural Sciences Neighborhood. The plan
proposes a redesign of the space and its roadways, lawns,
walks, and trees. With a continuous open greensward,
realigned service roadways, and walks at the perimeter, the
Sciences Green will create a useable and attractive campus
open space that integrates the buildings in this part of
campus with open vistas to the north and south. This new
greensward also has the potential to be extended north of
Ivy Lane as that area develops in the future.

SCIENCES GREEN PROPOSED IMPROVEMENTS

1   ADA accessible pedestrian path connection
2   Planting provides seasonality and mitigates the scale of the architecture
3   Recreational lawn
4   Additional reunion tent sites
5   Shared pedestrian and vehicular path connecting Ivy Lane into the Natural Sciences Neighborhood
6   Adjusted and leveled service access

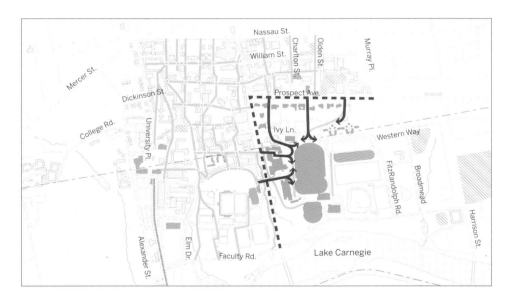

Existing buildings and varying land uses present several challenges to providing connections to the east edge of campus.

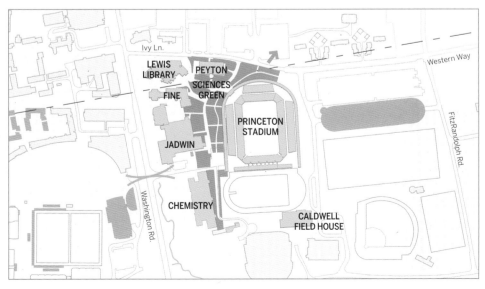

The proposed Sciences Green landscape design will unify circulation and campus character, and serve as a framework for future development, tying the new with the existing.

Campus aerial view, 1940

RE-ASSERT THE PRESENCE OF THE WOODLAND THRESHOLD

The wooded edge along Lake Carnegie and the remnant woodlands that follow the several tributary streams are important fragments of a complex ecological system. As the campus has grown, increases in the amount of stormwater being directed to the tributaries and the removal of woodland area has continued to put pressure on this already fragile ecology. In the interest of improving the campus environment, the campus woodlands are recognized in the plan as a valuable campus asset that needs to be protected, and in some cases restored.

This original woodland can still be partially seen as one uses the Washington Road and Elm Drive entrances to the University. The woodland that frames these entrances has become a familiar identifier of the Princeton precinct, as most visitors to Princeton now approach from Route 1. This remaining natural landscape creates a moment of arrival at Princeton (town and university) by establishing a clear separation from the suburban highways. Despite the diminished size of the overall woodlands, the concentration at the campus entrances provides a strong counterpoint to the refinement of the inner campus landscape.

Ecological health is sometimes a matter of establishing enough area to have a true woodland center, not just a series of edges. The breaks in the woodland area that have been created in the last few decades of development, have limited the continuity of the woodland canopy. Each significant break in this woodland mass creates more edge conditions which, as smaller fragments, lose stability as a woodland system and become exponentially more vulnerable to invasive species, more sensitive to climate change, and less self-sustaining. This last consideration is critically important in understanding that these woodland thresholds, if left to their own devices, will need some maintenance to remedy their current condition and will increasingly require even more care as they diminish in size and continuity. Maintaining or increasing the area and overall connectedness of the woodland will be of increased importance as the southern zone of campus continues to evolve.

Buffer landscapes

As part of the overall strategy of increasing the size and presence of the woodlands, the Campus Plan proposes new woodland plantings along Washington Road and Elm Drive. These buffers will create new recreational opportunities through nature paths, restoring the experience of Farrand's path systems and informally linking the University to recreational activities. From an ecological perspective, the proposed new woodland areas will act primarily as protection for the original fragments of native woodland. They will provide an important first line of defense against edge vulnerabilities like invasive plant species and establish exponentially greater opportunities for habitat. Building upon these woodland zones in overall size, complexity, and function is a priority of this plan. At every opportunity, Princeton should seek to construct woodland buffer areas.

At each of these buffers the planting can be designed to establish a density both of trees and ground plane plantings to help resist the influx of invasive species at the edge. These protective zones at the edge of woodlands are prime opportunities to create landscapes that absorb stormwater loads generated by the new projects. As has been recognized by employing this strategy in the design of the new Chemistry building, it is far easier to build these stormwater treatment landscapes as part of the construction of a major capital project than to wait until after a building and its associated site improvements are completed.

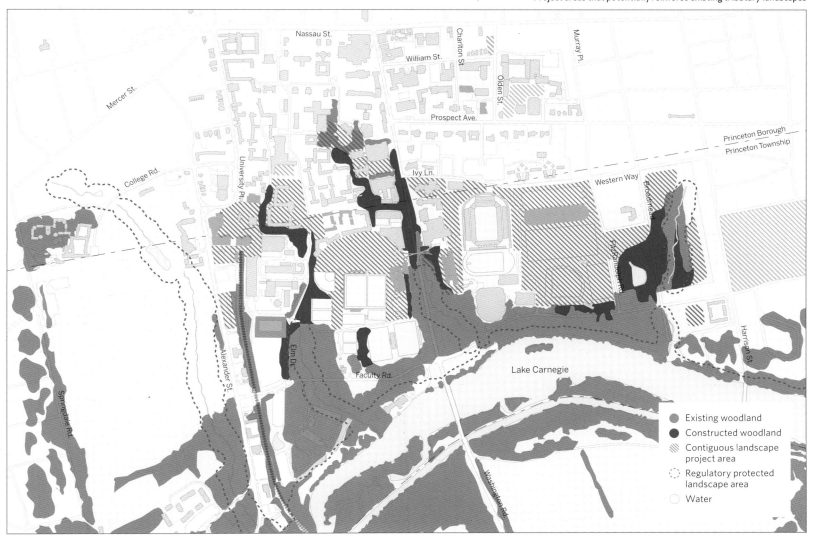

Legend:
- ● Existing woodland
- ● Constructed woodland
- ▨ Contiguous landscape project area
- ⬭ Regulatory protected landscape area
- ○ Water

Proposed constructed woodland along Elm Drive

PROPOSED IMPROVEMENTS

1 Reinforced woodland along existing stream
2 Understory woodland grasses
3 Inviting approach to the Ellipse
4 Pedestrian path connecting to Roberts Stadium
5 Constructed woodland planting

Hand watering is frequently used to save resources

ANTICIPATE THE IMPACT OF INCREASED LAND MANAGEMENT AND ENVIRONMENTAL PRESSURES

From a sustainable landscapes perspective, the ideal campus would consume no outside resources, present no hazard to adjoining natural systems, require no maintenance, and produce no waste. Although it is unlikely Princeton can ever achieve this goal, there is interest in seeking new ways to move closer to it. A major initiative of the Campus Plan has been to integrate the principles of sustainability into all aspects of the design, construction, and maintenance of the landscape. By striving to do better than just what is required by regulation, Princeton can become a national leader in sustainable landscape practices.

PLANTING

SOILS ←→ PAVEMENT

STORMWATER REUSE

In her work at Princeton, Beatrix Farrand acknowledged the challenges and rewards of working with a "living institution," in that each project she built at Princeton added another dimension to an already complex relationship between the operations of the campus and the built and natural environments. Farrand pioneered an approach to the efficient care and management of the campus environment, particularly by treating the basic mediums of landscape architecture—planting, soils, paving, and rainwater—not as individual issues but as components in a self-sustaining and integrated system. Although many of her techniques have become outdated and inefficient by today's standards, the idea that a modern, evolving institution should take this on as a challenge persists. With a campus already significantly larger than during Farrand's tenure and facing further growth, land management and sustainable development are more critical than ever, and the need to translate the spirit and intent of Farrand's work into modern techniques could not be more relevant.

Individually, each element of the landscape plays an important role in the development of the campus. Planting is one of the more visible manifestations of the campus ecology. Likewise, paving has a huge impact on the functioning of the landscape, and is also very much tied into the legibility of the campus as a unified whole. The plan supports the idea that there should be a multiplicity of paving systems on campus. Even if it were possible to standardize elements in an economical and attractive fashion, the extent of campus growth has led to divergent styles of architecture as one moves away from the historic core. This diversity

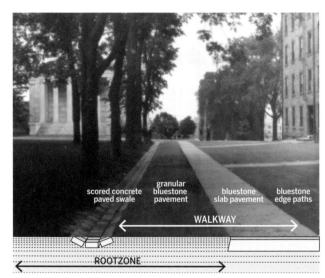

scored concrete paved swale — granular bluestone pavement — bluestone slab pavement — bluestone edge paths

WALKWAY

ROOTZONE

Historic pathway systems integrated stormwater reuse, paving, and horticultural sustainability

of image, the mixing of vehicular and pedestrian traffic on these surfaces, the increased variety of scales and types of open space, and the way that the paving contributes to the environmental health of the landscape, all need to be considered while knitting together the existing paths and creating a method by which the system might expand.

Soils are a less visible component of landscape health, but the functions that they perform are vital to addressing the increased pressure of larger campus populations and more intensive use, such as annual reunions. Similarly, the campus-wide approach to water, namely through stormwater reuse, is not highly visible, but is essential to the function of the landscape. Civil engineering and soils can both be employed to attain a goal of keeping as much rainfall as possible on site for reuse.

It is nearly impossible to speak of the performance of any individual landscape component, like planting, soils, paving, or stormwater reuse, in isolation because they are each intrinsically interconnected with the others. Innovations in landscape architecture have always emerged from

A more resilient landscape will increase resistance to damage from intensive activites, such as annual reunions

the study of the performance and interaction of these basic mediums. The Campus Plan proposes both big and small measures that will contribute to make Princeton a leader in this approach. Taken together, these efforts will result in a campus that recharges its groundwater; sustains healthy plants that, in turn, require less maintenance; and reduces stress on the regional ecology and performance of the tributary streams into which most of Princeton's stormwater runoff is released.

Princeton has always valued the overall quality of its campus landscape. Particularly during the period of rapid growth that characterized the Farrand years, the excellence of the campus environment, as expressed in its planning, design, construction, and maintenance, was very much a priority of university policy. A robustly beautiful and functionally sustainable landscape continues to be the ideal vehicle through which meaningful connections can be made between Princeton's history of landscape excellence and its ongoing expansion as a modern campus.

Prospect House garden, originally designed by Beatrix Farrand and recently restored by Lynden B. Miller Public Garden Design

Beatrix Farrand, one of America's finest landscape designers, worked on the Princeton campus from 1915 to 1941. Her deep understanding of plants and decades-long implementation of enhancements to the campus landscape have had a lasting impact on the beauty of this special place. Her legacy has endured thanks to the passing on of her design ideas from one University grounds manager to another over the years. That many of Mrs. Farrand's wonderful plants can still be found across the campus is also a testament to her understanding of what we now call the sustainable landscape. She added many fine varieties of trees and shrubs to the campus with an emphasis on those native to the Princeton area and of interest during the school year. Her work can best be seen in many of the beautiful trees, shrubs, and climbing plants that are still thriving at the Graduate College and Wyman House.

Beatrix Farrand believed that the beauty of the campus added to the mental growth and well-being of students. Generations of Princetonians have been devoted to their landscape. Because the campus is now used and enjoyed 12 months of the year, it is important to have plants for all four seasons. Expanding on a plan begun by Mrs. Farrand, we designed a garden within the walled upper garden adjacent to Wyman House. In the shade of enormous elm trees, we designed gardens around Maclean House, home of 10 Princeton presidents and now occupied by the Alumni Association. Inspired by Mrs. Farrand's dazzling displays at the Rockefeller Garden in Seal Harbor, Maine, which are still being maintained, we have added winter structure and many new plants to the Prospect House gardens and will continue to refine this garden in the future.

Working with the University's landscape team, we are designing new gardens and adding the very best plants around the campus. It is a great honor to be following in the tradition of Beatrix Farrand by continuing to enrich the Princeton landscape experience for students, staff, and visitors.

Lynden B. Miller
Garden Design Consultant
to Princeton University

Stormwater Management

Protect the lake and watersheds from the impacts of development by restoring the existing water system and establishing stormwater management principles.

. . . .

Princeton University belongs to the Stony Brook Millstone River watershed. Stream corridors, forest buffers, and other natural resources located on the campus are essential for preserving and maintaining a healthy, balanced eco-system and a natural flow of water.

As the campus and surrounding communities have grown over time, there has been a slow degradation of the watershed's natural resources and the ecology of the lake valley. Development has interrupted and altered natural pro-cesses, throwing the stable interaction between elements of the ecosystem out of balance.

Buildings, parking lots, roadways, and other structures within the watershed have increased the number of imper-vious surfaces that prevent rainfall from percolating into the soil where it replenishes the groundwater aquifer and feeds the streams and Lake Carnegie. Instead, rain falling on these surfaces moves across the land as runoff, where it is captured in constructed stormwater infrastructure and discharged directly into the streams and lake. Currently, most rain falling on the developed areas of campus is being converted directly to runoff, causing water pollution, erosion, and flooding.

The East Basin, 2006

A STORMWATER MANAGEMENT STRATEGY FOR PRINCETON'S CAMPUS

At present, the University primarily manages stormwater in two regional detention basins: the West Basin and East Basin. Each basin was designed and constructed to control stormwater runoff for future development projects, relying on a "banking" system established to deduct impervious development from the total available capacity. This method-ology was in line with the stormwater regulations at the time they were constructed, and many development projects on Princeton's campus have deducted capacity from the two regional basins. Unfortunately, most of the runoff from these development areas did not physically flow to either the east or west regional basin. As a result, the receiving stormwater systems and stream valleys that con-veyed these storm flows to Lake Carnegie have deteriorated.

The Campus Plan identifies several new campus-wide stormwater management projects that will not only make important contributions to the success of future development at Princeton, but will also comply with recent more stringent regulations. These projects are intended to mitigate and treat stormwater for near- and long-term initiatives on a localized basis in an attempt to alleviate the over-burdened storm drain and stream systems. Further-more, the Campus Plan proposes the use of sustainable design principles such as Low Impact Development (LID) techniques for all future development projects, to minimize adverse effects to the environment.

APPROACH AND ANALYSIS

The stormwater management strategy proposes a two-pronged approach to restore the watershed. First, a series of campus-wide strategies will restore the watershed and create capacity for future growth. Secondly, specific projects will meet the highest standards of sustainability, going above and beyond mitigating their own impacts in order to contribute to the enhancement and restoration of the watershed.

The East Basin offers little valuable habitat and is currently an eyesore to the surrounding area.

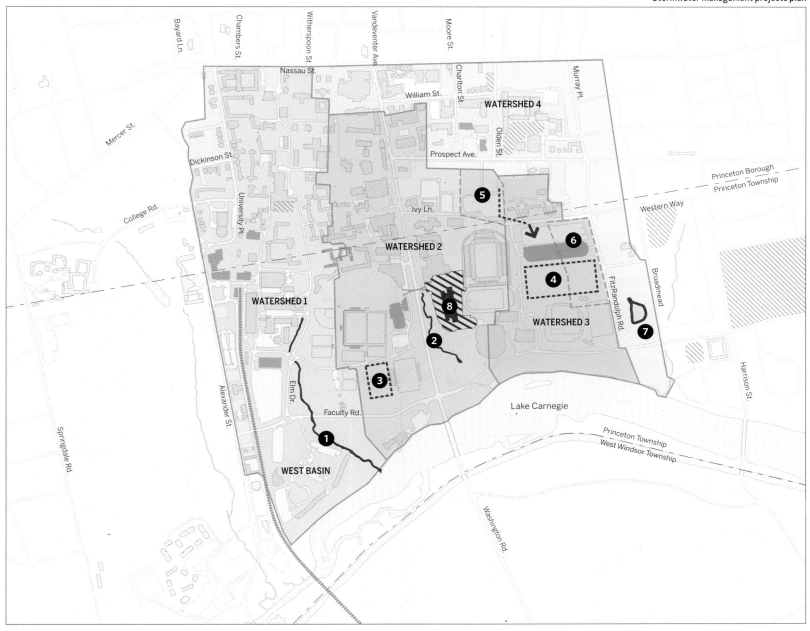

PROPOSED PROJECTS

Stream Restoration Projects
1 Elm Drive stream
2 Washington Road stream

Underground Detention and Infiltration
3 Bedford Field
4 New athletic fields

Re-piping and Shifting Watershed Boundaries
5 Ivy Lane parking lots
6 Eastern parking and fields

Basin Improvement Project
7 East Basin

Project-Specific Stormwater Management
8 Chemistry building (case study)

Four watersheds lie within the area of the main campus. The stormwater management plan proposes campus-wide strategies to improve the quality and reduce the rate of water runoff that passes through the watersheds and down to Lake Carnegie. These strategies fall under four main categories: restoration of the major natural streams on campus (**1, 2**), detention and infiltration of stormwater under new athletic fields (**3, 4**), re-piping and shifting of runoff to watershed three (**5, 6**), and improvements to the capacity of the East Basin (**7**). In addition to these campus-wide strategies, project-specific improvements will be implemented. See the Chemistry building case study (**8**).

CAMPUS-WIDE APPROACH

The campus-wide approach to stormwater management begins with a "sensitivity analysis" that identifies areas most affected by projected future development. The analysis first establishes a comprehensive hydrologic model of the entire campus to develop an understanding of the complex nature of the present-day watershed. Then data about planned campus-wide development is applied to the hydrologic model in order to understand what type of impact future building will have on current conditions.

The analysis evaluates the watershed's response and identifies specific drainage areas that are most sensitive to development. The campus-wide approach promotes sensible, localized stormwater management strategies, not a single solution.

For example, the central and western portions of Princeton's campus have experienced the greatest impacts from past development, resulting in erosion and degradation in the stream corridors. Based on the sensitivity analysis, various stormwater management strategies were identified that will not only mitigate anticipated adverse impacts of planned development, but also repair and restore the present-day degradation resulting from past development projects.

For areas where high density development is proposed and/or where existing drainage areas are highly sensitive to projected growth, the plan proposes designs that will mitigate the projected increase in stormwater by constructing systems that will detain and infiltrate it. Certain projects present the opportunity to create capacity for nearby future growth, such as two athletic field projects proposed at Bedford Field and the eastern athletic practice fields. Other proposed projects, such as the Ivy Lane parking lots, can alleviate an over-burdened sub-watershed area by "shifting" water runoff from one area to a nearby area that has available capacity.

In areas that are currently degraded and slated for high density development, the plan proposes landscape-based restoration projects that will help sensitive areas regain capacity as well as create additional capacity to accommodate future growth. The current degraded stream valleys (Washington Road and Elm Drive) and pond (East Basin) on campus present prime opportunities to implement watershed restoration projects. The stream valleys should be stabilized, re-established with native plants and enhanced with floodplains and wetland areas along the banks.

PROJECTS AND STRATEGIES

Elm Drive stream restoration

Portions of the Elm Drive stream channel will be restored by creating floodplains and wetlands, stabilizing the channel using bio-engineering techniques, and restoring buffer zones. Restoration of floodplains and wetland areas along the stream channel should provide capacity for development projects in the Arts and Transit Neighborhood or other development.

Washington Road stream restoration

The redevelopment of the Natural Sciences Neighborhood presents an opportunity to restore the buffer zone and habitat associated with this stream. The Washington Road project will expand the ecological area by recreating the buffer zone, enhancing and stabilizing the existing stream channel, creating floodplains, recreating habitat, and restoring the natural water balance. Creating floodplains could provide additional capacity for development, as well as contribute to the improved health of the watershed.

Bedford Field

The future reconstruction of this field southwest of the Neuroscience and Psychology buildings presents a stormwater mitigation opportunity. Layers of crushed stone will be constructed beneath the Bedford Field to store, mitigate, and infiltrate stormwater for Neuroscience and Psychology and other projects.

New athletic practice fields

The construction of the new athletic fields will provide stormwater mitigation for the project itself, as well as creating capacity for future development. The fields will be constructed over layers of crushed stone in order to store, mitigate, and infiltrate stormwater.

> To make a complex campus environment truly sustainable requires plans and designs that answer multiple challenges "at one fell swoop." This way better playing fields make room for better buildings and landscapes absorb stormwater away from civil engineering.
>
> —GUY NORDENSON,
>   PROFESSOR OF ARCHITECTURE

Elm Drive stream

Washington Road stream

Ivy Lane parking lots

Stormwater runoff from the Ivy Lane parking lots will be re-routed to the stormwater mitigation area located below the athletic fields. This shifting of the watershed boundary takes advantage of excess capacity below the fields, alleviating the Washington Road stream channel in the process.

East Basin

In order to accommodate future development in the eastern part of the main campus, the plan recommends a stormwater landscape project that will make significant improvements to the existing regional detention pond, referred to as the East Basin. At present, the detention pond is near its regulatory capacity. It lacks the important natural characteristics of a pond wetland that could provide stormwater quality treatment and groundwater recharge, as required by current state regulations. The physical improvements would be made mainly to the landscape, with the goal of providing water quality treatment for future development projects that convey stormwater to the basin. Additionally, the basin's capacity will be increased for managing the quantity of stormwater runoff.

Landscape projects

The Campus Plan's landscape projects also provide an opportunity to integrate stormwater management. By greening areas that are impervious as well as by improving soil and drainage conditions, these projects should reduce the peak rate and volume of stormwater runoff, thereby alleviating over-burdened downstream systems. The proposed projects will provide water quality treatment capacity using natural systems by integrating stormwater runoff with landscape design.

SITE-SPECIFIC APPROACH

New development projects present an opportunity to enhance sensitive watersheds by going beyond simply mitigating their project-specific impacts.

When selecting sites for new development, existing ecological resources should be protected to the greatest extent possible in order to maintain natural processes that store, treat, and infiltrate stormwater. Wooded areas, open space, and resource buffer zones should be preserved in order to maintain groundwater recharge that ultimately feeds wetlands, streams, and surface water bodies.

New development projects also provide opportunities to reintroduce natural systems into the built environment. By recreating systems such as streams, wetlands, floodplains, and vegetated buffers, natural processes can be restored to support a balanced ecosystem, improve water quality, and provide flood capacity for stormwater. Newly-created natural systems typically exceed stormwater management regulations specific to individual projects, thereby contributing to the overall sustainability of the watershed.

PRINCIPLES TOWARD SUSTAINABLE FUTURE DEVELOPMENT

Future development at the University will promote sustainability by minimizing negative impacts and enhancing ecological processes within the watersheds. Sites selected for new development projects should first and foremost respect the environment by protecting sensitive natural resources, buffer zones, forests, and other ecologically sensitive areas. Whenever possible, new projects should build on existing developed sites, improve the impervious cover condition, or make it greener by creating new natural areas, integrating stormwater within the landscape design, and promoting infiltration and rainwater reuse.

SUSTAINABLE STORMWATER MANAGEMENT PRINCIPLES

Water balance: *the mass balance of water essential to preserve natural flow and sustain a healthy watershed.* Development adversely affects the natural water balance because it changes the hydrologic cycle (increases runoff, decreases infiltration, etc.), ultimately causing downstream flooding, erosion, and groundwater depletion.

Ecohydrology: *water balance maintained by preventing changes to the hydrologic cycle.* Effective sustainable developments mimic the existing balance by maintaining runoff patterns and infiltration quantities. Ecohydrology recognizes the interaction between hydrology and ecology by encouraging the restoration and maintenance of the natural water balance.

Low impact development (LID): *avoiding adverse impacts and minimizing disturbance by closely simulating pre-development water balance.* LID is accomplished by using design techniques such as integrating stormwater and landscape areas and preserving or protecting sensitive areas such as riparian buffers, wetlands, steep slopes, flood plains, woodlands, and areas with permeable soils and mature trees.

Integrated management practices (IMPs): *design techniques that integrate stormwater and landscape.* IMPs address stormwater management in site-specific, practical, cost-effective landscape features rather than in traditional end-of-the-pipe facilities.

Biomimicry: *reintroducing natural systems into the built environment and rethinking the engineer's traditional "interference" response to development.* Biomimicry uses the principles of nature, rather than structured or engineered solutions, to manage stormwater.

Water conservation: *conserving water to contribute to the long-term sustainability of resources.* Water conservation techniques decrease the project's overall consumption of water and reduce the demands on the water supply and disposal.

The individual project goals for stormwater management should exceed local regulations requiring projects to match existing conditions. Projects should strive to reduce the rate and volume of stormwater runoff by 25 percent and demonstrate exemplary water quality treatment measures.

Rendering of landscaped biofiltration area west of the Chemistry building

Project-specific stormwater management at the Chemistry building

The design of the new Chemistry building presents an exciting opportunity to set a high standard for the future of sustainable development on campus.

The Chemistry building will be constructed adjacent to an ecologically sensitive area with a stream and steeply sloped bank along Washington Road. The redevelopment of this site will restore the buffer zone and habitat associated with the stream by locating the Chemistry building farther away from these areas than the Armory building that it replaces. By expanding the ecological area and recreating the buffer zone, the project will enhance the health of the watershed.

Redevelopment of this site will further demonstrate sustainability by incorporating the Low Impact Development technique of "greening"—the future site will contain more green (pervious) areas than the existing site. Greening is an important strategy for managing stormwater runoff for the project; a reduction in imperviousness will result in a lower stormwater runoff. The expected reduction in

stormwater runoff will also help to alleviate the adjacent stream channel's stressed condition.

The volume of runoff from the site will be further reduced via a rainwater harvesting system. Stormwater collected from half of the building's rooftop will be conveyed to an underground storage cistern where it will be stored and used to supplement the building's toilet flushing demand. This system will not only reduce the volume of stormwater discharged, but it will also demonstrate water conservation by reducing the amount of potable water consumed for non-potable uses.

Stormwater runoff from the project site and portions of the building rooftop will be directed to landscaped bio-filtration areas which promote natural treatment processes and infiltration. By dispersing stormwater throughout the site close to the source, the project is expected to alleviate the erosion and degradation caused by piped discharge to the stream.

Wayfinding

A new comprehensive wayfinding program will promote a better visitor experience and improve traffic patterns by providing essential information that people and residents need to find the University and navigate the campus.

Initially, Princeton developed as a tranquil enclave where students and faculty could together pursue their academic endeavors with minimal interruption. As the University grew and developed in the 20th century, the gates opened, and soon the number of visitors to programs and campus events swelled to over 700,000 a year.

Like much of the University's landscape and buildings, previous modes of signage were designed to serve the "private Princeton," home to an intimate community very familiar with the quirks of the Core Campus. But the modern campus needs an up-to-date, comprehensive wayfinding program that will communicate directions clearly and concisely to a wide variety of visitors seeking diverse campus destinations. Without creating visual clutter, this new generation of signage and other prompts will provide the necessary information that newcomers, and the entire community, will need to navigate their way to and around campus. An effective wayfinding system will deliver people to events, meetings, and classes without disturbing the experience and pleasure of their campus journey.

Princeton is a strikingly beautiful and distinguished academic setting that is confusing to navigate in spite of the campus' comparatively small scale. Visitors, returning alumni, and even members of the community have difficulty finding their way to a destination. There are four main reasons for wayfinding confusion:

Point of arrival What was historically the back of campus has become a front door for many visitors, as many now arrive not at the pedestrian gate on Nassau Street but through the winding vehicular routes and visitor parking areas in the south.

Lack of addresses Because it is largely pedestrian, typical street addresses don't exist for many parts of the Princeton campus.

Limited landmark visibility The topography and architecture of Princeton contribute to the confusion. The system of gothic courtyards and quadrangles, while beautiful and inspiring to visit, often disorients first-time visitors. The campus topography coupled with courtyards that limit long views, particularly when approaching from the south, compromise visitors' ability to understand where they are and where they need to go.

Lack of identification signs Inadequate building identification signage compounds the visitor's wayfinding challenges.

Historic gateway of Princeton: Nassau Hall in 1837

Current vehicular gateway: view approaching visitor parking garage

Current pedestrian arrival point: view of campus from Lot 7 garage

UNDERSTANDING THE CAMPUS

Princeton is a large campus made up of intimate spaces. It is a place more easily understood over time as intricacies and nuances that were initially confusing coalesce into the image of a single coherent space. The wayfinding challenge is to create a "language" that will facilitate giving directions to first-time visitors. This begins by breaking the campus down into smaller, more easily understood areas and implementing a system of check-points that will enable visitors to quickly reference their location for orientation purposes.

THE PRINCETON CAMPUS COMMUNITY

The Princeton campus population comprises undergraduates, graduate students, faculty, administration, and staff. All of these people were once first-time visitors who had to find their way to Admissions, student check-in, a meeting, or an interview for employment. Like the residents of any town, the members of the Princeton community have their prescribed routes and destinations. When they depart from those typical pathways, they may get lost or feel unsure about finding a particular destination. Changes to the campus over time mean that even alumni can feel disoriented in a place that they once knew intimately.

A WALKABLE CAMPUS

One of Princeton's most distinctive features is its landscape of beautiful tree-lined stone pathways and named walks. This network forms the basis of an effective and well-designed system that delivers visitors and residents to their desired destination. By lengthening and reinforcing this network with landscape improvements and new construction, the University will create a surrogate street system with recognizable reference points. This will support pedestrian wayfinding without changing the essential nature of the campus experience. By enhancing this existing asset with simple markers, the navigation system will overcome topographic limitations and short vistas. These pedestrian pathways comprise the primary organizing principle for a new campus wayfinding system.

700,000 VISITORS A YEAR

Princeton plays host to a diverse list of visitors each year who would all benefit from improved campus wayfinding.

Recent annual attendance counts:

Art Museum: 100,000
McCarter Theatre Center: 200,000
Other concerts and performances: 100,000
Athletics: 250,000 (all events)
Admissions: 26,000 (Orange Key Tours)
Conferences, camps, and summer academic programs: 30,000
Alumni Reunion events: 20,000
Firestone Library: 18,500
Commencement: 10,000

Campus Components

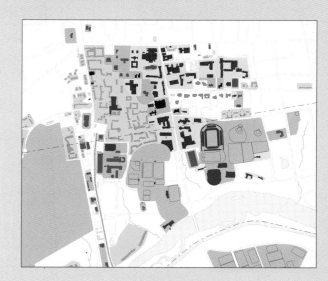

Buildings Like all campuses, Princeton can be comprehended as clusters of buildings. This simple classification is easily understood by different people in a variety of ways: by function (academic, residential, athletic, cultural), by form (such as a distinctive landmark), by name (as a location on a map) or as a destination in an event listing.

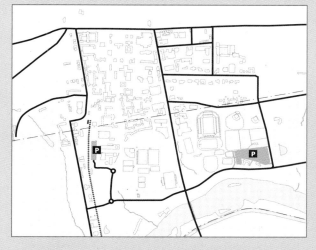

Roads The vehicular arrival routes to campus are the main arteries of the campus, the system that delivers most visitors and members of the community to the University.

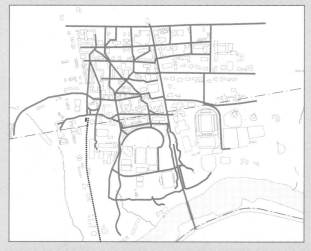

Pathways Once they have arrived, the visitors and members of the community encounter the network of pedestrian walkways that lead them from the edges into the core areas of the parklike campus and its intimate courtyards.

Generations of campus signage

Illegible carved sign

Campus map

Undersigned destinations

EXISTING CAMPUS SIGNAGE

At present, (1) Princeton is dotted with myriad signs representing many generations of styles and approach. What is missing is not necessarily quantity, but quality and consistency. There is a rich heritage of inscribed signs that lend character; while this tradition has been carried forth in some of the modern architecture on campus, understated execution (2) limits its usefulness. Other buildings are undersigned, most notably athletics facilities, like Jadwin Gymnasium (4), which has no visible exterior identification sign. A consistent "palette," a logical approach, and well considered sign placement will greatly improve both vehicular and pedestrian traffic flow. Previous signage efforts also included free-standing map cases spread around campus which serve as moderately successful wayfinding tools. Their effectiveness is undermined by poor execution and placement—with the maps (3) at the back of the case rather than close to the glass and the viewer—as well as their occasionally awkward locations.

SIGNAGE CATEGORIES

Vehicular The Campus Plan recommends improved state highway signage, a University marker along Washington Road to signal arrival, street identification signs, an expanded family of vehicular directional signs, and an improved system of parking lot identification and classification.

Pedestrian Pedestrian signs will consist primarily of directional signs attached to existing campus lampposts. Colored bands at the lamppost base would identify the major campus walks. Directional "finger" signs at key intersections will help visitors quickly find their way with minimal visual impact.

Identification The comprehensive and consistent identification of campus buildings will help visitors and new campus residents find a destination. Improving the visibility of existing inscriptions with guidelines for contrast and fill colors will also improve their legibility.

Information The creation of a new campus map will be essential for better campus orientation, as will the introduction of new information kiosks at key points of arrival that will help someone quickly plot a route or check an event's location. Whether messages are delivered via kiosk, pamphlet, website, or hand-held device the goal is to help people focus on the purpose of their visit rather than the frustration of being lost.

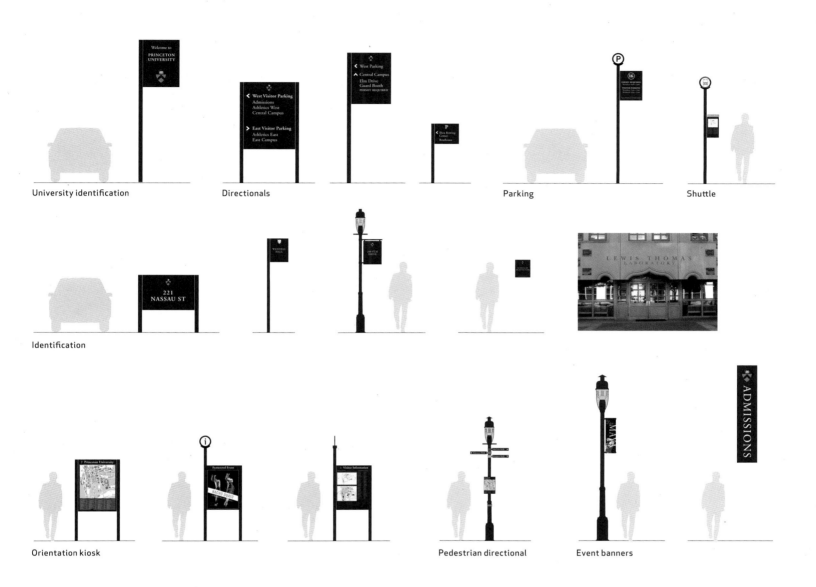

University identification

Directionals

Parking

Shuttle

Identification

Orientation kiosk

Pedestrian directional

Event banners

For more than 250 years Princeton's campus has grown to serve the needs of students, faculty, and society. A new wayfinding system will make it easier for the entire University community and our many welcome visitors to enjoy these beautiful grounds and buildings, and take advantage of the extraordinary resources to be found here.

—BRIAN J. MCDONALD,
  VICE PRESIDENT FOR DEVELOPMENT

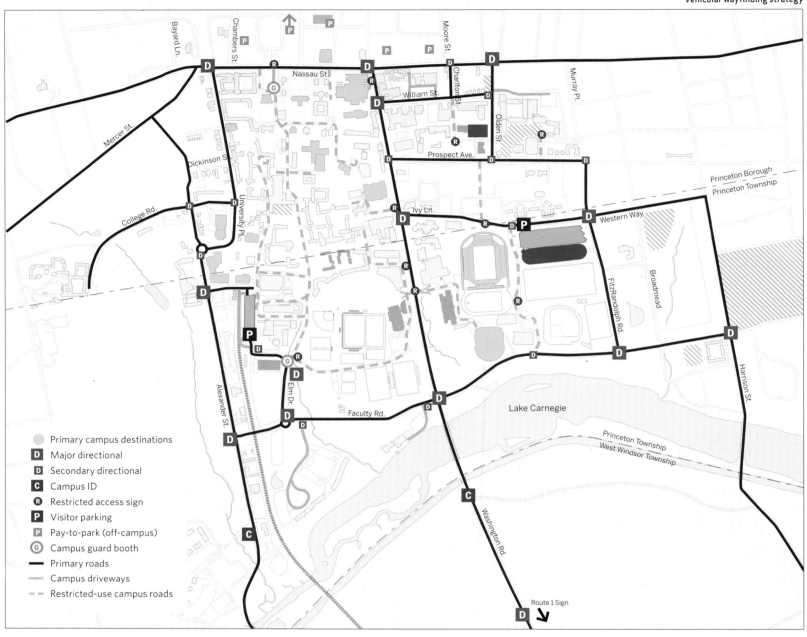

Primary campus destinations
D Major directional
D Secondary directional
C Campus ID
R Restricted access sign
P Visitor parking
P Pay-to-park (off-campus)
G Campus guard booth
— Primary roads
— Campus driveways
--- Restricted-use campus roads

VEHICULAR STRATEGY

Most modern-day visitors to the Princeton campus arrive by car. Though there are a variety of routes, the most direct and ceremonial is via tree-lined Washington Road. As one drives north, the road passes over the lake, then cuts through the campus, providing access to the west and east parking areas. The intersection at Faculty Road, currently undersigned, is an important traffic distribution point with access to both visitor parking lots.

Beginning at Route 1, a new comprehensive signage system will offer consistency and clarity. At present, messages for visitor parking at the Lot 7 garage change from "Admissions Parking" to "Parking Garage Entrance" and the garage is commonly referred to as "Lot 7" in conversation or printed driving directions. To avoid confusion and make giving directions easier, the new system will institute clear naming conventions across all media, from signage to print

to web and will divide campus visitors into those seeking destinations west of Washington Road and those heading east of Washington.

Additionally, the vehicular strategy will focus on providing a family of signs that will display information at key intersections in an attempt to direct cars in the right direction and prevent them from driving in restricted areas. For example, the current building identification signs along Washington Road imply access from that roadway that does not actually exist. The process of pausing to read, consider, and even turn at those signs creates potential hazards on an already congested route. Delivering visitors to the appropriate parking areas and seamlessly onto the campus shuttle will make the visitor experience memorable for all the right reasons.

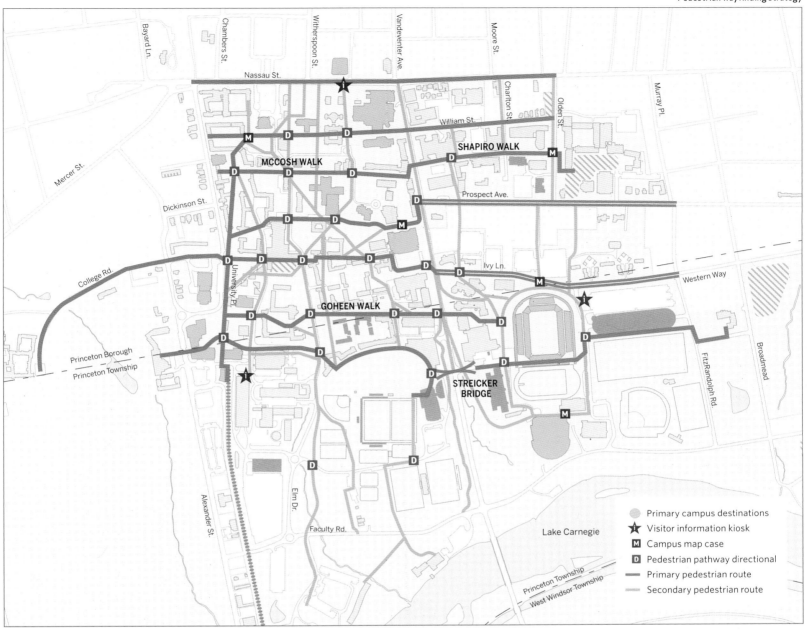

PEDESTRIAN STRATEGY

Princeton is largely a pedestrian-friendly campus with an intricate web of landscaped walkways that traverse the grounds from north to south, west to east. This system, implemented in large part by landscape architect Beatrix Ferrand from 1912 to 1949, is one of the University's most treasured assets. Everyone on campus uses these pathways, in conjunction with the campus shuttle, to get to classes, meetings, appointments, and events. But a first-time visitor can find weaving through archways, intimate interior courtyards, and past seemingly unmarked buildings, disorienting and confusing.

Spanning the campus are walks named after past University presidents—McCosh, Goheen, and Shapiro—as well as unnamed key routes. These serve to collect and distribute pedestrian traffic; they are an existing, well-integrated mechanism designed to deliver people efficiently on foot or bicycle to their destinations. The missing link is the user's ability to understand and reference this system. Renovations and additions to pavings and plantings will create a more complete set of recognizable pedestrian pathways, benefiting first-time visitors and long-time campus residents alike.

In tandem with improvements in the landscape, an integrated pathway signage program will introduce a descriptive language for routes and navigation that has been missing from the campus "dialogue." By utilizing existing elements in the landscape such as the prevalent campus light post, and introducing pedestrian-scaled "finger" signs, the wayfinding program will have a minimal visual impact on the overall campus environment.

The E-Quad garage

SUPPORTING THE CAMPUS

Parking

Traffic Planning

Shuttles and Transit

The arrival of the automobile in the early 20th century presented challenges to campus planning that eventually led to a ban on automobiles from locations designated in Douglas Orr's 1963 Plan. The ban was instituted in part to maintain the intimacy of the growing university's environment and retain the traditional ten-minute interval between classes. Today, the automobile is an unavoidable reality, and so the Campus Plan proposes sustainable ways to accommodate cars while preserving the integrity and pedestrian character of campus landscapes.

Parking

Developing sustainable strategies to address parking demand for a growing campus population

The Campus Plan addresses the inevitable presence of the automobile. Careful planning of the size, location, and design of parking facilities has aimed to preserve the walkable nature of the campus and the character of campus neighborhoods. In the plan, these goals are balanced against the necessity to provide adequate parking in a suburban setting that offers few alternative transportation modes. The Dinky is a valuable asset to the University and the community, but it does not connect the majority of campus commuters to their points of origin. Faculty, staff, students, and visitors who do not have easy access to mass transit consequently drive to campus. Dependent on their vehicles, these drivers are greatly affected by the location and convenience of their designated parking spaces.

The location of parking has a major impact on roadways and intersections in the immediate vicinity. It also determines the routes and frequency of shuttle service between the remote facilities and the commuter's campus destination.

PLANNING APPROACH AND ANALYSIS

As of 2006, the University had approximately 6,800 parking spaces on campus, mostly in surface lots. The total number of spaces included approximately 1,450 spaces at housing sites such as Butler Tract and Lawrence Apartments and approximately 150 spaces for campus plant vehicles, mostly at the MacMillan building. The remaining 5,200 spaces were allocated to faculty, staff, graduate students, and undergraduate students in numbered and lettered lots. Visitor parking is also factored into that number, mostly at Lot 21 and the Lot 7 garage.

Currently, the University provides employees and students with permits for parking on campus. Although there is enforcement of parking permits by the Department of Public Safety, parking facilities do not have gates, card readers, or any other controls to monitor usage. Vehicles entering the Core Campus via Elm Drive are expected to stop at guard booths in order to obtain clearance. Parking permits are free to all employees, and there is no charge for visitor parking on campus.

Based on a parking survey conducted in 2005, 84 percent of faculty, staff, and graduate students arrive on campus in single-occupancy vehicles. Graduate students living at University housing obtain parking at their housing sites; others receive permits to park on campus. According to University data, approximately 27 percent of undergraduate students have cars parked in campus lots (Lot 23).

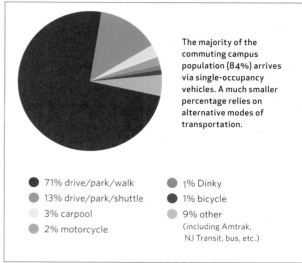

The majority of the commuting campus population (84%) arrives via single-occupancy vehicles. A much smaller percentage relies on alternative modes of transportation.

- 71% drive/park/walk
- 13% drive/park/shuttle
- 3% carpool
- 2% motorcycle
- 1% Dinky
- 1% bicycle
- 9% other (including Amtrak, NJ Transit, bus, etc.)

That does not include undergraduate vehicles parked in eating club lots. Freshmen are not permitted to have cars on campus.

Between 2006 and 2016, the campus population is expected to increase, and several parking lots will be developed into new buildings, resulting in the need to identify new parking sites to offset losses and meet additional demand. A significant portion of that demand stems from the approximately 1,000 spaces that are being displaced by new construction (see the map on the facing page). Visitor parking demand is also expected to increase. The Arts and Transit Neighborhood will draw more visitors, as will the growth in academic departments and the student population.

Along with commencement and reunions, large athletic and cultural events will continue to draw drivers to campus, requiring a parking strategy that addresses the demand for parking during evenings, weekends, and special events. Drivers arriving for events or lectures may not be as familiar with the campus as students or daily commuters are; therefore, wayfinding and signage are critical components in the planning and design of parking facilities.

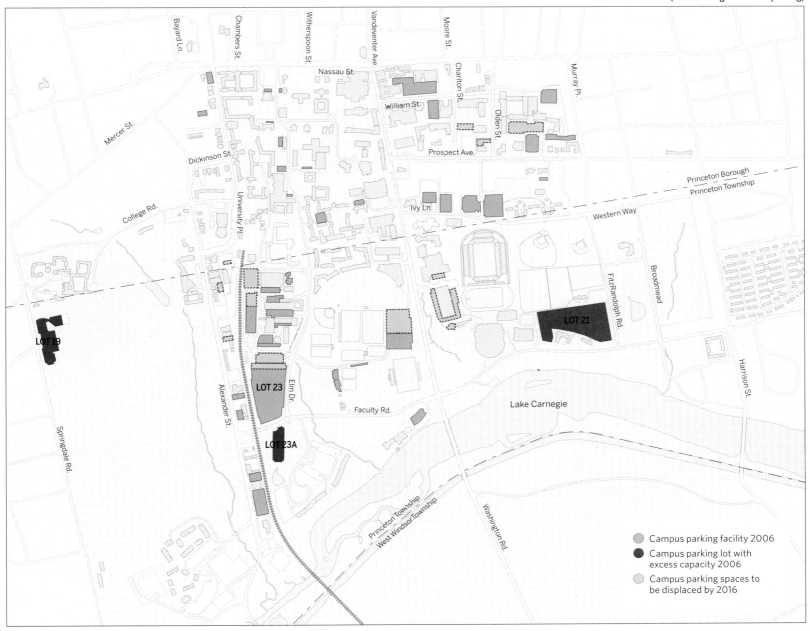

Campus parking facility 2006

Campus parking lot with
excess capacity 2006

Campus parking spaces to
be displaced by 2016

Parking facilities are scattered throughout the campus, though few are within the historic core. All parking lots are at full capacity except for the remote lots—namely, Lots 19, 21, and 23A. Several of the existing lots will be displaced in the next ten years as new buildings are developed in the Natural Sciences, the Arts and Transit, and the Prospect Avenue and William Street Neighborhoods.

RECOMMENDED PARKING STRATEGIES

To address anticipated growth and adhere to defined goals, the planning team analyzed and evaluated available parking options in terms of capacity, feasibility, cost, traffic, shuttle operation, design opportunities, environmental and community impacts, and long-term benefits. Based on surveys of existing usage and occupancy, three parking lots have extra capacity. Before any new parking is developed, the University will utilize this parking surplus. To ensure that the spaces are accessible and convenient, the campus shuttle service will be extended to serve the commuters newly assigned to these lots.

Currently there are approximately 850 parking spaces dedicated to sophomores, juniors, and seniors on campus. Starting in fall 2009, on-campus undergraduate parking will be limited to juniors and seniors, thus reducing the number of cars on campus. In spring 2010, some administrative staff members who are currently on campus will be relocating to a new building on Canal Pointe Boulevard. This will further transfer cars off campus and, in turn, reduce vehicle miles traveled since most of the commuters will be arriving via Route 1.

The University is also in the process of evaluating a variety of transportation demand management (TDM) strategies to reduce the overall number of cars on campus. This includes incentives to commuters to switch from single passenger vehicles to alternative modes. Some potential strategies include providing employees with tax-deductible transit vouchers, creating preferential parking for carpoolers, and improving pedestrian and bicycle routes to campus. When combined with a campus-wide education and public relations program, these incentives may realize up to a ten percent reduction in the number of cars on campus in the next ten years—the equivalent of a 1.5-acre parking lot.

Although the existing surplus can meet the demand for parking in the next few years, it cannot meet the full ten-year demand, especially as existing surface lots are displaced by new construction. A new parking facility on the east side of campus will increase supply by approximately 1,000 spaces. Rather than providing incremental annual increases in the form of scattered asphalt surface lots, the new facility satisfies ten years of parking demand at one time. It will accomplish this while converting the largest surface lot on campus (Lot 21) into athletic fields that are

Lot 7 garage

in character with adjacent open space and athletic uses. The new parking structure will take advantage of the sloping grade of its site to provide three levels of parking without significant visual presence on Western Way (see below). The structured parking is set back from Western Way deliberately to maintain a more landscaped buffer of terraced parking bays. The surface parking lot also provides potential long-term academic development opportunities along Western Way between the stadium and FitzRandolph Road.

Apart from offering design opportunities, the site has strategic advantages over other potential sites evaluated by the planning team. Since the destinations of the majority of faculty, staff, and off-campus graduate students are buildings off Washington Road or Shapiro Walk, it is highly desirable to locate the new facility on the east side of campus in order to be accessible by walking for as many people as possible. This location is within walking distance of the Natural Sciences Neighborhood and the concentration of academic buildings from the E-Quad to Firestone Library.

This location also promotes the use of Faculty Road for vehicular access, as Faculty Road has sufficient capacity to handle additional traffic volumes. A new "Stadium Road" will encourage commuters to approach via Faculty Road, thus minimizing garage traffic on adjacent residential streets. Some commuters who currently park on the west side of campus and shuttle to the east side will be reassigned to the new parking facility. This will free up spaces in the Lot 7 garage for visitors and commuters destined for the Arts and Transit Neighborhood.

By removing Lot 21 and shifting the parking closer to commuter destinations, the project will in effect consolidate athletics facilities around the Caldwell Fieldhouse. Thus, the project will trigger improvements to the University's athletic infrastructure, including a new baseball field, improved varsity practice fields, a new competition-level club sports field, and a more integrated athletics neighborhood.

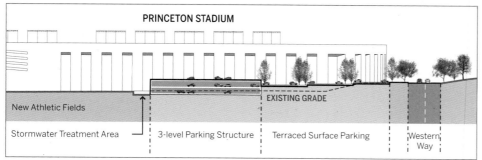

PRINCETON STADIUM

New Athletic Fields

Stormwater Treatment Area · 3-level Parking Structure · Terraced Surface Parking · Western Way

EXISTING GRADE

Schematic section of new parking facility
The proposed parking facility includes a terraced surface lot and a partially submerged parking structure that takes advantage of the existing slope south of Western Way. The profile of the garage also facilitates the treatment of stormwater runoff.

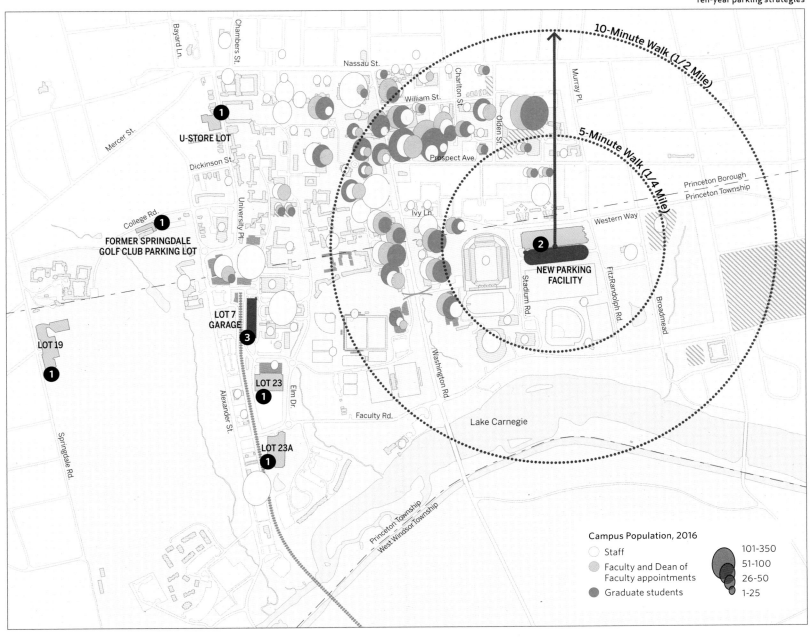

Campus Population, 2016

○ Staff
○ Faculty and Dean of
 Faculty appointments
● Graduate students

101-350
51-100
26-50
1-25

Prior to constructing a new garage, parking demand will be met at existing surface lots with additional or potential capacity (**1**). With the opening of the new parking facility (**2**) on the east side of campus, some of the commuters who currently park in the Lot 7 garage (**3**) will be reassigned to the new facility. This will vacate spaces in the Lot 7 garage so that they can be assigned to faculty, staff, and visitors in the Arts and Transit Neighborhood.

Traffic Planning

Optimizing vehicular, bicycle, and pedestrian
movement while reducing impacts on
residential neighbors

Controlling traffic movement in and through Princeton is a
challenge for two reasons: there has been and continues to
be significant growth in surrounding communities, and the
existing road network is inadequate to cope with the volume
of vehicles. Future growth is likely to shift the distribution
of both people and parking on campus, so the Campus Plan
takes into account both short-term and long-term traffic
projections and roadway improvements.

PLANNING APPROACH AND ANALYSIS

Based on traffic counts at all intersections in the campus
region, the planning team confirmed not surprisingly that
most of the regional peak-hour traffic uses Nassau Street,
Alexander Street, Washington Road, and Harrison Street.

Because of their configuration, the Route 1 intersections at Washington Road and Harrison Street experience
congestion during the morning and afternoon peak periods,
whereas the cloverleaf interchange of Alexander and Route 1
has a larger capacity to accommodate peak hour traffic.

Closer to campus, congestion occurs along Nassau
Street at various times of day. Because the five-point intersection of Nassau Street, University Place, Mercer Street,
and Route 206 is difficult to maneuver, drivers tend to use
University Place to travel northbound to Nassau Street and
Alexander Street to travel southbound from Mercer Street.
As drivers converge at the intersection of Alexander Street
and University Place, the conflicting movements of vehicular
and pedestrian traffic cause extensive delays and back-ups.
Farther south, congestion is typical during the peak hours
along Faculty Road between Alexander Street and Elm
Drive, especially as afternoon traffic exits the Lot 7 garage
and other parking facilities off Elm Drive.

Traffic volumes also tend to be high along Washington
Road, north of Ivy Lane. For the most part, this results in
a traffic-calmed condition at an area of heavy pedestrian
crossings. The combination of pedestrian traffic and the
constrained capacity of the intersection at Nassau Street
indicate that the traffic condition is not likely to change in
the future. However, as the campus grows southward, the
portion of Washington Road south of Ivy Lane will require
improvements (see the Traffic calming and pedestrian
safety section on page 155).

Due to these conditions, drivers gravitate to roadways
with less congestion and greater capacity to avoid problem
areas. For example, drivers shift to the Alexander Road
cloverleaf to reach Route 1 even if Washington Road or

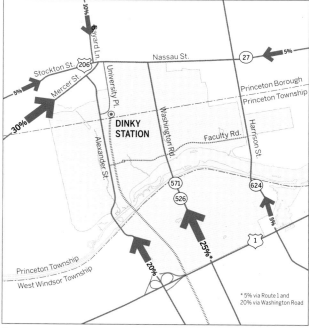

Commuter approach percentages
Staff, faculty, and graduate students who drive to campus rely on
roadways with the greatest capacity and the least congestion to arrive
at their destinations. For that reason, a large proportion of commuters
arrive via Mercer Street, Alexander Street, and Washington Road.

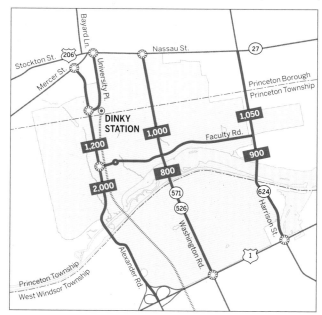

Major roadways and congestion areas
Traffic volumes (including University and non-University vehicles) on the three
major north-south roads (Alexander Street, Washington Road, and Harrison
Street) indicate that drivers rely on Faculty Road to avoid congested areas along
Route 1 and Nassau Street.

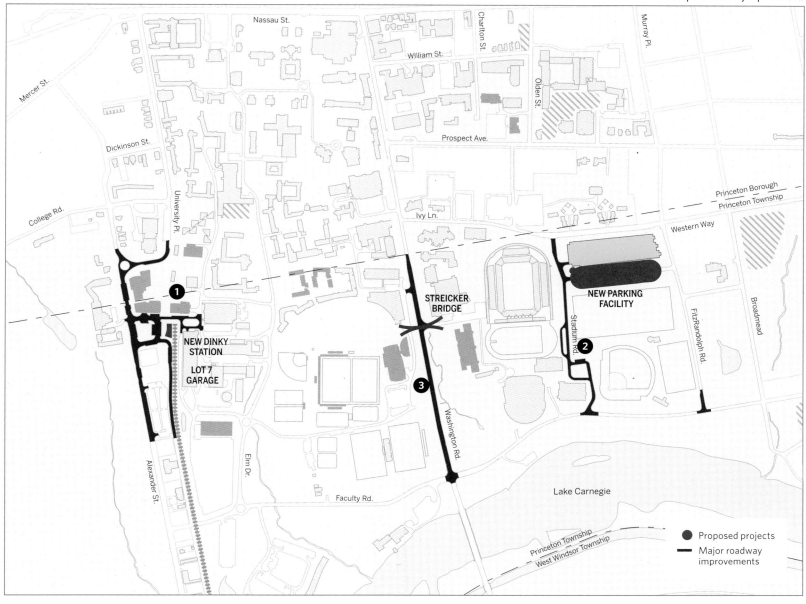

Harrison Street is the shortest route. Drivers use the convenience of Faculty Road to make these choices. This is clearly indicated by the shift in traffic volumes north and south of Faculty Road. Also, some of the drivers destined for the University or the central business district arrive via Mercer Street or Stockton Street if they are approaching from the west. This allows them to avoid the delays along Route 1.

The 2005 parking survey determined that approximately half of commuters approach the campus from the north and west—via Mercer Street and Route 206—and approximately half approach from the south—via Washington Road and Alexander Street. Unless the capacity of the Route 1 intersections at Washington Road and Harrison Street are increased, these approach patterns are likely to remain unchanged in the future.

New projects on campus will create opportunities to improve traffic circulation. The new Arts and Transit Neighborhood will address congestion at the intersection of Alexander Street and University Place and provide a Transit Plaza at the new Dinky station and direct access to the Lot 7 garage (**1**). Access to the new parking facility will be established via an improved Stadium Road (**2**) and FitzRandolph Road. Traffic-calming measures will be implemented along the southern length of Washington Road to reduce vehicular speeds and increase pedestrian safety (**3**).

Conflicting traffic, transit, and pedestrian movements exacerbate congestion at a heavily used intersection.

The reallocation of land uses, parking, and transit functions in the Arts and Transit Neighborhood will eliminate the cluster of conflicting movements and facilitate the circulation of pedestrians, shuttles, and vehicles.

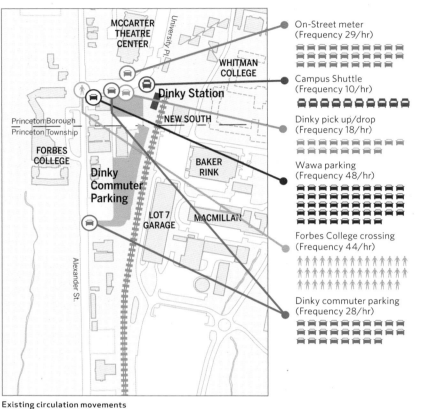

On-Street meter
(Frequency 29/hr)

Campus Shuttle
(Frequency 10/hr)

Dinky pick up/drop
(Frequency 18/hr)

Wawa parking
(Frequency 48/hr)

Forbes College crossing
(Frequency 44/hr)

Dinky commuter parking
(Frequency 28/hr)

Existing circulation movements

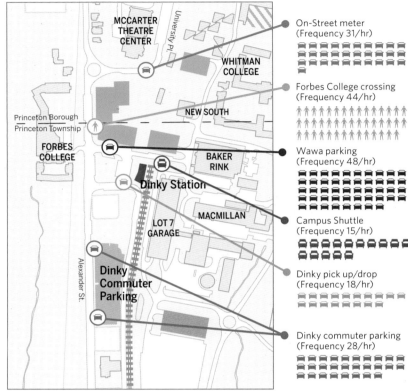

On-Street meter
(Frequency 31/hr)

Forbes College crossing
(Frequency 44/hr)

Wawa parking
(Frequency 48/hr)

Campus Shuttle
(Frequency 15/hr)

Dinky pick up/drop
(Frequency 18/hr)

Dinky commuter parking
(Frequency 28/hr)

Proposed redistribution of circulation movements

PROJECTS

Arts and Transit Neighborhood

The congestion problems at the intersection of Alexander Street and University Place are exacerbated by conflicting pedestrian and vehicular movements as well as by the concentration of on-street parking and drop-offs associated with the Wawa store and the Dinky station. The Arts and Transit Neighborhood features a newly reconfigured intersection with a roundabout in order to facilitate the natural movement of northbound traffic to Nassau Street and southbound traffic from Mercer Street. On-street parking, the Wawa, and the Dinky drop-off are relocated away from the intersection to reduce friction between local and through traffic. Furthermore, some of the campus surface lots off Alexander Street will be removed, thus reducing the number of vehicles that use these lots on a daily basis. A signalized pedestrian crossing for Forbes College will be created. A new Transit Plaza and roadway linking Alexander Street to the Lot 7 garage will centralize transit functions and facilitate visitor and commuter access to the garage. Direct access to the Lot 7 garage offers the added advantage of relieving some congestion on Faculty Road created in the afternoon by exiting garage traffic.

Faculty Road and parking access

A new northern access point to the Lot 7 garage will divert approximately half of the garage traffic away from Faculty Road. Improving the operation and capacity of Faculty Road would reinforce its role as a "collector-distributor" of campus traffic, thus preserving the equilibrium and circulation flexibility between Alexander Street, Washington Road, and Harrison Street. Faculty Road will also serve as the primary access route to the proposed new parking facility east of the stadium. Once improved, Stadium Road will provide garage access in the morning directly from Faculty Road. This route takes advantage of Faculty Road's capacity to handle additional traffic and deters commuters from using residential streets to access the garage. South of the garage, Stadium Road will be closed to garage traffic during afternoon peak hours, favoring pedestrians in the athletics neighborhood during practice times. The majority of exiting afternoon traffic will utilize Faculty Road and FitzRandolph Road or Ivy Lane and Washington Road.

Traffic calming and pedestrian safety on Washington Road

In addition to the Forbes College crossing on Alexander Street mentioned above, pedestrian safety is a concern along Washington Road. As a main gateway into the heart of campus, it serves vehicles and pedestrians, the campus, and the region. In order to ensure pedestrian safety and the smooth flow of traffic, a series of street crossing and traffic calming strategies are recommended, especially along the southern portion of the road. Based on an analysis of existing conditions and accident reports, the planning team determined that the portion of Washington Road south of the borough-township line poses the greatest risk for pedestrians and cyclists. This section of the road has a higher speed limit, wider travel lanes, and lower lighting levels. Based on three years of accident data, the highest rate of pedestrian, bicycle, and vehicular accidents occur at the intersection of Faculty Road and Washington Road.

Streicker Bridge, an elevated pedestrian bridge connecting the new Chemistry plaza to the Ellipse, will provide a safe crossing where one does not currently exist. In addition to the planned bridge, the Campus Plan recommends a median that would extend between Goheen Walk and Faculty Road. Although much of the median will be composed of a flush textured paving system that does not obstruct emergency vehicles, segments of the median will feature raised landscape areas and pedestrian refuge areas, especially at Goheen Walk and Faculty Road.

In addition to slowing traffic and providing safer crossings, the Campus Plan proposes improving north-south pedestrian pathways that parallel Washington Road and form a "ladder" from the Natural Sciences Neighborhood up to Nassau Street (see the Natural Sciences Neighborhood section). In the spirit of protecting the integrity and safety of pedestrian pathways on campus, the plan also recommends restricting non-University delivery and service vehicles from main campus pathways. Dedicating and centralizing delivery and trash collection locations will reduce the number of vehicles that currently use pathways to access buildings across campus.

Bicycle routes and storage

In order to ensure cyclists' safety and to encourage cyclists to commute to campus, the plan recommends that dedicated bicycle routes be created along major routes leading to the main campus. The main campus area will be a shared facility zone in which pedestrians and cyclists use the same pathways. Beyond this area, a set of roadways will be targeted for new or improved bike lanes, signage, and shared roadway improvements (see the adjacent map). In addition to these routes, the plan recommends that an off-road shared path be extended along Alexander Street to connect the main campus to the new administrative neighborhood on Canal Pointe Boulevard. This plan is being implemented by West Windsor Township. Supplementing the bike racks at major campus buildings, two bike centers are recommended for additional security, storage capacity, and minor maintenance. One facility would be on the west side of campus, in the vicinity of the new Dinky station. A second would be incorporated into the new parking facility on the east side of campus.

Washington Road crossing

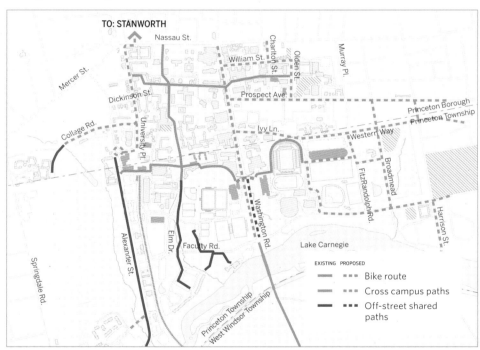

Bike plan

Cyclist on campus walkway

Working with the borough and township, the University will identify desirable bike routes within the immediate vicinity of the campus.

Shuttles and Transit

Improving transportation options to promote accessibility and support regional connectivity

SHUTTLES

Although some parking facilities are close to campus destinations, many (including Lot 7 garage and Lot 21) require shuttle service since they lie beyond a comfortable walking distance. The first shuttle route (the Orange Line) was instituted in 1989. It runs along Elm Drive, transporting commuters from Lot 16 and the Lot 7 garage to the Core Campus. Two additional routes were instituted in 2003. The Blue Line primarily serves Lot 21, and the Green Line serves the graduate housing areas. Ridership on the three lines has increased steadily since the program's inception. The Campus Plan recommends a revamped shuttle program to create a unified transit system that will respond to the changing distribution of campus facilities over time.

Approach and analysis

As part of a study to improve shuttle service and respond to anticipated campus growth, the planning team facilitated focus groups of shuttle riders and community residents to solicit feedback about the existing service. In light of the steady increase in ridership, many users, especially graduate students, requested greater frequency and connectivity to different quadrants of campus and to off-campus destinations, such as shopping areas. Community residents voiced concerns about shuttle routes along residential streets—especially William Street and Prospect Avenue—and the size of the vehicles. Also, in order to allow off-campus staff at an administrative building along Canal Pointe Boulevard to get back and forth to the main campus, additional shuttle service will be necessary, possibly in collaboration with the Princeton Theological Seminary.

Proposed routes

Starting in 2008, the campus shuttle system will be developed into a more comprehensive and user-friendly set of routes serving the Core Campus and new growth areas, the daily campus community, and the visitor population. Based on feedback from the focus groups, new routes will be diverted away from residential streets where possible and onto campus and commercial thoroughfares. As a case in point, routes will be redirected off William Street to Nassau Street. Improved service will reduce travel time and increase signage and accessibility. Four new shuttle routes will allow passengers to access all parts of campus (see the adjacent 2008 shuttle routes map). New shuttle stops, maps, and logo designs will create a consistent and identifiable image for the new campus transit system. With small adjustments, these routes will accommodate campus growth over the next ten years to serve a new Dinky station and the proposed new parking facility east of Washington Road (see the adjacent map of potential 2016 routes).

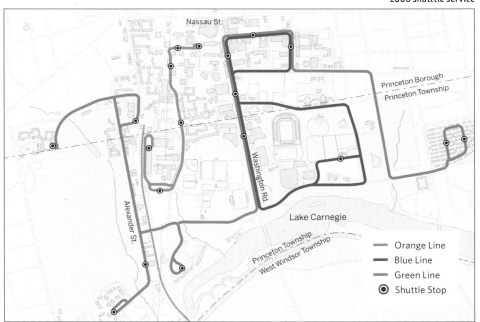

2006 shutttle service

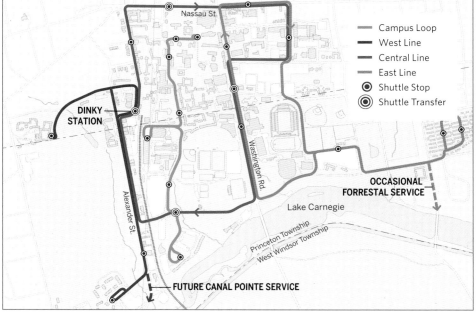

2008 planned shuttle service

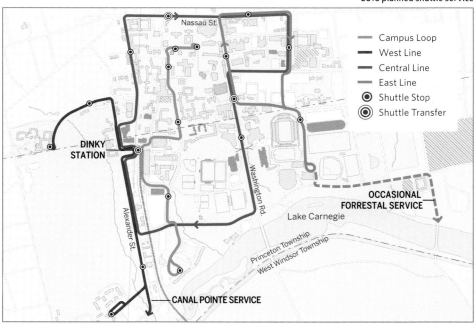

2016 planned shuttle service

Campus shuttle, 2007

Dinky station

TRANSIT

Like many small towns, Princeton lacks an extensive public transit system. As the most heavily used form of public transit in the region, the existing New Jersey Transit Dinky line is a crucial service for the campus and surrounding communities. Serving commuters, shoppers, students, visitors, and theater-goers, it links Princeton University, Borough, and Township to the New Jersey Transit and Amtrak rail corridor between New York City and Philadelphia. It also carries historic charm and symbolism even to those who may not utilize it on a regular basis.

From the University's and the community's point of view, investment in alternative transportation modes—especially as part of a more comprehensive transportation demand management strategy—is likely to reduce the need for road widenings, additional signals, larger parking facilities, and other costly and energy-intensive improvements. It also has the benefit of reducing carbon emissions, fossil fuel dependency, and impermeable surfaces that adversely affect soil and water quality.

NJ Transit/Dinky station

Based on a 2006 Dinky Rider Survey, approximately 40 percent of the riders are University-affiliated. Over half of all riders walk to the Dinky station—approximately 375 walkers per day in each direction. The Arts and Transit Neighborhood would anchor the Dinky station within a mixed-use district while accommodating a possible future bus rapid transit (BRT) service along the Dinky right-of-way. A Transit Plaza has been designed to accommodate a variety of transit modes that link to the Dinky and potentially the BRT, including campus shuttles, a planned community jitney, taxis, and single passenger vehicles. Refer to the "Arts and Transit Neighborhood" section, in this chapter, for additional information on the proposed Transit Plaza and Dinky station.

Community jitney

Princeton Borough is currently developing plans for a community jitney service that would link the Dinky station and the community via a regularly scheduled route that would run through the borough and provide easy access for residents and commuters to several locations in downtown Princeton. The plans for the Transit Plaza make accommodations for this service as part of a multi-modal transit hub that provides links to the campus, the community, and the central business district.

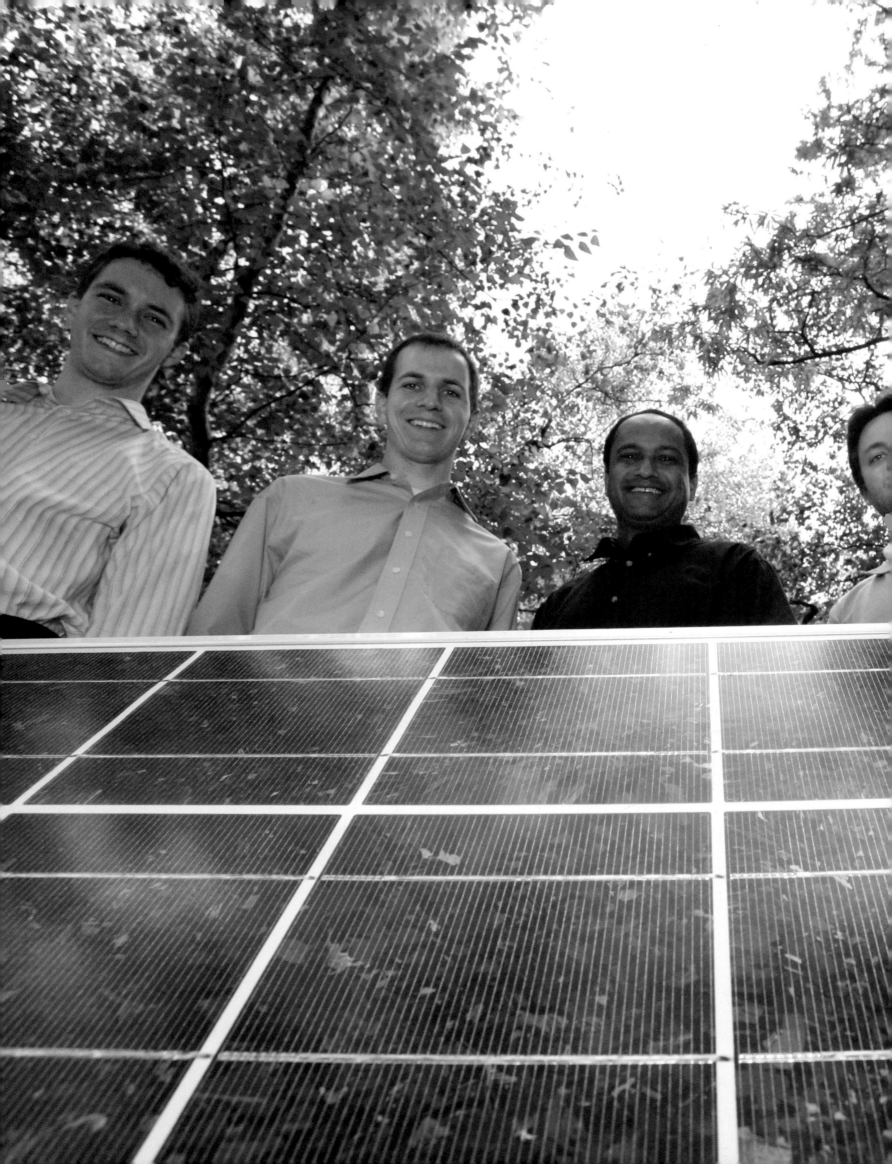

CHAPTER 6
A SUSTAINABLE CAMPUS

Universities today bear the same responsibility to confront environmental challenges as other institutions, municipalities, and countries around the world, but they can make unique contributions through research, teaching, and student initiatives. Universities also have many opportunities to practice sustainability, through such activities as campus operations and the housing, feeding, and transporting of people. Curbing greenhouse gas emissions tops the list, so in anticipation of increased power demands required by almost two million square feet of new development in the next decade, the Campus Plan recommends strategies to decrease Princeton's "carbon footprint" during this period. Famous for its scenic greenery, Princeton's walkable campus will soon become even "greener" through greater emphasis on transportation initiatives, recycling, conservation education, and better water management.

Sustainability: "meeting the needs of the present without compromising the ability of future generations to meet their own needs" —The United Nations

Sustainability at Princeton

Becoming a dynamic working laboratory to help inspire exemplary global citizenship

Princeton has declared the pursuit of sustainability an institutional priority in its Campus Plan. The University has developed a comprehensive framework to bring that priority into focus on areas that represent its major sustainability challenges. The framework is organized into three themes that complement the existing operational and academic structure: 1) greenhouse gas emissions, 2) resource conservation, and 3) education, research, and civic engagement. Within each theme are specific subject areas managed by the Princeton Sustainability Committee with student, faculty, and staff participation. This committee is responsible for assessing current and historic performance, defining metrics for tracking performance over time, and setting targets that coincide with the current Sustainability Plan timeline.

The National Spherical Torus Experiment at the Princeton Plasma Physics Laboratory

PRINCIPLES

Reduce campus greenhouse gas emissions by implementing alternative energy technologies, energy conservation programs, green building techniques, transportation demand management strategies, and commuter alternatives, while increasing the size of the campus by two million square feet.

Improve natural resource conservation by taking an ecosystems approach to development, integrating landscape and stormwater management strategies.

Foster civic engagement by representing sustainability principles in the built environment, as well as the social, academic, and research environments on campus.

HISTORY

Princeton has a long history of energy and environmental innovation dating back to the founding of the campus in Princeton. The stewardship of the University lands drove the design of the University's first buildings and later Beatrix Farrand's landscape design. The campus hosts one of the nation's most efficient and cost-effective central power facilities, with cogeneration in place since 1996 and chilled water storage since 2006. Princeton installed a 100-well geothermal system in 2003 to serve 207 units at Lawrence Apartments. Diligent maintenance over the years has ensured that the steam and chilled water delivery infrastructure operates at maximum energy and economic efficiency, aided by a real-time computerized central monitoring and dispatch system. Reflecting these efforts, in 2007 the energy plant received an EPA Energy Star CHP (combined heat and power, or cogeneration) Award. The University's CHP system requires approximately 21 percent less fuel than typical onsite thermal generation and purchased electricity, reducing carbon dioxide emissions by an estimated 18,000 metric tons per year, according to the EPA. Energy efficiency initiatives have also been a part of standard operations for many years, including lighting retrofits, window upgrades, improved insulation, and Energy Star appliance use.

In the research arena, Princeton is co-located with more climate change and energy research facilities than any other university in the country:

- Civil and Environmental Engineering— School of Engineering and Applied Science
- Carbon Mitigation Initiative— Princeton Environmental Institute, Geosciences, Ecology and Evolutionary Biology
- Woodrow Wilson School of Public and International Affairs
- Princeton Plasma Physics Laboratory
- Geophysical Fluid Dynamics Laboratory

CHALLENGES FACED BY THE CAMPUS TODAY

The biggest sustainability challenge the campus faces today is reducing greenhouse gas emissions while adding over two million square feet of built environment by 2016. Princeton is not unique in its growth projections, but it is unique in its effort to decrease its carbon footprint with activities on its own campus.

Some 85 percent of the University's carbon footprint is generated by the central power facility that provides power, heating, and cooling to campus buildings. Although additional development would normally require added capacity, the University plans to add two million square feet without an addition to the central plant. This goal will be accomplished through conservation efforts in existing buildings and by providing capacity with energy alternatives that produce no net carbon dioxide or other greenhouse gases.

There are a number of promising options currently being studied for onsite use, including ground-source heat pumps ("geothermal"), biofuels for the central power plant, and solar electric power. Another contributor to the carbon footprint is transportation, including employee commuting, University-related travel, and the on-campus fleet. It is important to note that reducing carbon dioxide emissions requires a multi-faceted effort. Truly addressing sustainability requires a shift in economic models, behavior patterns, political perspectives, international relations, and rewards systems. A combination of social, economic, and energy policies will ensure that the University will succeed in cutting emissions to the levels required given the current scientific consensus.

INTEGRATION WITH ACADEMIC PROGRAMS

Sustainability at Princeton enjoys very close ties with academic programs. In fact, students and faculty are a critical driving force behind important campus initiatives.

With support from the Office of Sustainability, campus-based research projects are increasingly being integrated into courses, the results of which will provide data for both the ongoing campus assessment program as well as the overall sustainability movement. Recent or upcoming class projects include an evaluation of impervious surface area changes on campus over time, studies to evaluate the effectiveness of vegetated rooftops ("green" roofs) for insulation and rainwater filtration, sustainable agricultural practices, and strategies for communicating these issues to the general public.

Princeton's cogeneration system typically runs at about 78 percent efficiency compared to the local power grid efficiency of about 40 percent.

Biodiesel testing

Infrastructure is the invisible, literal lifeblood of a campus. A well designed set of support systems allows a campus to grow sustainably and efficiently, making it possible to use limited resources to better support the core mission of the institution.

—MICHAEL MCKAY,
VICE PRESIDENT FOR FACILITIES

ADDRESSING GREENHOUSE GAS EMISSIONS

Scientific consensus indicates that developed nations must control emissions within the next decade and reduce emissions dramatically by 2050 to avoid the worst consequences of climate disruption. Reducing greenhouse gas emissions on campus involves all areas of campus operations, but is primarily focused on heating, cooling, electricity, and transportation. The goal of sustainability efforts in this arena is to reduce emissions to 1990 levels while the campus expands dramatically.

Energy efficiency

The Campus Plan recognizes that the first step toward curbing emissions is conserving the energy resources the University currently uses. Examples include: lighting retrofits featuring specialized sensors and more efficient bulbs, research into advanced technologies such as highly efficient LED lighting, tests of alternative lighting such as solar concentrator skylights, window upgrades, replacement of leaking steam traps, steam and chilled water pipe insulation, installation of low-flow bathroom fixtures, and upgraded metering. Princeton's conservation programs benefit from additional programmatic support provided by many student educational initiatives such as "Pull the Plug," a program encouraging students to turn off all sources of power in their rooms when leaving for breaks.

On-campus thermal energy storage plant

Geothermal well drilling at Lawrence Apartments

Alternative energy

The campus will soon benefit from aggressive research into zero- or low-carbon energy sources such as geothermal, biodiesel from sustainable sources, and solar electric power. In addition to the geothermal system at Lawrence Apartments, Princeton has already committed to a 400-kilowatt solar panel array on one of its Forrestal Campus warehouses. Consultants are conducting a ground source heat pump (geothermal) study for the main campus to assess its potential for increasing heating and cooling capacity without burning additional fossil fuels. The University is also testing the feasibility of including biodiesel as a fueling option for the central plant.

Transportation

Commitment to a sustainable transportation infrastructure will impact not only the quality of the campus environment, but also that of the region. Commuter miles, all University-related travel, and the on-campus fleet are included in Princeton's transportation emissions inventory as well as small motors used in vehicles caring for the grounds. Cars and delivery vehicles contribute pollutants, require large amounts of impervious paved surfaces, infringe on pedestrians, and cause expensive deterioration of roadways. However, vehicles are also essential, especially for emergency needs, so careful transportation planning is critical as the campus becomes denser. To this end, the Campus Plan has recommended ways to discourage single-occupant driving, enhance links to public transportation, support carpools and emergency ride home programs, and implement transportation demand management strategies.

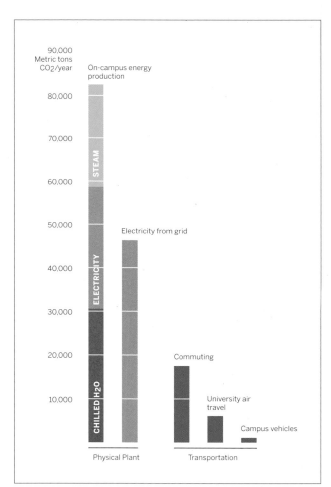

Princeton's greenhouse gas emissions, 2006

CONSERVATION

Green construction and renovation

The University requires sustainability performance in its new buildings and major renovations as outlined in the Sustainable Buildings Guidelines. These guidelines require, among other things, a minimum level of energy performance in the building design that is 50 percent better than national code requirements (ASHRAE 90.1). The benefits of an efficient building include downsizing all mechanical systems, reducing the energy demands of the building, and decreasing greenhouse gas emissions. The guidelines also require life cycle cost analysis of major proposed building systems and innovative green design options as well as evaluation of all aspects of building design and performance, from stormwater management to materials choices. The University currently uses the U.S. Green Building Council's Leadership in Energy and Environmental Design (LEED) checklist to help guide that process, with the goal that every building and major renovation achieve, at minimum, the equivalent of LEED Silver.

Creating high-quality pedestrian and cyclist environments

Promoting quality pedestrian and cyclist environments across the campus not only reduces dependency on vehicles and pollution in the air and on the ground, but also encourages increased physical activity for better health. To achieve these improvements the Campus Plan proposes: extending the existing pedestrian and cyclist circulation network to new areas of campus and employee residential clusters near campus; improving the network in areas where it is deficient; enhancing existing pathways; and instituting an extensive program of landscape design and wayfinding improvements.

Growing vibrant landscapes

Natural and cultivated landscapes across campus play a critical role in maintaining a healthy ecosystem. While plantings and vegetation keep soils healthy, they also contribute to cleaner air and water, provide shading and improve energy efficiency for buildings, and provide habitat for New Jersey wildlife. The Campus Plan embraces the opportunity to integrate the campus more fully into the local natural landscape through restoration efforts and additional plantings. Robust natural landscapes provide pervious surfaces, thereby improving groundwater recharge, preventing soil and stream bank erosion, and protecting nearby surface waters.

The Campus Plan proposes an extensive series of design improvements that include strategic woodland plantings in degraded areas and stream restoration. Historically, Princeton has irrigated minimally on campus, instead relying on robust plantings that require little maintenance, chemical input, and watering. This approach is a historically sustainable one, requiring far less fossil fuel input than extensive annual or sensitive specialty plantings. While limited specialty plantings are an integral part of the campus character, Princeton will maintain its traditional approach to general landscaping. Goals will emphasize: preserving native soils, increasing pervious surfaces, installing plantings adapted to the local climate and soil types that

In the U-Bikes program, students repair abandoned bicycles and loan them to the University community

McCosh Courtyard

Princeton has a long and rich tradition of sustainable landscapes—a tradition that will be reinvigorated over the next ten years. Systems of collecting and distributing rainwater to irrigate plantings naturally, using native plants in logical ways that don't require chemical fertilizers and pesticides, and restoring and expanding our green areas and woodlands are key strategies for our stewardship of a sustainable campus.

— NATALIE SHIVERS,
   ASSOCIATE UNIVERSITY ARCHITECT

require minimal maintenance, favoring organic approaches, and irrigating as an exception rather than a rule. The end result is a campus landscape resilient to most weather fluctuations and therefore more sustainable, efficient, and cost-effective. In keeping with these goals, new buildings on campus are being strategically placed over existing parking lots to enhance green spaces and minimize impervious surface area.

Improving water quality and ecological balance

The Campus Plan identifies stormwater management as one of the most critical and strategic means to promote campus sustainability. Although the campus looks and feels very "green," large areas of impervious parking lots, roadways, and roofs contribute to increasingly overtaxed stormwater basins, eroded stream banks, polluted water, puddles on campus pathways, and flooding. The proposed landscape-based approach to stormwater management relies on bio-engineered techniques rather than hard infrastructure that disturbs the landscape.

Dining services and sustainable food systems

Dining Services has set specific targets for purchasing improvements. Current initiatives include buying: ecologically friendly seafood in partnership with the Monterey Bay Aquarium Seafood Watch program; fairly traded and socially responsible coffee; expanded organic produce selections; hormone-free and grass-fed meat options; and more local Jersey Fresh produce.

Dining Services also intends to minimize landfill waste by diverting food scraps to a local pig farm, using Green Seal Certified cleaners, and installing high-efficiency dishwashing equipment. The department has also been a key partner, working closely with students and the Office of Sustainability, in the launching of Princeton's first student-run organic garden. Students were instrumental in creating the campus' first farmers market, initiated in 2007.

Students at Mathey dining hall

Student organic garden at Forbes College

Green purchasing

Procurement of goods for the campus is a vital part of operations. It is also a source of influence on the consumer market. One of Princeton's most aggressive green purchasing initiatives is its 100 percent post-consumer chlorine-free recycled paper policy for all standard printing and copying on campus. The goal is to reach 90 percent campus compliance in 2008 with this policy, up from a 2007 compliance rate of about 72 percent. In 2007, this program resulted in an emissions savings equivalent to keeping 40 cars off the road per year.

Conservation of potable water resources

Drinking-quality water is typically used for a wide range of functions on campus, from irrigation and toilet flushing to water fountains and showers. As the campus grows, unless the University conserves, the campus will increase its demands on local resources. The goal of the Campus Plan is to conserve potable water and test alternatives. At the new Chemistry and Butler College building projects, Princeton is installing rainwater capture and reuse systems for, in the case of Butler, irrigation, and in Chemistry, for flushing toilets. Other conservation efforts in all new construction and renovations include installation of low-flow showerheads, toilets, and faucet fixtures, as well as water-free and ultra-low-flow urinals. Students in WaterWatch and Greening Princeton are actively involved in water conservation education in the residence halls and in the larger campus community.

Recycling and reuse

Princeton currently recycles approximately 38 percent of all household items, including bottles, cans, cardboard, paper, scrap metal, and food scraps. The goal is to reach at least 50 percent by 2012. Strategies to increase recycling rates include introducing more uniform and visible labeling for all containers, expanding receptacle locations, and augmenting year-end recycling services for student move-out. With a 38 percent recycling rate, the University consistently performs better than any other Ivy League school in total recycling and per capita recycling. Contributing to these efforts, Forbes and Mathey colleges recently chose to refinish rather than replace most of their dining hall furniture. Student ecology representatives ("Eco-Reps") also help in the effort through active leadership in the residential colleges.

On campus farmers market

COMMUNICATING SUSTAINABILITY

Sustainability initiatives are never fully successful until local and national communities learn about them and what they can achieve. In an effort to engage the student body in communicating its experiences in sustainability, the Office of Sustainability began the Princeton Student Environmental Communication Network (SECN) in the fall of 2006. Students learned how to produce professional-level radio programs that were subsequently aired nationally and on regional radio networks. The program is being developed into a spring 2008 student-initiated course that will cover both radio and video production as well as academic study of ethics in journalism and the development of the environmental communication field. The long-term SECN goal is to establish a true network, engaging institutions of higher education across the nation. The "Sustainability at Princeton" website was launched in 2007 and can be found at www.princeton.edu/sustainability.

THE CAMPUS AS AN ENVIRONMENTAL LABORATORY

There's a good chance that sometime last winter, a team of undergraduates measured the heat escaping from the windows of a campus building, while inside, a group of professors and graduate students huddled together, discussing ways to strengthen international agreements to control global climate change. Such is the nature of environmental studies at Princeton—investigations that span a wide spectrum of disciplines, from the sciences to the humanities, and which operate across a wide range of scales, from the local to the global. Moreover, if the findings of the undergraduates result in more energy-efficient windows on campus, while the deliberations of the faculty members and graduate students result in a more effective successor to the Kyoto Protocol, then both groups will have fulfilled the University's pledge of service to the nation and the world.

Interest in environmental issues at Princeton is on the upswing, as reflected by growing enrollment in courses with environmental themes, increased participation in campus organizations devoted to environmental causes, and more and more research projects devoted to understanding and solving environmental problems. We have seen such upswings before, but what distinguishes the current one is the way in which it permeates our campus.

Two years ago Princeton became the first major university to switch entirely to recycled paper for all our basic uses. Observant diners may note that virtually all of the seafood served at campus dining facilities now comes from sustainably harvested species, the result of a partnership between Dining Services and student activists. The University has made energy efficiency a requirement in the design of new buildings. Meanwhile, faculty and students continue to study a wide range of environmental issues relevant to their daily lives and to international policy. Which is preferable—organic produce that is flown in from California or conventionally-grown produce from here in New Jersey? How does air pollution in China affect public health in the United States? Will the increased use of biofuels result in the destruction of tropical forests?

The bottom line is that we have far to go in our efforts to address environmental issues on campus and around the world. There is no justification for complacency. But there is plenty of reason for optimism.

David Wilcove
Professor of Ecology and
Evolutionary Biology and Public Affairs

CHAPTER 7
LOOKING TO THE FUTURE: BEYOND 2016

Joseph Hudnut, prominent 20th-century architectural critic, stated in 1947 that a university is "a growing organism whose form lies partly in the past, partly in the future." Princeton's past established a unique "sense of place" that endures through beloved traditions and the beauty of its historic campus. Princeton's continued success as a vital institution hinges on preserving this unique character while modifying the campus as necessary to meet the demands of new student populations and academic disciplines. Although this Campus Plan covers a ten-year period, the basic planning frameworks and principles it offers are flexible enough to apply well past 2016, ensuring the best use of existing properties before expansion south of Lake Carnegie or elsewhere becomes necessary.

Students at Commencement

Beyond 2016

The first goal of the Campus Plan is to prepare the University for the next decade of anticipated growth. The projects and policies described in previous chapters are based on known initiatives for academic, residential, campus life, and administrative expansion, and quantifiable needs for parking, traffic, utilities, and other services to support these initiatives. The plan provides a framework for the realization of these objectives.

But what can, or should, be said about the future of Princeton's campus beyond ten years? Is it useful to speculate about long-term growth, since specific needs for the future cannot be accurately predicted? Many current initiatives, such as the Neuroscience Institute and the Peter B. Lewis Center for the Arts, were not predicted or allocated space by the previous master plan in 1995. Some earlier long-range plans have been left unrealized or incomplete, as changing needs caused their obsolescence. A study of Princeton's campus planning history reveals a hidden wealth of unbuilt visions and ideas; a phantom cartography based on the philosophies and perceived needs of each era. Much of the richness of the campus design, as well as some of its weaknesses, derive from the unfinished layers imagined by planners and architects from the colonial period to the end of the 20th century. How then should this plan foresee future stages of campus evolution?

While specific needs cannot be known, it is safe to assume that the University, and thus its campus, will continue to grow as it has for 250 years. Academic programs, deriving from ever expanding fields of human knowledge, will continue to multiply and expand. As diminishing available land causes the campus to approach its capacity, each new project must be carefully and strategically located to preserve options for the future. Maintaining the ability to grow within the campus for as long as possible is an important goal; it reduces expansion pressures in areas immediately surrounding the campus, and avoids premature consideration of off-site development, such as the University's West Windsor lands. Concentrating growth within the walkable campus will also reinforce Princeton's unique intimacy and collaborative academic culture.

Surrounding regional growth, continuing at a rapid pace, impacts the campus as well. Over time the University must continue to recognize the regional impact of its decisions on traffic congestion and the environment.

For these reasons, the Campus Plan has studied the potential for long-range development with these objectives:

- Quantify the remaining available land for development on the main campus (generally the area between Nassau Street and Lake Carnegie).

- Identify a range of sites for the location of future buildings, to create predictability for the University and its neighbors.

- Ensure that the actions of the next ten years do not preclude opportunities for coherent campus growth in the future.

- Create a general framework for the long-range build-out of the campus, while maintaining sufficient flexibility to allow for new and changing needs.

- Develop principles for the sustainable long-range growth of the campus through the management of traffic, environmental, and other impacts.

The long-range planning effort has affected current thinking. The plan seeks to avoid the common error of the expedient meeting of an immediate need without understanding its consequences for future generations, in terms of site planning or demands on infrastructure. Many projects in the ten-year plan have been modified to ensure that they allow for sustainable future growth and favorable development patterns over the next 20 to 30 years. For example, the Arts and Transit Neighborhood anticipates mixed-use redevelopment of the Alexander Street corridor, and plans for the Natural Sciences Neighborhood and the new parking facility anticipate academic development along Ivy Lane and Western Way.

The next few pages describe options for the long-range arrangement of land uses and infrastructure. Future growth can be leveraged to create improved open spaces, pedestrian linkages, infrastructure, and environmental sustainability. The ideas shown here are meant to serve as a general guide and inspiration for the future stewards of the campus and its continued transformation.

> Princeton today is a very fluid, complex educational institution that demands new, imaginative building types that must be designed and situated in ways that enhance their mutual interactions. The University's setting is no longer an "affluent suburb" but rather one of the fastest growing "edge cities" in the United States. Taken together, these developments suggest that Princeton can achieve its goals only if it possesses a prescient, dynamic campus plan.
>
> —ROBERT GUTMAN,
> LECTURER IN ARCHITECTURE

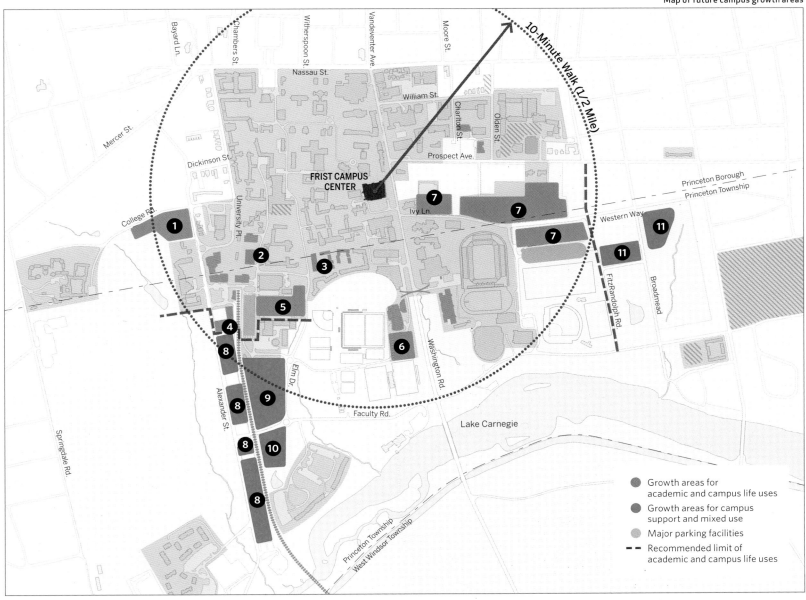

Legend:
- Growth areas for academic and campus life uses
- Growth areas for campus support and mixed use
- Major parking facilities
- Recommended limit of academic and campus life uses

CAMPUS CAPACITY

The map above illustrates the long-term development capacity of the main campus and immediate surroundings, showing remaining sites that could be redeveloped before consideration of off-campus development, in West Windsor or elsewhere, would be required. It is important to note that the areas shown in color are not buildings, but general areas for development that would include a combination of buildings, open spaces, drives, and pathways.

While the scale of development at these locations will depend on many factors including future needs, open space, infrastructure, and local zoning, the map demonstrates that additional capacity for growth within the walkable main campus, beyond the ten-year Campus Plan, does exist. The greatest opportunities for campus growth are in the Ivy Lane and Western Way Neighborhood and the Alexander Street corridor. These areas are discussed in greater detail on the following pages.

Future growth of the campus is divided into two basic categories: academic and campus life uses, which must be close to each other and within a ten-minute walk of the Frist Campus Center; and support uses, including administrative offices, graduate housing, campus utilities, parking, daycare, and others. The map defines proposed limits for the expansion of the first category of uses, to maintain a walkable main campus in support of the University's primary mission.

The areas outside these limits include potential sites for support uses which are compatible with their surroundings. For example, the proposed daycare facility in the Broadmead area can fit within the context of a residential neighborhood, and housing, retail, and administrative office space on Alexander Street can support a mixed-use vision for the corridor. The Campus Plan also recommends that some support uses be relocated out of the central campus area to create new spaces for academic and campus life uses on limited available land.

POTENTIAL LONG-TERM GROWTH AREAS

1 North of Forbes College
2 New South
3 Elm Drive/Butler College
4 Arts and Transit Neighborhood expansion
5 MacMillan building
6 Lot 20
7 Ivy Lane/Western Way
8 Alexander Street corridor
9 Lot 23
10 Lot 23A
11 Broadmead

East Neighborhoods

The eastern area of the Princeton campus provides the greatest potential for future growth of academic and campus life uses. This area has been identified due to its close walking proximity to other main campus areas, access to parking, and the flexibility available for future development sites. A large consolidated area for potential growth can be developed gradually over time as land becomes available, ultimately resulting in the creation of a coherent, rather than haphazard, campus neighborhood.

A significant benefit of academic development on Ivy Lane and Western Way is the ability to create a physical and intellectual "bridge" between the applied sciences neighborhood to the north and the natural sciences neighborhood to the south. Academic collaboration between these areas is currently inhibited by a gap created by parking lots and a lack of pedestrian pathways. With new development, the entire campus east of Washington Road can become more strongly connected.

New development in the Ivy Lane and Western Way neighborhood will, however, also bring campus uses closer to neighboring residential areas. It is therefore recommended that FitzRandolph Road be established as the eastern limit of academic and campus life uses, which also ensures that these activities continue to be located within a ten-minute walk of the Frist Campus Center. Surface

A second pedestrian bridge at the Frist Campus Center would strongly link the Core Campus to the neighborhoods east of Washington Road, including future development along Ivy lane and Western Way.

parking lots on the north and south sides of Ivy Lane and Western Way will be available for potential development by 2016. Also the Data Center at 87 Prospect Avenue will have been relocated, and stormwater capacity will have been increased. In order to maximize flexibility for future development with a gracious campus layout, the plan also recommends the eventual relocation of the Ferris Thompson housing complex. While academic uses hold the highest priority, student residential and campus life facilities would contribute to a mixed-use neighborhood, bringing the vitality and vibrancy associated with the western areas of campus into this area, thereby truly integrating it into the existing campus.

East of FitzRandolph Road, support uses that are compatible in scale and character with the surrounding residential neighborhood are appropriate. By 2016, a new daycare facility will be located at Broadmead field. The site can also accommodate future expansion of childcare facilities, creating a daycare "village." Parking can be minimized by taking advantage of the nearby parking facility.

The new parking facility, part of the ten-year plan, lays the groundwork for future development by drawing pedestrian flows to this area of campus, reducing its isolation, and relocating athletics fields in preparation for future development along Western Way.

Planning principles

- Maintain the buffer zone specified in the E3 zoning ordinance north of Prospect Avenue.

- Reinforce the architectural integrity and student orientation of Prospect Avenue, through re-use of existing buildings for student activities.

- Establish FitzRandolph Road as the eastern limit of future academic growth south of Prospect Avenue.

- Create flexibility for future campus growth within walking distance to main campus areas and parking.

- Relocate existing and outdated facilities along Ivy Lane and Western Way to create land for future development.

- Utilize landscape and pedestrian strategies to connect future growth to existing campus areas, extend the sense of campus, and link natural and applied sciences.

- Maintain and enhance the natural landscape buffer of the Broadmead stream valley between campus areas and the residential neighborhoods along Harrison Street.

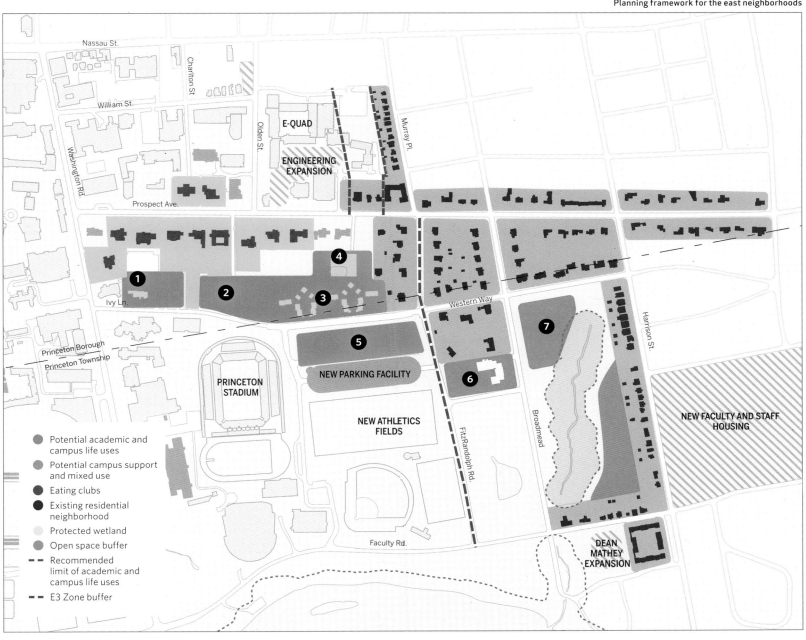

Nassau St.

William St.

Charlton St.

Washington Rd.

Olden St.

E-QUAD

ENGINEERING
EXPANSION

Prospect Ave.

Murray Pl.

①

②

④

③

Ivy Ln.

Western Way

⑤

Princeton Borough

Princeton Township

PRINCETON
STADIUM

NEW PARKING FACILITY

⑥

⑦

Harrison St.

Broadmead

NEW FACULTY AND STAFF
HOUSING

NEW ATHLETICS
FIELDS

FitzRandolph Rd.

Faculty Rd.

DEAN
MATHEY
EXPANSION

- Potential academic and campus life uses
- Potential campus support and mixed use
- Eating clubs
- Existing residential neighborhood
- Protected wetland
- Open space buffer
- – – Recommended limit of academic and campus life uses
- – – E3 Zone buffer

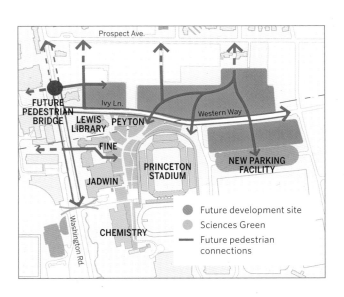

Prospect Ave.

FUTURE
PEDESTRIAN
BRIDGE

Ivy Ln.

LEWIS
LIBRARY

PEYTON

Western Way

FINE

JADWIN

PRINCETON
STADIUM

NEW PARKING
FACILITY

Washington Rd.

CHEMISTRY

- Future development site
- Sciences Green
- Future pedestrian connections

By creating additional pathways between Prospect Avenue and Ivy Lane/Western Way, and linking new open spaces to the Sciences Green, the entire eastern area of the campus can become better connected and establish a stronger campus character.

POTENTIAL LONG-TERM GROWTH AREAS

1. 5 and 7 Ivy Lane
2. Lots 4 and 25
3. Ferris Thompson apartments
4. 87 Prospect Avenue
5. Surface parking lot
6. 171 Broadmead
7. Daycare expansion

West Neighborhoods

Unlike the east neighborhoods, potential long-term development on the western edge of campus is less contiguous with the main campus, separated by existing infrastructure such as the rail line and the co-generation plant. However, the advantages of development in this area are its proximity to mass transit, including the Dinky and potential bus rapid transit, as well as to the new Arts and Transit Neighborhood, and the concentration of graduate student housing, which presents an opportunity to support a mixed-use neighborhood. The Campus Plan has identified three precincts for long-term growth in the western areas of campus including a northern zone within walking distance of the Core Campus, an area south of the Central Plant and east of the tracks, and the Alexander Street corridor.

The presence of the Graduate College and Forbes College and the close proximity of Princeton's residential core make the area immediately north of Forbes College an appropriate site for a future residential college or graduate student housing. Residential development on this site would be in keeping with the surrounding neighborhood.

The MacMillan building site is another key opportunity for academic and campus life growth. Since the power plant and other utilities are located just to the south, this site forms the southwestern limit of the walkable main campus. Given its proximity to undergraduate residential areas, the Arts and Transit Neighborhood, the Ellipse, and the Dinky station, the campus plan recommends that the MacMillan building site be redeveloped in the long term for academic, residential, or campus life facilities such as Health Services.

The Arts and Transit Neighborhood may be expanded in the future, near the planned Dinky commuter parking lot, and on the site of a demolished or re-purposed New South building. Redevelopment of New South or the MacMillan building would follow the principle that support uses such as administrative office spaces be relocated farther from the campus core, to accommodate academic and campus life growth on limited available land.

Further south, the Central Plant and a possible new Data Center will comprise a services neighborhood on campus. Expansion capacity for the Central Plant and potential Data Center is provided on their adjacent parking lots. Concentration of vital services in this area will reduce redundancy while maximizing security and oversight. If the MacMillan building site is redeveloped, the campus will be in need of a new facilities and maintenance building, and parking for associated plant vehicles. The Campus Plan recommends that Lot 23 be considered for these uses.

The University-owned properties along the southern portion of Alexander Street present an opportunity to develop a mixed-use and higher density corridor with administrative, commercial, and residential uses. In order to optimize the development of these sites, a new zoning framework is recommended to increase the allowable floor area ratio and reduce required parking ratios. With public transit options and reasonable walking proximity to campus, parking requirements could be lower than an average suburban development. The location of this corridor along a potential bus rapid transit line could also make it convenient to Route 1, Nassau Street, and the Dinky.

The Alexander Street corridor has three zones: in Zone 1 between the Arts and Transit Neighborhood and Faculty Road, academic or administrative uses are recommended. Zone 2 between Faculty Road and the Helm Building could provide a transition between administrative and residential uses. Zone 3 south of the Helm Building is recommended for residential uses, due to its adjacency to existing graduate student housing and a potential future bus rapid transit station stop. Some community-oriented service uses, such as the existing gas station, should be maintained in the corridor, and retail uses can be added to support existing and new housing. A recent study has shown that a significant demand for retail exists, partially due to the concentration of graduate students in the area. Overall, the corridor presents an opportunity to improve a significant gateway to both the University and the Princeton community.

Planning principles

- Consider the area north of Forbes College as the possible location of a new undergraduate residential college or additional graduate student housing, while creating new pedestrian linkages from this area to main campus

- Take advantage of the MacMillan building site's proximity to the Core Campus for academic or other core uses.

- Utilize the concentration of infrastructure in the southwestern services neighborhood of campus to expand needed capacity for utilities and support facilities

- Develop the Alexander Street corridor as a mixed-use area, potentially including retail to support nearby graduate student housing.

- Through redevelopment, strengthen the Alexander Street corridor as a gateway to the University and to the township and borough of Princeton.

Planning framework for the west neighborhoods

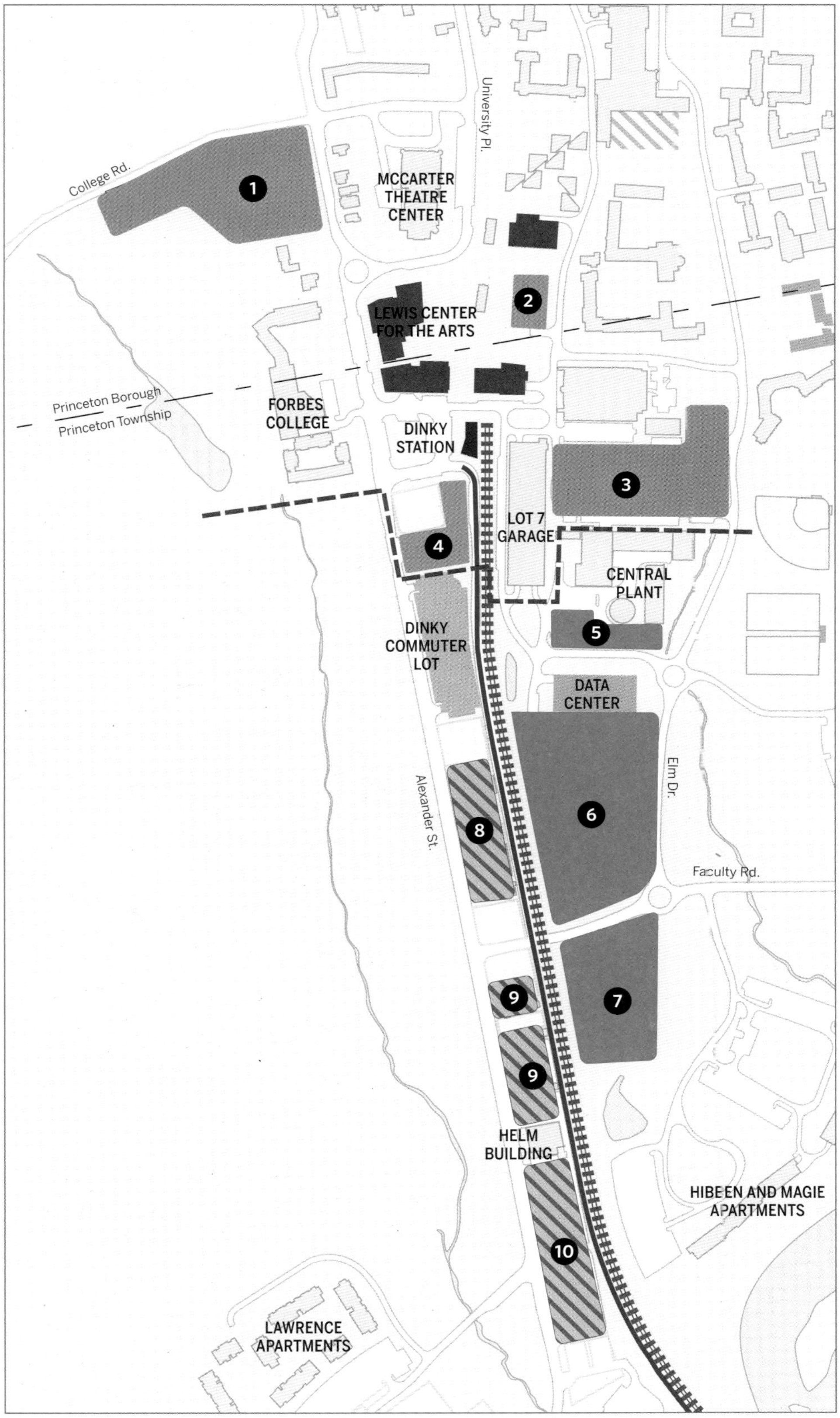

POTENTIAL LONG-TERM GROWTH AREAS

1 North of Forbes College
2 New South
3 MacMillan building
4 Arts and Transit Neighborhood expansion
5 Central Plant expansion
6 Lot 23
7 Lot 23A
8 Alexander Street zone 1: potential administrative uses
9 Alexander Street zone 2: potential mix of administrative and residential uses
10 Alexander Street zone 3: potential residential uses

- Arts and Transit Neighborhood buildings
- Academic and campus life uses
- Potential campus support uses
- Mixed use corridor
- Transit facilites
- Dinky Commuter parking lot
- Recommended limit of academic and campus life uses
- Potential bus rapid transit line

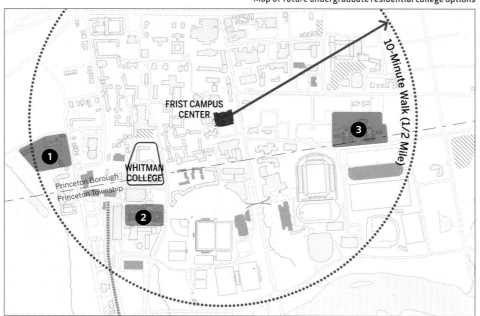

Map of future undergraduate residential college options

POTENTIAL RESIDENTIAL COLLEGE SITES

1   North of Forbes College   2   MacMillan building   3   Ivy Lane and Western Way Neighborhood

Map of future parking options

- ● New parking garage
- ● Potential future parking site
- ||| New Jersey Transit service
- --- Potential shuttle route
- -- Five minute walk (1/4 mile)

POTENTIAL PARKING SITES

1   Expansion of new parking facility   2   Lot 23 parking garage   3   Remote parking at West Windsor

RESIDENTIAL OPTIONS FOR THE FUTURE

The ten-year Campus Plan does not provide for additional growth in the undergraduate student population beyond the planned addition of 500 students accommodated by the new Whitman College and reconstructed Butler College. In the future, however, it is likely that additional undergraduate residential colleges may be needed. Looking at the long-term growth possibilities in the previous pages, only a few sites are suitable for the large footprint required to construct an undergraduate college. For size comparison, refer to the footprint of Whitman College in the map at left.

A logical location would be near the dense cluster of existing undergraduate residential neighborhoods on the western side of campus. Two potential sites, north of Forbes College and the MacMillan building, are possible, though the latter is constrained and may result in an unacceptably dense layout. This would follow the original "zoning" of the campus, conceived by Ralph Adams Cram in the beginning of the 20th century, which located all residential to the southwest and all academic to the northeast.

Another possible site is in the Ivy Lane and Western Way Neighborhood. With a mix of residential and academic uses, this neighborhood could develop a vibrant character in keeping with the historic core, with actively used open spaces and a diverse daily population of faculty, staff, and students. A new college could also be planned to ensure its compatibility with nearby community residential areas. This strategy would contribute to the goal of uniting the campus across the two sides of Washington Road.

PARKING OPTIONS FOR THE FUTURE

Many of the future developments are likely to be on existing parking lots. The resulting loss of parking spaces and a growing campus population will require a comprehensive strategy that identifies convenient, sustainable, and cost-effective parking solutions. Similar to the current ten-year plan, future strategies must maintain expedient connections between commuter arrival points, their parking locations, and their ultimate destinations on campus. The scarcity of parking sites within or near the core campus will also underscore the need to expand transportation demand management programs to reduce the number of vehicles on campus.

On the main campus, there are two potential future parking sites. One option would be to create underground parking just north of the new parking facility on Western Way, which would be, in effect, the basement level of future buildings along Western Way. This location has the advantage of proximity to academic neighborhoods and reduced reliance on shuttle service.

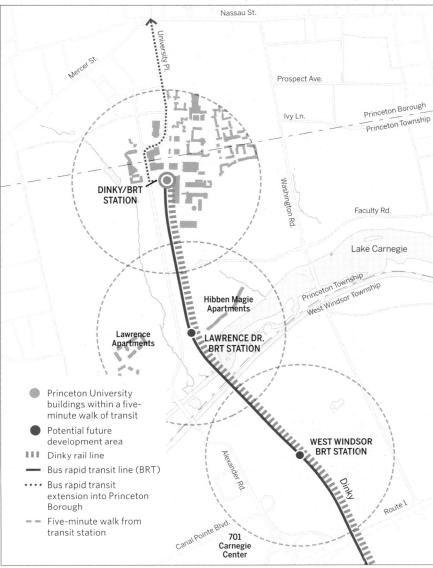

Map of transit-oriented development opportunities

Nassau St.

University Pl.

Mercer St.

Prospect Ave.

Ivy Ln.

Princeton Borough
Princeton Township

DINKY/BRT
STATION

Washington Rd.

Faculty Rd.

Lake Carnegie

Hibben Magie
Apartments

Princeton Township
West Windsor Township

Lawrence
Apartments

LAWRENCE DR.
BRT STATION

○ Princeton University
buildings within a five-
minute walk of transit

● Potential future
development area

▮▮▮ Dinky rail line

— Bus rapid transit line (BRT)

•••• Bus rapid transit
extension into Princeton
Borough

— — Five-minute walk from
transit station

WEST WINDSOR
BRT STATION

Alexander Rd.

Dinky

Route 1

Canal Pointe Blvd.

701
Carnegie
Center

THE OPPORTUNITY OF TRANSIT-ORIENTED DEVELOPMENT

The Dinky is a remarkable and unique asset to the Uni-versity. Rarely does a major university enjoy direct and convenient access to mass transit service, much less with a connection to the Northeast Corridor, linking the campus to major cities as well as Newark Liberty International Airport. Although this service established at the turn of the 20th century has been supplanted by cars as the primary mode of transportation to and from campus, it continues to serve as a vital link for a wide range of users, and can be embraced as a powerful means of reducing Princeton's dependence on automobiles, with corresponding environ-mental benefits.

In consideration of the benefits of reducing automobile traffic through increased transit ridership, New Jersey Transit is in the process of developing a bus rapid transit (BRT) system for the central New Jersey region. BRT consists of express buses running in dedicated lanes, with boarding platforms and ticketing facilities similar to a train. The advantage of these systems is the ability to avoid traffic and maintain fixed timetables, creating a reliable option for commuters. One component of the proposed concept is a line running parallel to the Dinky, supplementing the Dinky train service with more frequent rapid bus connections between Princeton and Princeton Junction. This additional level of service would provide greater convenience for riders, and could include a proposed extension of the bus routes north into the Princeton community.

One of the most interesting opportunities created by the BRT, however, is the potential to provide additional stops along its route, which is not possible with the current train service. Two possible station locations would be catalysts for long-term growth. A station at Alexander Street and Lawrence Drive would connect graduate students living in Lawrence Apartments and Hibben and Magie apartments to the center of campus, as well as employees in the Helm Building and future mixed-use spaces along Alexander Street. A second potential station in West Windsor would create an entirely new location for growth, convenient to 701 Carnegie Center where an off-campus administrative neighborhood is proposed as part of the ten-year plan. A West Windsor station could also connect new parking, athletics facilities, and housing to the core campus, and could be the starting point for potential future campus development on the West Windsor lands. By using transit as leverage, the walkable campus can be extended beyond its current borders.

Another option would be to create a new parking facility on the west side of campus on Lot 23. As part of a campus services neighborhood, this new parking facility could be developed in conjunction with a new building to house the facilities and maintenance offices currently in the MacMillan building. A portion of the new parking facility would be dedicated to plant vehicles that need to maintain direct access to all main campus buildings.

Because of physical, environmental, and traffic constraints, these on-campus parking facilities are not likely to be large enough to satisfy the entire parking demand of future campus growth. Inevitably, an off-campus parking facility will become necessary in the future. The most logical location for such a facility would be in West Windsor off Alexander Road. This location has convenient access from Route 1 and a potential connection to New Jersey Transit service along the existing Dinky right-of-way. A shuttle would connect this parking area to main campus via Alexander Street or via Faculty Road to Washington Road.

Physics Professor Daniel Marlow teaching in the Icahn Laboratory

It is the nature of a university to grow and change as the fields of human knowledge grow and change. The pace of institutional development will vary as a result of many external factors, from global events to the local economy, but it is the commitment to advance learning, scholarship and research that drives university expansion.

Although growth and change at a university may be inevitable, they are not always predictable. In the early 1960s Architect Douglas Orr produced a Master Plan for Princeton that imagined its full "build-out". Although the intervening forty years have been a time of unequaled growth and change, most of Orr's predictions have not been realized. On the other hand, the 1996 plan by Machado Silvetti was more modest in its objectives and most have already been accomplished. In this Campus Plan, Beyer Blinder Belle and University planners have again pursued a ten-year horizon to identify projects and objectives that are of the highest priority to the institution and clearly attainable…with an appropriate stretching of energies and resources.

What may happen after ten years cannot be drawn or imagined clearly. Just as a vision of our campus today would have confounded President Aaron Burr when he and his family moved to Prince-Town in 1756, we would surely be startled and amazed by a glimpse of Princeton University 250 years from now. For that reason, the long-term objective of this Campus Plan has been an exploration of growth strategies for no more than several decades rather than a visionary speculation of very long-term growth. If this plan does not propose specific solutions for an unpredictable future, it does suggest a framework that will allow our successors to make future decisions wisely, when they know a lot more about future needs than we can possibly know today.

As much as it has changed over 250 years, or even 25 years, our evolving campus has been able to maintain a strong continuity with its rich architectural legacy. As architects ponder and plan the physical spaces for academic disciplines that were unknown a few decades ago, President Tilghman and her advisors will guide the course of the University in Nassau Hall (c.1756), humanists will advance African-American scholarship in Stanhope Hall (c.1803), scientists will conduct ecological research in Guyot Hall (c.1912), and students will learn to live with each other in dorms constructed between 1877 and the present day. It is our privilege to preserve and celebrate these diverse layers of architectural history as new ones are added. Indeed, the Princeton campus evolved as a living record, not only of growth and change in higher education but of the architecture of America. This Campus Plan is dedicated to a thoughtful continuation of that record.

Jon Hlafter
University Architect
Princeton University

Acknowledgments

The richness of any planning effort springs from the imagination, clarity of vision, and commitment of the leaders, experts, and community members who participate. Princeton University's campus planning exercise benefited from strong participation in all three categories.

In the spring of 2005, President Tilghman asked me to serve as the executive sponsor of this two-year campus planning effort. Our first step was to establish a campus planning steering committee to provide broad oversight for the effort, advise on key decisions, and make sure that our planning was fully aligned with the University's overall strategic goals. The committee met in whole or in part every other week for two years. Chaired by President Tilghman, it included Provost Chris Eisgruber, Vice President and Secretary Bob Durkee, Vice President for Development Brian McDonald, former and present chairs of the Grounds and Buildings Committee of the Board of Trustees Neil Rudenstine and Karen Magee, Dean of the Architecture School Stan Allen, two members of the architecture faculty, Guy Nordenson and Bob Gutman, Vice President for Facilities Mike McKay, and myself. Sadly, Bob Gutman did not live to see the publication of this report. Bob's scholarly work prepared him well to be the conscience of this planning effort, and we all will miss his insightful questioning and dry wit.

The planning effort was ably directed by University Architect Jon Hlafter and Associate University Architect Natalie Shivers, with support from Bob Barnett and Paul LaMarche, the former and current vice provosts for space planning and programming. Kristin Appelget, the University's director of community and regional affairs, also played an important part ensuring that community views were carefully considered in all of our deliberations. This intensive dialogue among senior management, faculty, and trustees not only set the direction for the planning exercise, but provided constant guidance and feedback for our consultants.

We were very fortunate to have chosen a consulting team led by Neil Kittredge, a partner at Beyer Blinder Belle Architects & Planners, to lead this effort. Neil brought to this role a combination of vision and practical knowledge of our environment along with an exceptional ability to listen carefully, think creatively, and explain clearly. With his team of Marc Sharifi, Dale Riedl, Rayna Huber Erlich, and Nisha Baliga as well as Sapna Advani, Mia Sidonie Berberat, Marcello Ferri, Marie Hines, Lars Moestue, Edward Piatt, Maithili Raut, Gretel Schwartzott, Dia Sheriff, Elizabeth Shrum, Carolyn Straub, Jenny Tommos, and Hilary Verni from BBB, along with Stephen Cassell, Megumi Tamanaha, Arthur Chu, Craig Muller, and Elizabeth Stoel from Architecture Research Office, Neil created a comprehensive and integrated plan for the University that will serve as a blueprint for campus development for the next ten years and more.

Creating a campus plan that is both comprehensive and integrated is not easy. To achieve both objectives and engage the numerous issues that our plan needed to address, Neil assembled a team of consultants that not only invested significant energy and innovative thought in Princeton, but also integrated its visions into a unified whole. First among equals was Michael Van Valkenburgh and his team, led by Gullivar Shepard and including Matthew Urbanski, Jennifer Bolstad, Justine Heilner, Rachel Gleeson, Anita Berrizbeitia, Leor Lovinger, Yoshi Mishima, and Tim Kirby from Michael Van Valkenburgh Associates. It was clear from the history of the Princeton campus that landscape architecture and its relationship with the built environment would be a threshold theme of the planning effort. The strategy developed by Michael and his team exceeded the University's high expectations. Neil and Michael augmented the landscape architecture team with Lynden Miller and Catherine Redd from Lynden B. Miller Public Garden Design, Stephen Benz, Nicole Holmes, and Sandra Brock from Nitsch Engineering, and David Gibson, Ann Harakawa, Anthony Ferrara, Alexandria Lee, Darlene Levy, Andy Ng, Laura Varacchi, Julie Park, and Vijay Mathews from Two Twelve Associates. Lynden deftly conceived a path to reintroduce the glorious tradition of Beatrix Ferrand to our campus; Steve infused the landscape plan with higher sustainability initiatives; and David developed a comprehensive system of wayfinding that will enhance the feeling of being welcome on campus for years to come. We are also grateful to David's team for overseeing the design and production of this book, the accompanying brochure, and the campus plan website, as well as Juanita Dugdale for writing and editing, Peter Roper for renderings, and Fred Charles, Ari Burling, and Sesthasak Boonchai for photography. This book would also not have been possible without the significant investment of time by Ruth Stevens, executive editor in the University's Office of Communications.

The planning process was also enriched by consultants on transportation, parking, civil engineering, retail, and real estate. No planning exercise in the State of New Jersey can succeed without a thoughtful approach to these issues. Georges Jacquemart and Alireza Rabiee from BFJ Planning along with Frederick Gorove, Dan VanPelt, Charles Teuer, and Deanna Donahoo from Gorove Slade Associates; Barbara Chance, Guillermo Leiva, and Chris Jurek from CHANCE Management Advisors; Tom O'Shea from Van Note Harvey; Kate Coburn and Tom Moriarty from Economic Research Associates; and Karen Backus, Steve Jacobs, and Lori Matsukuma from K. Backus and Associates led these efforts respectively. We are especially thankful that both George and Barbara aggressively advocated for environmentally sustainable approaches to their respective challenges.

There were hundreds of students, faculty, staff, alumni, and community residents who actively engaged in many meetings and forums, both on and off campus. These campus and community conversations were the sources of some of the planning exercise's most important ideas and helped to refine others.

Finally, this planning process benefited enormously from the sustained and close attention of our trustees. In addition to providing regular briefings for the Grounds and Buildings Committee, we engaged the full board in discussions at Committee of the Whole meetings and at a board retreat. Through these conversations the trustees provided helpful guidance and encouragement at each stage of the planning process.

Princeton University owes deep gratitude to all who are mentioned above and its campus is significantly enriched by their investment of diligence, creativity, and vision.

Mark Burstein

Executive Vice President
Princeton University

CAMPUS PLAN TEAM

PRINCETON UNIVERSITY STEERING COMMITTEE

Shirley M. Tilghman, President of the University and Chair
Christopher L. Eisgruber, Provost
Mark Burstein, Executive Vice President
Robert K. Durkee, Vice President and Secretary of the University
Brian J. McDonald, Vice President for Development
Karen Magee, Chair of the Trustee Committee on Grounds and Buildings
Neil Rudenstine, Former Chair of the Trustee Committee on Grounds and Buildings
Stanley T. Allen, Dean, School of Architecture
Robert Gutman, Lecturer in Architecture
Guy Nordenson, Professor of Architecture
Paul LaMarche, Vice Provost for University Space Programming and Planning
Robert Barnett, Former Vice Provost for University Space Planning
Michael McKay, Vice President for Facilities
Jon Hlafter, University Architect
Natalie Shivers, Associate University Architect

CONSULTANT TEAM

Beyer Blinder Belle Architects & Planners LLP
led by Neil P. Kittredge, Partner-in-charge, with

Michael Van Valkenburgh Associates, Inc.	Landscape Architecture
Architecture Research Office, LLC	Architecture
Two Twelve Associates, Inc.	Wayfinding and Graphic Design
Nitsch Engineering	Sustainable Site Strategies
Gorove/Slade Associates, Inc.	Transportation Planning
BFJ Planning	Transportation Planning
CHANCE Management Advisors, Inc.	Parking Strategies
Lynden B. Miller Public Garden Design	Horticulture and Garden Design
Van Note-Harvey Associates	Civil Engineering
Economics Research Associates	Retail Planning
Juanita Dugdale	Editorial Advising
K. Backus & Associates, Inc.	Real Estate

IMAGE CREDITS

Campus photography courtesy of the Princeton University Office of Communications, University Archives, Office of Athletic Communications, Princeton Plasma Physics Laboratory, and the Campus Plan consultants.

Peter Roper	Renderings
Sesthasak Boonchai	Campus Model Photography

First Published 2008 by Princeton University
Copyright © 2008 The Trustees of Princeton University
In the Nation's Service and in the Service of All Nations

Printed and bound in the USA
Designed by Two Twelve Associates

ISBN 0-9773544-5-8
Library of Congress Cataloging-in-Publication Data available